Asian Legal Revivals

THE CHICAGO SERIES IN LAW AND SOCIETY
Edited by John M. Conley and Lynn Mather

Also in the series:

Additional series titles follow index.

Asian Legal Revivals

Lawyers in the Shadow of Empire

YVES DEZALAY AND
BRYANT G. GARTH

THE UNIVERSITY OF CHICAGO PRESS   CHICAGO AND LONDON

YVES DEZALAY is director of the Centre National de la Recherche Scientifique.

BRYANT G. GARTH is dean and professor of law at Southwestern Law School. His most recent books (with Yves Dezalay) are *The Internationalization of Palace Wars: Lawyers, Economists, and the Contest to Transform Latin American States* (University of Chicago Press, 2002) and *Global Prescriptions: The Production, Exportation, and Importation of a New Legal Orthodoxy.*

The University of Chicago Press, Chicago 60637
The University of Chicago Press, Ltd., London
19 18 17 16 15 14 13 12 11 10   1 2 3 4 5

ISBN-13: 978-0-226-14462-7 (cloth)
ISBN-13: 978-0-226-14463-4 (paper)
ISBN-10: 0-226-14462-3 (cloth)
ISBN-10: 0-226-14463-1 (paper)

Library of Congress Cataloging-in-Publication Data

Asian legal revivals : lawyers in the shadow of empire / Yves Dezalay and Bryant G. Garth.
    p. cm.
    Includes bibliographical references and index.
    ISBN-13: 978-0-226-14462-7 (cloth : alk. paper)
    ISBN-13: 978-0-226-14463-4 (pbk. : alk. paper)
    ISBN-10: 0-226-14462-3 (cloth : alk. paper)
    ISBN-10: 0-226-14463-1 (pbk. : alk. paper) 1. Law—Political aspects—Asia.
2. Lawyers—Political aspects—Asia. I. Dezalay, Yves, 1945– II. Garth, Bryant G.
    KM50.A853 2010
    340.023′5—dc22   2010007679

Contents

Acknowledgments

We are very grateful for the support of the American Bar Foundation, which allowed us to conduct the research that went into the manuscript and our other works related to the globalization of law. We also obtained the helpful support of the National Science Foundation, grant no. SES-9818796, for this project, entitled "International Strategies, Law, and the Reconstruction of Asian States." Bryant Garth is thankful to many individuals at Southwestern Law School who encouraged him to find time in the midst of administrative duties to help bring this work to fruition. As in our other collaborative works, we have been fortunate to have friends and colleagues who have helped us learn about the people and places that we are studying. Among others, we would like to mention Carol Jones for Hong Kong; Upendra Baxi, Mona Bhide, and Marc Galanter for India; the late Daniel Lev for Indonesia; and Jae Won Kim, Seong-Hyun Kim, and the late James West for South Korea. We would also like to thank the roughly four hundred individuals who allowed us to interview them. Their voices and accounts of career trajectories are central to the analyses in this book.

CHAPTER ONE

Introduction: Studying Law and Lawyers in Asia

The Role of Law in Asia

Discussions of the role of law and lawyers in Asia often start with some defensiveness (e.g., Ginsburg 2007; Ohnesorge 2003). The threshold question for many is whether the Asian state or the Asian economy does or does not have some cultural affinity with "Western" law, whether some version of the "rule of law" is necessary or inevitable in the region, or whether there is instead some competing "Asian model" of governance and regulation that may indeed triumph over what the West has produced. Scholars in the early 1990s made much of the idea that there was a Confucian model of development that was simply inconsistent with the Weberian model of law and state associated with Europe and the United States (e.g., Jones 1994). Prime ministers of rapidly growing Asian economies trumpeted Asian values in opposition to the individual rights consciousness of Western democracies. The World Bank at one point commissioned a study of the East Asian Economic Miracle to determine whether Asian economic development relied on a different economic model than that promoted by the World Bank's economists (World Bank 1993). The Asian Development Bank funded an extensive study to show that law really did matter in promoting economic development in Asia (Pistor and Wellons 1998).

We start with a competing set of issues. Law and lawyers are very present in the lives of the Asian states. One of the inventors of the idea of competing Asian values was Lee Kwan Yew, a British-trained barrister who learned Chinese only when he was well into his political career;

and the election in 2002 in the Confucian stronghold of South Korea involved on one side a human rights lawyer, Moo–Hyun Roh, and on the other a former Supreme Court justice, Lee Hoi-chang, who was the son of a public prosecutor. More generally, leaders of movements for independence in all the former Asian colonies were lawyers, and law has played a major part in the construction of these Asian states. Even the exceptions, notably China and Japan, came to law in part through a counterstrategy meant to modernize their nations while holding back the colonial powers, and one result was the implantation in Asia—including Korea as a Japanese colony—of a kind of Bismarckian model of lawyers in a strong state.

Furthermore, we see in all these countries a kind of legal revival, in two senses. One is a return to the old colonial roots, as in the revival of a theater production. The colonial imprint of law provides the core that defines the revival. The other sense of revival is the religious sense of a collective expression of belief, appropriately identified, for example, with a series of "great awakenings" in the United States. The rule of law is now deemed an article of faith for good governance in Asia and elsewhere (Ohnesorge 2007; Trubek and Santos 2006; for an historical reading that looks in a different way at Asian antecedents for the rule of law, see Ocko and Gilmartin 2009).

Our research begins with an examination of Asian colonial relationships—the geneses of law in Asia. We cover a good proportion of the ex-colonies in South and East Asia, including Hong Kong, India, Indonesia, Malaysia, the Philippines, Singapore, and South Korea. The countries we have selected include most of the Asian dragons celebrated for their rapid economic growth, and our selection includes the major colonies of the American, British, Dutch, and Japanese in the region. Drawing on these studies, we will also offer a few comparative observations about the role of law in other Asian countries, namely China and Japan. Certainly there is considerable activity in China and Japan that could be characterized as a renewed focus on law, and our findings based on the other countries may also suggest some issues and approaches useful in understanding China and Japan. Our principal aim, however, is to explore what can be learned about law in Asia from the seven case studies that we develop in some detail.

One of the reasons that scholars have trouble examining the role of law in Asia is that the usual categories of analysis are those that come from within the legal profession—for example, courts, bar associations, law firms, and faculties of law. It has been difficult for scholars to find ways to link the study of those entities as such—separately or combined in some fashion (Halliday, Karpik, and Feeley 2008)—to the role of lawyers in the state and in the economy. It is relatively easy to see that lawyers invest in politics. The colonial origins of legal professions in Asia through the co-optation of elites already possessing political power ensure that law and politics will mix. Again, our approach to law and politics is different. We examine the role of law and lawyers in building legitimacy. In particular, we examine strategies to produce a belief in law and in the legitimacy it provides to a national state or a colonial relationship. As in our prior work, we draw on Pierre Bourdieu (e.g., 1998) and use the concept of strategy not to suggest a conscious or necessarily self-interested plan, but rather to refer to actions taken by individuals making sense of a field in which they operate. One task of empirical research is to relate individual "strategies" to the "rules of the game" which shape activity within a given social arena—or "field" in Bourdieu's terminology.

We also focus on the relationship between social and legal capital, examining processes through which different kinds of capital go into the law, including family capital. In order to understand the evolving role of law in Asia (as elsewhere), it is essential to explore the relationship between family and other social capital on one side and legal universals on the other. We see in Malaysia, for example, that legal capital not fortified with family and state capital is relatively weak by itself to assert the law against authoritarian state power. On the other hand, where legal capital and social capital are strongly intertwined, as in India and the Philippines, lawyers could mobilize much more strength when opposing an authoritarian state.

The key to the relationship between law and the legitimation of state power, according to Kantorowicz in his classic study of the notaries and the King (1997), is the double agency of the lawyers serving strong rulers at the same time as they moderate them. The double-agent strategy can be linked to the currently fashionable literature drawing from rational choice theories. In crude terms, lawyers must succeed in selling the idea that they can provide credible legitimacy to the dominant holders of economic and political power without threatening that dominant position. In Barry Weingast's well-known formulation (1997: 260), "The survival of democracy and the rule of law requires that political officials have incentives to honor a range of limits on their behavior." We do not need to see this relationship as the product of rational actors choosing instrumentally to put law in this place. The concepts of strategy and field that we employ provide more subtle explanations of what leads actors to particular activities. But lawyers have long been specialists in brokering relationships where political and economic elites give up some portion of their power in exchange for credibility in the guise of the rule of law. Incentives for the exchange include the legitimacy that is provided for positions of power and the application of rules that help to secure that power.

Lawyers in Asia and elsewhere invest in state politics and then to a greater or lesser degree profit from that investment. They may become the experts in the rules and procedures that the state produces and also take up roles asserting and brokering political power. The connection between the two roles is apparent for all who look for it, but lawyers have an interest in affirming a basic difference between law and politics. Legally oriented scholarship tends to focus on the import and export of specific legal technologies and knowledge, exemplified by the civil codes from France or Germany or constitutional courts from the United States or Europe. The scholars look to see if the supreme courts are building a larger role or asserting more independence, for example. In fact, however, these imports and exports only make sense in relation to more general strategies used to build positions in the field of state power. An increased scholarly focus on courts, for example, does not necessarily lead to greater understanding of the position of law. As Martin Shapiro notes about a range of globalization scholarship that embraces law, "one is tempted to say that the word 'juridification' applies more aptly to the study of comparative politics than to the actual politics being studied" (Shapiro 2008: 329). The narrow focus on the institutions of the law as such supports professional ideology, but it makes it difficult to see the collective strategies through which lawyers seek to maintain and build their position in the field of state power.

The process that allows lawyers to gain state power is especially complicated in the histories of Asian colonies. Law came with colonialism, and therefore models established in Europe of the relationship between law and state were brought to Asia, and they were then transformed and further hybridized in relation to colonial politics. They were used by the colonizers in part to co-opt local elites into protégé statespersons in training for leadership of dependent states (Benton 2002). Colonial elites could justify their local positions in part by their possession of prestigious learned capital acquired abroad, for example, in the law faculties of Oxford and Cambridge and the Inns of Court in Britain, and in the equivalents in the other colonial powers. Accordingly, one strategy of lawyers in the colonizing countries was to call on the dominant state to put more law and legitimacy in the colonial systems of governance. This co-optation process had much in common with other colonial relationships, including those typical of Latin America, but the early lawyers in Asia were for the most part facilitators of trade and commerce, whereas in Latin America they were initially designed to be agents of the Crown (Perez-Perdomo 2006). The Asian colonial developments also occurred much later and for a shorter duration than those in Latin America. In both cases, of course, the process of co-optation has also allowed the local elites to transform the model as it serves them in a particular local context. The strategy of allying with colonial elites continues. John Bresnan, writing about his experience in the Ford Foundation in the 1950s and 1960s, notes that India received the most money outside the United States, and that many new ideas began there because, in his words, "Its sophisticated elite made it the most likely place for the Foundation to enter any field of activity for the first time" (2006: 26).

Northern Competition and the Production of Law in Asia

Any replication of European models of law and politics in Asia was further complicated by transformations within the colonial powers and in the competition among them. The Dutch and English empires competed in the region for centuries, and the United States entered the fray in the late nineteenth century with the Spanish-American War and the takeover of the Philippines. The competing European colonial powers lost some their power over the course of the twentieth century in relation to the growing global hegemony of the United States. There was also competition between the Soviet Union and the West that culminated in the Cold War. These competitive processes helped shape the role of law and lawyers and the construction of states more generally. Odd Arne Westad's recent book on the Cold War (2005), for example, details the relationship between third world countries, movements for independence, and the global activities of the Soviet Union—as well as those of the United States. The Soviet Union also had influence over the legal systems of Communist countries generally, including Communist China (Conner 2010). Because of the importance of law and lawyers to the international strategies of the United States and the hegemonic power that the United States was able to assert in the region, we focus particular attention in this book on the role of the United States, especially in the period after World War II.

During the Cold War, as we shall see, the United States forged alliances with authoritarian states combining military, economic, and technocratic elements, and those alliances had definite impacts on the position of law and lawyers. The post–Cold War period then brought a renewed U.S. emphasis on the rule of law, both as a political strategy as a way to build trade and commerce according to a U.S. view of globalization. The latter part of the book concentrates on these U.S. influences and relationships. It remains true, however, that there are other countries competing for influence not only in Asia but also throughout the globe. What happens within the dominant powers as well as in the competition among them will continue to play a major role in determining what role law and lawyers play in Asian states (for a fascinating look at renewed Japanese interest in foreign investment in law in Asia, for example, see Taylor 2005).

The focus on the importance of global competition raises scholarly issues examined by Wallerstein and the "world system theory" he pioneered (Wallerstein 2000). Going beyond a traditional comparative sociology of national professional fields, a Wallerstein-inspired perspective leads to analyses of relationships between national and international competition. We therefore examine strategies whereby elites seek to redefine an international hierarchy of expertise while at the same time building the dominance of their own state and its approaches. This approach highlights a double competitive logic: one that involves competing expertises seeking universal credibility, such as law versus economics, and another that represents a competition between imperialisms.

The logic of the competition between imperialisms is seen in professional networks structured around the new hegemonic power—the United States—competing with those built by the old "imperial societies" of Europe (Charle 2001). The competition in the exportation of expertise that is evident in the politics of development assistance is therefore played out in a triangular dynamic, where the "imported states" (Badie 1992) from the periphery represent the stakes and a laboratory to try out new technologies of governance.

World system theory provides lines of inquiry to build on the sociology of professional fields—including studies of the internationalization of the reproduction of the "state nobility" (Bourdieu 1998) and on the genesis of the international field of state power (Bourdieu 2002). The hypotheses and issues that derive from this sociology of globalization nicely extend Bourdieu's observations made about the "Esprits d'Etat" (1993) and the reproduction of the "Noblesses d'Etat" in the French national setting (1998). In this international competition over universals, the elites who dominate national professional fields mobilize resources of the national state—accumulated through more or less lengthy and more or less successful investments in the construction and perpetual reactualization of the state. The authority of these competing professional expertises, and thus their value on the international market of symbolic import and export, therefore quite depends on their success in shaping debates on state institutions at home.

The confrontations between different hegemonic powers seeking to diffuse their model of the state to other countries—as a basis for an emerging international field of state power—must be analyzed as elitist fights contributing toward the acceleration of the internationalization of the reproduction of national elites. This internationalization helps to compensate for the increased competition among national university graduates by helping revalorize the linguistic and cultural capital of the descendants of the old cosmopolitan elite (Dezalay 2004). As in our prior work (Dezalay and Garth 2002), therefore, we focus our attention on the "palace wars" involving elite actors whose activities have disproportionate weight in shaping the role of law in the state.

Accordingly, our study is not a study of the "legal profession" in the countries that we examined. Such a study would spend much more time on ordinary practitioners and courts, on the gender and ethnic make-up of the rank and file of the profession, and on diverse legal careers. The legal profession in all these countries has grown substantially, and there are important divisions within the legal professions. One increasingly common feature is the growing divide between the elite of the profession and the masses of lawyers educated at the law schools that have proliferated in Asia in recent years. Our focus is on the elites, many of whom, as we shall show, are descendants from the elites trained under colonialism. But the elites, as we shall also see, are not homogeneous or united by any particular approach to state governance.

Our approach also does not focus on transformations within Islamic Law or on the recent "revival of Islamic law" seen in Asia and elsewhere. Our general approach suggests that there are colonial linkages and hegemonic competitions at the national and transnational level that merit detailed study as a basis to understand these transformations (see Hussin 2007). It will suffice for this study, however, to focus more generally on the role of lawyers historically and in brokering global (and especially U.S. influenced) legal imports. Many Islamic lawyers are of course part of our study, but their connections to economic and state power were not based specifically on their connections to Islamic law.

Consistent with our focus on the role of palace wars in the North and the South, our analysis of the global competition involving hegemonic and colonial states and types of expertise takes into account the internal divisions within individual states. Even if we can point to British imperial models or general U.S. approaches, for example, the crucial determinants of a colonial relationship may be which local groups shape colonial policy at a particular time and in a particular place. In particular, as the work of George Steinmetz illustrates, it is necessary to pay close attention not only to different groups in any colony but also to the different fractions within the colonizing powers (2007; 2008). Those differences shape developments at different times and in different sites (2007; 2008). As we shall see, the British approach in Hong Kong, India, and the Malay Peninsula shared some evolving concern with legal institutions and legitimacy, but local factors and different agendas among those in charge of colonial policy led to very different outcomes.

Lawyers and Asian States

Commentators and scholars see an increasing role for law and lawyers in the state as part of a more general global trend. The trend is described variously as a movement toward "juristocracy" (Hirschl 2004), the spread of a "rights revolution" (Epp 1998), or even just a "legalization" of international politics (Goldstein 2001). Much of the scholarship has a strong normative dimension. Recognizing this dimension, William Alford notes critically that "American scholars and policy-makers . . . share a deep faith in the value of China developing a legal profession that operates as we would like to think our own does" (2007: 287). Lawyers are assumed in this literature to be the natural architects and custodians of the national and transnational states—statespersons by definition. The role of lawyer statesperson has a long history in the United States (as we shall see in chap. 4), and it is not surprising that it reverberates in scholarship and policy prescription finding favor on U.S. campuses. In the Philippines at the turn of the twentieth century, U.S. colonial administrators responded to their encounter with colonialism to seek to build a governing elite of lawyer statespersons, and similar efforts continue today in multiple Asian settings—again with the goal of building a larger role for law and lawyers.

Our research supports a broad narrative that is in many respects consistent with the normative goal of an increased role for law and lawyers in Asia. As we shall see, however, there are also many other elements that are inconsistent with that account and prognosis. According to this narrative, the story begins in the colonial era when colonial powers in varying ways saw the need to co-opt local elites. One prominent strategy was to train them in the law, make them lawyers, and use them as part of delegated governance. The local elites, in turn, bolstered their own power by serving as double agents serving themselves and their colonial masters (Benton 2002). Their local status was tied to the status of the expertise that they acquired in legal academies abroad. They in turn co-opted the colonizing powers to their own ends even as they served those powers and their law. Lawyers then became key leaders in movements for independence and the architects of the new states. In various ways, according to this narrative, they lost their power in the state to authoritarian governments or developmental states and only recently made a comeback to state power through a revaluation of their position. The revaluation is associated with globalization and a renewed emphasis on law in the governance of the economy and the state. It is also consistent with a U.S. approach to governance, as we have noted, and with the prescriptions of the World Bank, the International Monetary Fund, philanthropic foundations, and governmental programs supporting development. These globalization agents, in addition, including new generations of lawyers whose expertise now comes in part from study in the United States, have promoted market-led rather than state-led economic growth, which makes the legal comeback evident less in the state as such, and more in strengthened courts and imported entities such as corporate law firms and human rights NGOs—the "civil society" of much of the literature.

This narrative—and the rule-of-law literature behind it—suggests a pattern that will unwind in Asia and elsewhere. The first point, therefore, is to emphasize that Asian legal revivals are not inevitable. What happens in any given place is path dependent. When lawyers play roles in politics and state governance, the activity takes place on the basis of the historical emergence of law and lawyers in relation to each of the Asian states. Even very recent developments are built out of the history that includes the colonial relationship and subsequent historical developments. It is also not simply a matter of a European model taking root in the colonial setting and mimicking the pattern determined by the colonial power. There is a decoupling of the historical approaches shaped in Europe when they are moved in some fashion to the colonies. In important respects, there is a reenactment in the new setting of much of what was seen in the European geneses. Each setting produces its own history of law, social capital, and the state. Despite very different national experiences, however, our general analysis of the Asian countries featured in this book aligns with a positive story of the development of the rule of law in recent years in Asia. This general finding is consistent with recent literature on the relationship between lawyers and the state.

Our theoretical framework differs from most of the literature, however, and it leads to a very different assessment of the inevitability of this trend. If lawyers are seen as the natural architects of the state, as many scholars posit, then the theoretical focus of research will tend to be on the public activities connected to the legal profession itself—moving toward independence and state building, for example, or resisting authoritarian states in the name of democracy and human rights. Halliday, Karpik, and Feeley, for example, have recently produced an excellent volume looking at the activities of various components of the "legal complex" in promoting or at times failing to promote political liberalism (2007). They insist that this activity is a key feature—almost a universal component—in the behavior of the legal profession and the actors connected to it. Karpik and Halliday initially developed this theoretical approach to show that "politics matter" for the legal profession. Arguing against classic works by Richard Abel (e.g., 1981; 1988) and Magali Sarfatti Larson (1977), they insist that lawyers as a group are not only interested in enriching themselves by creating a monopoly and building up the market for their services. They also have a natural and desirable role in politics.

Politics do matter for lawyers from our perspective, but not because lawyers reject market logic in the name of political principle. Their political strategies are intimately connected to markets for legal representation and expertise. The oppositional dichotomy between politics and markets makes sense as a matter of professional ideology, but it obscures the potential double profits of the political strategy. The ideology of a fundamental division is one that many wish to encourage, since it promotes political activities and portrays them as part of a moral commitment to public service. In fact, however, professional rewards are built into the strategy of political investment and the ideology that celebrates it.

As stated above, it is important to see the connections between legal investment in the state and its legitimacy and the markets for legal services. A narrow focus on the political activities of lawyers misses the relationship of lawyers to social, political, and state capital. It misses, therefore, key factors that explain particular political investments, successes or failures in resisting authoritarian developments, or even the connections of lawyers to authoritarian regimes or regimes that come under the label of "crony capitalism." There is a familial and social logic that facilitates the reproduction of legal elites, shapes their professional clientele, and determines their political allies. This more general focus reveals that there is nothing inevitable about lawyers' commitments to liberalism or democracy.

Our research strategy relies on explorations of the histories of law and state and on interviews with legal elites and their competitors. The early part of the book is mainly historical. We begin the discussion with the production of a legal profession in Europe and the United States that was ostensibly transplanted to their colonies. The study of the geneses of the political role of lawyers in Europe, in European colonies including the United States, and in the U.S. approach to colonies reveals the complex mixing of markets and politics throughout the history of the legal profession. Chapter 2 accordingly begins with the origins in Europe of the complementary relationship between lawyers and the state. A close rereading of the European history of lawyers and the state, beginning in Renaissance Italy with the emergence of the city-states, shows the need to see the construction of the European relationship among lawyers, markets, and states as part of one historical whole. Drawing on studies of Renaissance Italy, eighteenth-century France, eighteenth- and nineteenth-century England, and nineteenth-century Germany, this chapter maps out the different European colonial models and policies and the basic roles that lawyers have worked out as mediators, spokespersons for causes and groups, and clerks providing legitimacy to governmental institutions.

Chapter 3 moves ahead in time and across the oceans to see what happened when European countries took their legal approaches abroad

to Asia, using India and Indonesia as the major examples. For comparative purposes, the chapter also explores some similar developments that
occurred in Japan and China at the turn of the twentieth century. Again
we see contrasting examples with both similarities and differences in approach. India and Indonesia both began as colonies devoted to trade,
and the initial legal investment was strictly in the service of trade and the
economic exploitation of the colonies. In the latter part of the eighteenth
century, however, the British began to focus much more on law and on
governance to legitimate the colony at home and abroad. India became a
showcase colony for the British Empire. The legal profession in India obtained a strong and lucrative position linked to politics and the colonial
state. In contrast, the Dutch invested in law and legal legitimacy in the
late nineteenth and early twentieth centuries—relatively late in the colonial relationship with Indonesia. In contrast to India, therefore, Indonesia experienced a colonial relationship that set the stage for a relatively
small and weakly established legal profession.

Chapter 4 then brings the United States and its colonial approach into
the picture, showing what brought the United States into the practice
of colonialism alongside Europeans. The history of the United States
and its ambivalent relationship to the European empires produces a U.S.
model of law and empire. The approach itself and the leading purveyors
of that view grew out of the initial experience in the Philippines at the
turn of the twentieth century. In order to understand this approach, we
begin the chapter with the colonial development of the legal profession
in the North American colonies and then show the relationship between
the rise of the corporate law firm and the evolution of the U.S. imperial
approach. The United States merits this detailed attention because, as
noted before, variations on the U.S. approach asserted a powerful impact
in Asia and elsewhere after World War II and especially in the 1980s and
1990s. That impact is quite clear in parts 3 and 4 of this book.

These early chapters draw considerably on legal and colonial histories. Our purpose, however, is not the usual one seen in legal scholarship. Legal scholars typically examine histories of particular institutions
in order to build them into a narrative that adds weight and legitimacy to
present arrangements. A grand tour of the origins of ancient traditions
in this manner contributes to the credibility of approaches that are anchored in a long historical narrative. We do not aspire to a grand theory
of law and lawyers past, present, and future, nor are we suggesting that
what we see today is the inevitable result of an unwinding narrative.

Any historical narrative, including the one we use in this book, tends to impose a logic that appears natural and inevitable, but our venture into these histories is meant to show roads that might have been taken as well as those that were pursued. There are similarities as well as differences in roads opportunistically pursued as lawyers have continued in different periods to make strategic alliances in the field of state power—building law out of politics. The old European models that we describe thus reveal patterns and enduring legal roles that help organize and make sense of current practices. The relationship between lawyers in the city-state of Florence and the powerful condottieri, for example, is replicated in the ways that lawyers in Latin America have served Latin American generals and caudillos (Perez-Perdomo 2006). The replication in Latin America of one model, similarly, is a reminder that the situation in Asian countries also relates to the colonial progeny of European models exported and at the same time reinvented in colonial settings. Lawyers provide legitimacy to authoritarian states on the one hand, and they seek to gain power by representing dissident groups on the other. How lawyers take advantage of opportunities at different times and in different places may differ substantially, but it is important to see that even the modern variations build on long-established patterns through which lawyers and states shape and profit from each other.

Part 2 traces the different approaches and their consequences for the early construction of the legal fields in the different and competing colonial settings. It begins with examples where lawyers thrive under the colonial relationship and accrue considerable power over time. The two leading examples are the long period of investment by the British in law in India (chap. 5) and the sustained effort of the United States over a shorter period of time in the Philippines (chap. 6). The following chapter (chap. 7) in this part then examines the results of colonial relationships leading to much less investment in the law and lawyers—Indonesia, Malaysia, Singapore, and South Korea, the recipient of the least legal investment. The legal legacy from colonialism was much weaker in these countries than in India and the Philippines.

Part 3 focuses on a second historical moment, which involves challenges to the political role of lawyers. This period also connect to the U.S. role in the Cold War. The United States, despite its earlier investments in building up law and lawyers as part of it foreign policy agenda, was more interested in this period in building alliances against Communism. The U.S. agenda included the support of military and authoritarian governments aligned with Western-trained economists and characterized by relatively little respect for law and lawyers. In this context, as chapter 8 shows, the countries with the least colonial legal investment—Indonesia and South Korea—correspondingly had the weakest legal resources to resist marginalization in the period from independence through the Cold War. Chapter 9 focuses on two other countries that moved toward authoritarianism during the same period—the Philippines and Singapore. For somewhat different reasons, the chapter shows, lawyers and authoritarianism went hand in hand in these countries. Lawyers prospered and provided a legal façade to legitimate the regimes. In contrast, as chapter 10 shows, the legal profession offered varying levels of resistance to marginalization in India and Malaysia. They mobilized relatively early against authoritarian activities.

The subject of part 4 is a third moment—the rebuilding of the role of law and lawyers after the Cold War pressures abated. We see the relatively successful challenges to the authoritarian regimes in India under Indira Gandhi and in the Philippines under Ferdinand Marcos (chap. 11). Both cases show the impact of the strong colonial legal legacies. In contrast, we see the relatively unsuccessful rebuilding of the role of law and lawyers in Malaysia, Hong Kong, and Singapore (chap. 12) related to the relatively weak historical legacies.

The next chapter then focuses on relative success stories that relate not only to colonial investment but also to the cold war and the U.S. stake in the particular country (chap. 13). In India and the Philippines, not surprisingly given the strong historic role of lawyers, we see a story of continuity and moderate change, moving toward a new generation of social entrepreneurship. The story of continuity returns us to the linkage between social capital and legal capital. When the legal profession regains its stature and place in the state, it brings and relegitimates what is embedded in the law—elite families and close connections with foreign countries, for example, and, especially in the Philippines, close ties to the traditional oligarchy and the Roman Catholic Church.

The more surprising developments are in Indonesia and South Korea, where the very weak legal profession has regained a political role that also involves producing a new generation of social entrepreneurship. More generally, we find in these countries a basis to regrow the role of law and lawyers in the field of state power after years of marginalization. One feature of this third moment in all the countries is the maintenance or construction of links between cosmopolitan law merchants—business and corporate lawyers—and those who use law to fight authoritarian regimes or to build public interest law.

The seemingly paradoxical link of corporate lawyers to moral causes is of course reminiscent of Wall Street lawyers both serving and taming the robber barons in the United States. The complex legal histories in Asia involving agents of traders and lawyer statespersons may make this large fraction of Asian countries surprisingly comfortable with a U.S. legal model—hybridized in different ways in different settings. The concluding chapter (chap. 14), finally, brings the chapters together with a more general analysis of international, legal, and social capital in the various Asian legal revivals.

Our theoretical approach emphasizes the construction of legal capital out of learned, social, political, and state capital. This theoretical framework is not meant to provide a single grand theory. Rather, as we shall see, it accommodates the very different pragmatic strategies that are found in different settings—the results of different political circumstances linked to path dependency. At the same time, however, there are some common features that can best be explained by again using the concepts of capital and capital conversion associated more with economics than sociology. In particular, as discussed in the concluding chapter, we can refer to quasi-cyclical processes that begin with an initial accumulation of legal capital as a mix of imported material and converted local social capital. Next is a consolidation and valorization of the market for legal expertise through investments in institutions and knowledge, thereby reinforcing the claim of autonomy. Sustained investment over a long period helps to accumulate social capital and build up a degree of legal autonomy.

Our examples then reveal a process typically characterized by the obsolescence and creative destruction of legal capital. The devaluation may come from profiteering by legal elites thriving in crony capitalism, as in the Philippines, or reaping the rents of a monopoly on conveyancing in small city-states where land is scarce and rapidly appreciating. It may also come from new competing expertise, such as economics. Competition between colonial powers and changing balances of power within colonial or neocolonial powers are also part of the process. The ascendency of U.S. approaches to law in some settings undermined approaches linked to European countries, and the end of the Cold War made it more difficult for lawyers to claim legitimacy for their support of authoritarian anticommunist states, such as Indonesia or South Korea.

Finally, to continue with the cyclical model, we often see a kind of legal revamping either through the traditional path developed in Europe of lawyers as political moderator of authoritarian regimes, or in the period after the Cold War through the importation more specifically of a U.S. model of law firms and social justice entrepreneurs. We see this latter importation especially when the United States is highly influential and finds an elite willing to embrace U.S. approaches to build up their power at home. South Korea and Indonesia offer particularly good examples of U.S. influence in corporate law and in social entrepreneurship. The decline in the value of legal capital is not inevitable, however, nor can one count on the revamping of legal virtue when that capital has declined. The decline presents opportunities that may be seized by a new generation of lawyers. A political strategy may revive the credibility and value of law, which may lead again to decline.

In contrast to the earlier chapters that rely on historical accounts, the chapters on the challenges to and revivals of the role of law and lawyers rely to a great extent on personal interviews that we conducted in the countries that we studied. The interviews focus on the career trajectories of elite lawyers and competitors in the field of state power, in particular economists. They reveal the social background of lawyers, their investments in politics and the state, their relationships to business, their links to foreign contacts and expertise, and the strategies that they individually and collectively use to build professional credibility.

We conducted more than fifty interviews in each of the countries that we studied. We obtained names from a wide range of sources, including academic and journalistic accounts of the work of notables such as NGOs and activists, from publications and Web sites describing corporate law firms and NGOs, and from projects of court reform. We interviewed the deans of major law schools and business schools and the chairs of economics departments. We interviewed judges and individuals who had served in governmental roles. We made particular efforts to meet with the founders of leading institutions to see what factors and people came to produce a particular organizational innovation, such as corporate law firms or pioneering NGOs.

The detail of the interviews, as we stated above, makes it possible to get beyond the dichotomy of politics or markets. Legal professionals—

whether they are denoted activists, academics, corporate lawyers, judges, or politicians—cannot be understood apart from the web of local, national, and international relationships within which they operate. Challenges to law and lawyers and revivals of law and lawyers both depend on the social capital embedded in the law.

PART I

Introduction: Geneses of Law and State in Europe and Their Relationship to Colonial Ventures Abroad

Our inquiry will proceed through series of layers, each of which is necessary to understand the history and current situation in the Asian states we examine. We start in Renaissance Italy to make sense of the European genesis of the legal profession and to show its strict connection with the creation of the state (chap. 2). We see the emergence of certain models in other European countries as well, setting up organizational patterns that were carried by agents of colonialism into their colonial domains throughout the globe, including Asia. Chapter 3 looks especially at the paradigmatic colonial origins through trade and economic exploitation by the Dutch East Indies Company in what became Indonesia and the British East India Company in the Indian subcontinent. Unlike the situation in Latin America, which we studied in our earlier work (Dezalay and Garth 2002), law came to Asia initially through trade rather than through investment in colonial governance. The investment in governance came later in Asia with the exception of the Philippines under Spanish rule, which more resembled Latin America. Chapter 4 puts the U.S. approach to colonialism and law into the picture by examining how law came to North America and how lawyers and the legal profession came to play such a key role in the governance of the state and economy. As was the case in other colonial settings, the United States used its resources to try to pattern colonial governance on U.S.

governance—with a strong role for lawyers and markets and a relatively weak role for the state. In each case, the local result depends as much on local factors as it does on the model of law and state that the colonial power seeks to export.

CHAPTER TWO

European Geneses:
Models of Law and State Power

The structuring of legal and political spaces (and their relationship) in states shaped by colonialism, including those in Asia, is strongly marked by their colonial geneses and by the competition between imperial societies. The basic political strategies that structured legal fields in the periphery emerged initially in Europe and can be traced to specific histories of the European legal fields. The early histories show how configurations of political strategies crystallized into national models defining the profession and professional excellence in Europe. Europe is the starting point for law and the legal profession in other places, including in the United States and Asia. The European geneses that we see in this chapter were later translated and reenacted as colonial geneses.

Our purpose in this chapter is to introduce European approaches to law and state. It draws on a few leading sources rather than an extensive review of the literature. In addition to establishing the European approaches, we seek in this chapter to illustrate our basic problematic on the complementary relationship between law and politics—which is evident already in Renaissance Italy. This analysis of the origins of the legal profession and the state sets up the subsequent chapters focused more on the construction of that relationship through colonial experiences in Asia.

The European models for the relationship between lawyers and the state depicted in this chapter should be seen less as ideal types and more as the product of specific historical paths. We will nevertheless distinguish several models for that relationship, each of which highlights a particular legal strategy. There are many hybrids, however, and the hybrids proliferate in the Asian colonies discussed in this book. The models highlight dimensions that will also be seen in the Asian settings.

European Beginnings: Law and the Emergence of the City-State in Renaissance Italy

The very concept of the European state emerges from feudal society in tandem with lawyers playing double strategies that serve themselves and the emerging political powers. Legal expertise develops and is given value through investments in new institutions of state power. Rather than a dichotomy between law and state politics, both law and politics only make sense if one sees the mutual construction and transformation of each. The legal field serves as a crossroads where different forms of capital meet, circulate, and exchange. The processes of exchange and construction are characterized by double games of simultaneous investment in both politics and law, in oligarchic power and academic learning, and in local and international contexts. We see this with the emergence of the state in Italy.

The classic exposition of the emergence of law and state in Europe is Lauro Martines's book on *Lawyers and Statecraft in Renaissance Florence* (1968). The book examines the construction of the modern state through the development of city-states during the Italian Renaissance, and therefore shows also the growth of legal markets through early state investment. Martines shows how different types of capital—including economic, learned, cosmopolitan, political, and religious capital—are combined at the core of the legal field. The legal field facilitates the circulation of capital between different social groups and the exchange of economic capital into learned capital placed in the service of key institutions of the state. The relational capital and notoriety that come from the link to the state can then be turned into profits in the legal market and in the wider field of economic activity.

Martines's book can now be read in conjunction with James Brundage's recent book on *The Medieval Origins of the Legal Profession* (2008). Brundage reviews the establishment of Roman law in ancient Rome, and shows how, despite the fall of the Roman Empire, learned investment in this highly formalized law continued to attract elites who could put it in the service of dispute resolution and other activities. The key to developing what he calls a legal profession, however, was the establishment of the faculties of law, in particular the University of Bologna. The University of Bologna was operating by the second quarter of the twelfth century and was thriving in conjunction with a recognizable legal profession by the middle of the next century.

Study at the University of Bologna, which was essential to become a lawyer, lasted six to ten years and required competence in Latin and Greek. The length of the program alone made it costly even for very well-to-do families. The wealth requirements were also underscored by the very high cost of the opulent ceremonies associated with the doctorate. The very high barriers to entry therefore meant that access to the legal profession—including lawyers, judges, and professors—was in practice restricted to members of the aristocratic oligarchy or the wealthy bourgeoisie (Martines 1968: 41, 70).

The law degree appealed both to old families and to ascending ones ready to turn their economic wealth into the learned and cosmopolitan capital that was essential to enter the field of political power even at the local city-state level. Family and wealth mattered further in defining the elite of the legal profession. For the most august legal positions, such as that of an ambassador capable of negotiating treaties, appearing in papal courts, or handling arbitrations, it was necessary to have a famous name, family titles, and even greater financial resources.

Social mobility through the law was therefore highly limited and gradual—evolving over generations (Martines 1968: 68). New entry was initially limited to positions requiring less social and learned capital such as notaries and *procuradors*, which then facilitated the accumulation of more capital and access to higher positions (Martines 1968: 32). The strong connection between family capital and learned capital can be seen as a means to preserve the preeminence of the aristocratic and bourgeois families who had accumulated a diversified portfolio of symbolic capital. The new lines of entrepreneurs and merchants had to invest in learned and cosmopolitan capital in order to gain recognition in the field of political power. Thus, the notaries (eight to ten times more numerous than the lawyers) were not only underrepresented in the leadership ranks of the guilds but also handled the less prestigious and influential positions in the state—never serving as ambassadors or leading advisors, for example.

We can analyze this articulation between family capital and learned capital as part of the circulation of capital and resources. New accumulations of wealth are invested in institutions for the reproduction of legal learning. In return, those who possess the valued learned capital gain access to the most important positions in the legal field and in the field of state power. The grand professors were themselves well paid for their learned credentials. The same was true for those who negotiated treaties as ambassadors or handled disputes among merchants, state powers, or religious groups. In an era of economic and political turmoil, legal investment provided insurance for family capital. One could cash in on connections and family prestige (Martines 1968: 76), ideally by accumulating the positions of grand professor, lawyer, ambassador, and judge—or by providing advice or legal opinions in important matters of state.

Politics and markets of the law were strictly connected (Martines 1968: 107). The key to a great political career was the "relentless and able aggregation of clients, positions and offices" (1968: 112). Those from the newly ascending families, for example, sought a political sponsor as the best way to attract clients (1968: 393–94). The clients in turn sought a lawyer not only for legal expertise but also above all for the lawyer's ability to command authority in matters of importance in and around princely circles.

More particularly, the account of the relationship between lawyers and the emerging city-states makes it clear that it is far too simple to assign lawyers the role of architects of the modern state. Their role was more modest and complex. Rather than building the state, they instead provided legitimacy to princes who drew on their military and commercial power to conquer their political autonomy from the pope and from ecclesiastical authorities. They used their learned expertise to find ways to make that rule more legitimate. Among other things, the lawyers made themselves useful in state construction by finding doctrinal ways to bolster the position of princes, including reinterpreting the fundamentals of sovereignty according to Roman law.

The complexity of the role stems in part from the fact that the legal agents placing their expertise and social capital at the service of the new states were themselves also the products of the developing new state (Martines 1968: 476). Multiple turf battles among different and overlapping jurisdictions operating at the time provided one of the major markets for experts capable of interpreting texts to justify the claims of one or another client—including the councils of the Signoria in Florence or even the papal courts. Legal knowledge was a useful weapon on both sides in these battles (Martines 1968: 251).

More importantly, the lawyers were not content simply to take part in the competition among the different state powers—exacerbated by struggles for influence between families and clans who used various jurisdictions to serve their own private interests. They also helped to grow and transform the particular jurisdictions. As Martines shows, the new structures of state power were constructed "by raiding existing judicial power" (1968: 473). The modern state was constructed by absorbing more or less autonomous judicial organs constructed by feudal societies. New functions of the state could be served by renovated institutions through the expertise of lawyers. The value of legal expertise in the field of the major state institutions therefore came from the fact that it facilitated one of the principle strategies for the centralization of state power—the appropriation of judicial prerogatives that had been created within the older political regimes.

It might seem paradoxical that the elites of the legal field promote restrictions on the autonomy of the existing jurisdictions. But in fact the jurisdictions tended to be more seigneurial, communitarian, or religious in terms not only of who served as judges, but also the norms and operating procedures that were employed. Therefore the lawyers' strategy can be seen as the protection of judicial power in their own (and their families') interests by placing themselves in the front ranks of advisers to the new holders of state power—at the same time accelerating a process of legal rationalization again benefiting the representatives of legal science. The double game in this way was perfectly coherent with the earlier strategy of using legal expertise to inscribe and reconvert family capital into the new mechanisms of state power developing at the level of the city-states.

This double role and double identity of notable and jurist was therefore taken into account by the princes and the civic authorities that they employed. Indeed, more generally, the highest functions of the state were reserved to the lawyers belonging to the most prestigious families. And since the new leaders, notably in the case of the condottieri or those emerging in the battles between clans, had reasons to distrust the political ambitions of legal patricians possessing substantial family and economic capital, they often appealed to foreign lawyers having similar social and legal capital. Lacking the connections to a network of local familial power, foreign lawyers were more malleable and trustworthy in their service to those who hired them. Martines shows this process as it played out in Milan, where warrior leaders such as Visconti or Sforza gained power at the expense of the old family lines.

The major lesson of these descriptions, once again, is that it is necessary to go beyond the simple opposition between legal power and state power. The Italian historical example provides a kind of formula for the reproduction of lawyers as merchants of peace that we see repeated in numerous settings and with many local variations. According to this formula, there is an initial mix of family social capital and financial capital, which then provides the means to acquire—in effect, to convert—some of those resources into internationalized academic capital centered on Bologna during the time of the Renaissance. The resultant mix of academic and social capital provides access to powerful rulers and thus the further accumulation of political and relational capital, in demand as the basis for a profitable monopoly in markets for legal expertise and dispute resolution.

Three Models

The complex intermingling of state and law contains the basis for at least three models that tend to become paramount at certain times in particular sites. They contain emphases on one or another aspect of what we saw in the Italian history of the emergence of lawyers with the city-states. The models, as we have stated above, are the concrete products of opportunities and constraints of particular social contexts. Each model emerges during one historical period, crystallizes into certain recurring patterns, becomes central to the legitimacy and legitimating ideology of the legal profession, and then provides the basis for the reproduction of the model into subsequent generations. Three types can be specified as such and then related to historical examples approximating the models.

The first figure is the lawyer as a clerk in the sense given by Kantorowicz (1997). The clerk draws on learned capital to become a technician providing legitimacy to religious, royal, political, or other power. Kantorowicz highlights the particular case of the French notaries providing legitimacy to the crown. This first type is for the most part oriented externally, drawing on such activities as keeping books, providing statistics, serving bureaucratic functions, or even engaging in diplomacy or negotiation. The activities in the service of political power signal to the outside world that the power is being exercised according to legitimate criteria related to the expertise of the clerk.

The second figure or model is the mediator combining learned and relational capital to serve as intermediary or broker between different powers or as manager of social conflicts. The model develops in particular where the power is more fragmented rather than centralized in one leader. Thus lawyers in England served as agents and intermediaries between the papacy and English royalty or different feudal interests (Prest 1986), and there is a general pattern that we have already seen of lawyers brokering among interests in trade, business, land, and state.

The third type is the lawyer serving as a tribune or spokesperson for emerging groups. The representation serves to help those interests gain recognition from dominant social groups directly or through legal arguments or media campaigns. The French lawyers for the Jansenists and later the philosophes (Bell 1994) exemplify this model, which prefigures the "cause lawyers" seen in the United States and elsewhere (Sarat and Scheingold 1998).

We have already seen key elements of the first model in our account of Renaissance Italy. It is similar also to what develops subsequently in Portuguese and Spanish colonies in Latin America. Wealthy and aristocratic families invest in legal knowledge such as that initially produced for the Italians at the University of Bologna and later for the Latin Americans educated in Spain or Portugal. The legally educated elites put their legitimate expertise—acquired at some travel and expense—at the service of strong rulers such as the Italian condottieri—later the Latin American caudillos. In addition to providing the classic role of legitimating that rule, they also typically use their positions to mediate and provide diplomatic service both within and between city-states. They acquire considerable political capital and influence that can be converted into commensurate profits as they advise, negotiate, and handle disputes.

Great Britain provides another example of a second model that is a variation of the lawyer as clerk in the service of power (e.g., Prest 1986). The barristers since the fifteenth century were trained at the Inns of Court through a process that could last ten years and could be compared to education at a "finishing school" (Prest 1986). Those who accumulated sufficient social and learned capital were predisposed to serve as agents and intermediaries for the monarchy or for the landed aristocracy defending its independence against royal or religious power. They provided advice and resolved disputes, serving also as Justices of the Peace. The autonomy of the bar was therefore constructed on the basis of capital and activities attuned not only to legitimation but also to maintaining equilibrium within the field of political power. The activities of these

learned gentlemen as civilizers and guarantors of moderate power crystallized as a legitimating legal ideology. This highly successful strategy
became institutionalized in the barristers' monopoly on litigation and in
the production of learned legal knowledge.

France can be credited with the invention of the third model—public
advocates serving as spokespersons or tribunals of emerging social
groups (Bell 1994; Karpik 2000). In the case of the Parisian bar, the ar-
chetype of this kind of engagement, the initial embrace of the heretical
Jansenist cause in the early eighteenth century came from complex reasons. One cause was the monarchy's decision to raise money by selling
legal offices, preventing all but the richest lawyers from acquiring public offices (Bell 1994: 70). The less prosperous members of the bar then
had to find other strategies to valorize their competence. They increased
their investment in professional, scholarly, and civic strategies. This was
the period when disinterestedness was promoted, for example, by Henri
François d'Aguesseau (who died in 1751).

The defense of the public and the "citizen"—an ideal created as part
of these activities—became new sources of prestige,[1] especially as the
printing presses began to multiply and publications proliferated in part
around the Jansenist divide: "Young barristers saw participation in these
causes célèbres as a quick way to make names for themselves. . . . God
has put the church of Christ itself amongst your clients" (Bell 1994: 83).
Lacking the power to gain the perquisites of the state, the lawyers reconverted into pamphleteers, first in the service of the Jansenist bourgeoisie, and later serving the educated bourgeoisie of the enlightenment:
"Thus the career of barrister suddenly began to seem attractive not only
to upwardly-mobile bourgeois and would be Jansenist priests, but also
to would be philosophers" (Bell 1994: 83). The new developments also
led to recruitment to the bar of a more educated group. But contrary to
their elders seeking to be "high priests of the law" valued for their technical facility and political wisdom, the new arrivals sought above all to
gain access to public tribunals through rhetorical and theatrical abilities:
"genius, a good voice and the art of touching hearts" (Bell 1994: 94). As
a result, "barristers' careers reached new peaks as a result of the public's
endless taste for sensational causes célèbres" (Bell 1994: 94).

1. According to Bell, "Given that barristers could no longer aspire to high office, or
hope to influence royal policy, the late seventeenth century also saw the publication of a
flurry of works aimed at providing the bar with new professional ideals" (1994: 83).

The success of the strategy led to its extension to new causes célè-bres emerging from Enlightenment thought, then against the authoritarian regimes that came with the restoration of the empire. Even if the causes changed, the emerging strategy was fundamentally the same. It involved legal defense accompanied by a major investment in publicity, transforming the court into a tribunal for public opinion. The repeated process promoted both the lawyers and the tribunals into leaders of a public opinion that they of course helped to craft. Strengthened by the resultant notoriety, they became central to the markets in political representation.

The long pedigree of this strategy and its application to new contexts and themes made it appear natural and inevitable, as if the French bar had progressively discovered its true social function as champions of liberalism against arbitrary state power (Burrage 2006; Karpik 2000). This role took root in a variety of institutions, expertise, moral norms, and professional hierarchies, further making this role appear natural. By definition—or at least because of the manner of the construction of the profession and its discourses—the vocation of lawyers in France was to give voice to civil society against arbitrary acts of state power. This civic duty was seen as a moral obligation collectively inscribed in an ethic of disinterestedness. The pattern embedded in French professional hierarchies, in addition, did slow investment in more commercial markets, but there were nevertheless very clear rewards—economic and otherwise— from this professional strategy.

Further, the fame of the French Revolution, fed by lawyers reconverted into professional representatives of the public, favored the exportation of this model in which legal expertise and media campaigns reinforced each other.[2] The notoriety of arguments in the courts of the major

2. The same phenomenon could be found in Britain at the same time even though the model that ultimately predominated was closer to the lawyers serving and moderating state power. As Pue states, for example, "Nineteenth century English Barristers frequently acted much like their counterparts across the Channel . . . framing their argument in relation to issues of great national importance, translating individual grievance into constitutional cause and employing the privileged sanctum of the courtroom as a podium from which to address a wider public" (Pue 1997: 186). Similarly, "A high profile on circuit . . . could provide an excellent foundation from which to launch a political career of either an establishment or a radical sort" (Pue 1997: 186). As with respect to the lawyers supporting the Jansenists from the Paris Bar, their radical counterparts from the Inns of Court also encouraged their political allies to invest in the judicial scene: "Radicals of this era made

capitals paid dividends for launching political careers. Public recognition also translated into professional clients. The key point, however, is that the legal accumulation of political capital served to infuse legal capital with a greater social value. Put simply, lawyers succeeded in building their position as merchants of social peace. They could demonstrate to potential clients that it was worthwhile to invest in lawyers and legal representation for particular causes or conflicts. In this way, legal markets and politics sustained and nourished each other.

This model became a tremendous symbolic success, exported almost universally and serving to shift hierarchies in the legal field. The bar could be seen as the natural champion of liberal values embedded in civil society against the excesses of autocratic rulers. Access to justice in this way became one of the rallying cries and legitimating ideologies of the bar. And the privileging of public advocacy helped to place lawyers tied too closely to commerce relatively low in the French legal hierarchy.

Germany can be credited with the development of a Prussian model that provides a contrast to the three linked to the Italian history of the city-state (Rueschemeyer 1997). This model could be termed "professionalization from above" or the "disciplinarization of legal expertise." Lawyers serve as experts and agents on behalf of state power. The construction of the centralized Prussian state in the nineteenth century came through the dismantling and bureaucratization of decentralized aristocratic justice. There was first a purge and then bureaucratization compensated for by the relative monopoly that was created. The failed mobilization of the bar in the liberal revolution and divisions in German society (anti-Semitism as one) helped contribute to a separation between the state bureaucracy and the private bar that reemerged in Germany. Legal elites were able to rebuild their credibility through reinvestment in academic knowledge. Law as science (e.g., Friedrich Carl von Savigny) contributed to the reversal of a long decline of legal academia and the creation of a new model of law as a policy science in the service of a strong modernist ruler. Here again there was great success in the international export of this model, notably to Meiji Japan, China, and Korea. We also see basic features of this model in a more general usage as an aspect of a cold war strategy to encourage "modernizing states," often led by the military.

---

the fullest use of law to advance their goals . . . using the law pro-actively in their own interests" (Pue 1997:187).

A return to Italy illustrates some of the hybrid variations on the European models that continued to take shape. Italy at the time of the Resorgimento in the nineteenth century, as Maria Malatesta has shown (2002), saw considerable prominence go to the lawyer-politician as a broker between private (family) capital and public institutions. Neopolitan lawyers played a role as importers of the French/Napoleonic model. Then they became reexporters as part of a diaspora that took place when the restoration of the Bourbon monarchy in Naples forced them into exile. In exile, many converted into political and ideological agents of unification led by the Piedmont monarchy. Lawyers served as brokers between landowning families and the state in order to invest in and profit from growing state intervention: public construction of housing, roads, and railways on private land, for example—a process that takes place all over Europe (Kostal 1994) and indeed throughout the world. The brokering experience at both the local and central political levels led to the accumulation of relational capital later valorized and consolidated in political careers. Lawyer-politicians were in this manner able to control state bureaucracies through clientelist practices and then sell this key resource of contacts to propertied clients—fueling the growth of a profitable professional market for those able to gain the position of power brokers.

In all these cases we see efforts by the elite of the bar to gain the position as the state nobility or noblesse d'état, endowed with a double legitimacy—one as the agent for the rationalization of governmental practice, the other as civilizer, mediator, and moderator of political struggles around state power. Nevertheless, even if these models in practice converge toward the same objective, the strategies and the paths followed vary significantly. The variations can be traced to national political histories and national variations in the ability to mobilize learned capital combined with elitist social capital (United Kingdom), bureaucratic capital (Germany), or political capital (France). We now explore what happens when the products of these histories both in terms of the laws and the state move to colonial settings, mainly through expatriates and traders.

CHAPTER THREE

Expatriates and Traders in Early Colonial State Building in Asia

Colonial states are imported states (Badie 1992) in the sense that they are produced in substantial part by the activities of lawyers and laws exported by the colonial powers. Following the chapter on European origins, we now turn to the movement from Europe to Asian colonies. The exported and imported models are "texts without context" (Bourdieu 2002). The legal institutions exported into the colonial settings look very similar to the European models, but they are structured and function with notable differences. The differences relate to three features typical of the colonial settings and the lawyers and legal institutions transplanted there.

The first feature is that the legal field in the colonial settings favors elites even more than was seen in Europe. One reason is the heightened importance of cosmopolitan capital in the local colonial contexts. Elites must have a way to engage and relate to the European colonial powers, and those with cosmopolitan capital are better equipped for that engagement. A second reason is the very high cost of access to the rather few positions available to gain a legal education, particularly when it required travel abroad to colonial faculties of law. It was very difficult to acquire the learned capital requisite for the law degree, and privileged groups were much more likely to gain access to that capital. Finally, colonial governments seeking to delegate and legitimate their administrations often quite consciously sought to co-opt local elites as their protégés.[1]

---

1. Building on the work of Nathan Brown (1995), Ronen Shamir (2000: 108) wrote, "If we wish to understand colonial legal systems, we must pay more attention to local elites."

A second feature of the colonial settings is an even closer connection and intermixing between law and the field of political power than that which existed in Europe. The members of the legal elite in Asia were especially likely to be characterized by the accumulation of different forms of capital, by multiple positions in the state and the economy, and by close family connections within a ruling oligarchy. It was typical for the colonial elite, for example, to be lawyers, professors, and politicians (or even leaders of the military) at the same time.

The third feature is that the production and legitimation of learned capital remained centered in the capitals of the European colonists. The colonial relationship and the distance between center and periphery ensured the dominance of European producers of learned legal capital. Identities at the periphery might also be fragmented and loyalties accordingly further divided. It was therefore more difficult to build the autonomy of colonial legal practices from the fields of power in the European center or from those in the colonial periphery. A cause and reflection of these characteristics is that the activities of the notables of law in the colonial settings were strictly intertwined with major battles for the control of state power.

The features that were typical of colonial relationships were echoed by a similar process seen in certain Asian countries not associated with the specifically colonial export of law and lawyers. Countries that were dominated or threatened by imperial politics elected to import European legal models as a strategy of fighting fire with fire. The strategy was typically implemented by local elites seeking to strengthen their hand in modernization and in the construction of a strong state. Brown notes, for example that "law might serve to rob imperialism of its ideology" (Brown 1995: 115). Countries could "civilize" through law before being forced to by colonial powers. The process allowed national elites to push aside colonial pressures and even play on the competition among colonial powers.

The result generally was a decoupling of the transplants in the colonial contexts that was also a reenactment of the European geneses described in the previous chapter. Law served as an instrument of imperialist strategy resting in large part on the co-optation of local elites recruited on the basis of their social capital—exemplified by the "pure Christians" in Latin America, the Indian Brahmins, the Malay aristocracy in Malaysia, the *ilustrados* in the Philippines, and the Javanese aristocrats in Indonesia. Legal expertise tied to the colonists served as local political capital. Law faculties abroad, as we shall describe in subsequent chapters, typically produced key statesmen who were able to occupy major roles in the field of state power.

The heteronomy of the legal fields at the periphery was reinforced by the geographic distance from the centers for the (re)production of legitimate legal knowledge. In the classic model, therefore, innovation in legal expertise in the periphery became controlled by local notables of the law. Innovations produced in the European capitals were carefully reinterpreted in light of local conditions and the strategic position of the importers—part of the actual process of "decoupling." Another reason for the general lack of autonomy for the local institutions—courts, faculties of law, and the bar—was that they were relatively new and under the control of local elites. The process then led to a double role for local elites investing in the construction of nations. In India, Indonesia, Malaysia, the Philippines, and Singapore, in particular, they reconverted from colonial agents into founding fathers.

The key point is not that the transplants into the colonial settings "failed" because they were turned to the interests of colonial elites originally co-opted into the colonial system. What occurred in the colonial settings was less a failure than a reenactment of the genesis of the legal fields within fields of state power in Europe. There was a kind of telescoping effect in political-legal practices that moves back to the European prehistory. By the time of colonization, there had already been a relatively long process of autonomization of the legal field in relation to the political field in Europe. For reasons already explored, the colonial settings were not characterized by much autonomy between law and politics. The role and importance of law depended on the mobilization of key players in the field of state power. The extent of that mobilization depended on the valuation of legal capital at particular times within specific colonial powers and according to the approach to governance of any given colony.

This reenactment in the colonial setting, moreover, was marked by the circumstances that brought lawyers abroad from Europe. Indeed, a fundamental divide in exploring relationships between law and the state is not that between common law and civil law, or between different images of empires. It is between law in the service of trade and law as an aspect of colonial governance. The reenactment in Asia did not replicate specifically the path that led to the three models and strategies given in the preceding chapter, although all could be found in the Asian colonies.

The founding lawyers abroad in Asia started as traders and only later re-converted toward investment in state building.

This feature of lawyers in Asia provides a basic difference with the situation in Latin America, in particular. In Latin America, lawyers from the beginning served primarily as agents to implement the policies of the Spanish and Portuguese crowns. There too, relatively late in colonial history, after the colonial powers invested more in law and legal legitimacy as part of a counteroffensive to legitimate their colonies, lawyers began to assume a greater role in state building (Perez-Perdomo 2006; Brown 1995). While lawyers in Latin America and Asia both developed a role in state building, the differences in origins have continued to produce differences in the structures of the professions and their role in the state. We trace these origins in Asian colonies in the following sections of this chapter.

Trading Companies and Colonial Outposts: Early Geneses of Colonial Law and Lawyers

Trade and commerce characterized most early legal investment in the Asian colonies. The paradigmatic examples are the Dutch East Indies Company and the British East India Company, whose activities we examine in shaping the colonial origins of Indonesia and India, respectively, but similar stories are found throughout Asia. The major exception in the colonial origins of law is the Philippines, which as a Spanish colony had an early colonial history similar to that in Latin America. We provide detail on the Philippines in chapter 4, but the focus of this chapter is on the role of the trading companies.

There were many similarities, not surprisingly, between the approaches characteristic of the British East Indian Company in the Indian Subcontinent and the Dutch East Indies Company in Indonesia (Leue 1992). The genesis in each case related specifically to the commercial companies exporting their models into the trading settings. As Leue notes, "The Europeans carried their law with them wherever they went" (1992: 137). They created the "merchant-judge" as a counterpart to the justices of the peace familiar to them, and they conferred a similar mix of powers on them. In Leue's words, "The governor of an English presidency town was at once head of the executive, legislator, chief justice and a big trader in his own right, and the same holds true of high company functionaries everywhere" (1992: 154). Furthermore, "like the squires some 'trading justices' turned their position to financial profits," yet in general the colonial judges were "too rich to be corrupt," "proud to do hard public work," yet "often ignorant and prejudiced" and "a law unto themselves" (Leue 1992: 157). The merchant-judges, as the quotations indicate, were above all merchants and administrators with little familiarity with the actual law of their home countries. As Mines (2001) points out for Madras, "until near the end of the . . . eighteenth century, justice in Madras was administered by merchant judges who were Company servants whose principal purpose in India was trade." In the assessment of Leue, this justice developed out of the idea that merchants-judges-administrators, like captains of their ships, had to be "masters of their house" in territories that could be vast and often dangerous as well. Their aim was to amass a fortune as quickly as possible, and their personal interests were therefore often in conflict with those of the companies they served (Leue 1992: 140).

The merchants working for the trading companies created systems of dual justice. There was one system of European justice with decisions recognized within the colonizing states—decisions with respect to financial payments and the repatriation of inheritances to the metropolis, for example. It was necessary to keep these matters aside from indigenous customs and adjudications. The merchants also sought to avoid strictly indigenous conflicts that were thought to be of lesser importance, stepping in only to take on challenges to their authority within their enclaves by external sovereigns. They had mayors' courts that functioned as appellate courts—often staffed with notable indigenous people who could rule on local or ethnic customs. As a rule, in short, they left the "adjudication of petty cases in the hands of the native hereditary village headman" (Leue 1992: 133). Examples included "caste arbitration" and the work of "Chinese captains" or "choultry judges."

Nevertheless, there was a relative porosity between the two systems of justice, and the European courts were popular among the indigenous populations, perhaps because they were able to make and enforce legal orders rather than seeking the consensus and compromise associated with other local processes (Leue 1992: 149). This basic approach translated to a dual system involving the recognition and delegation of small disputes among indigenous people to notable representatives of the groups charged with doling out "traditional" justice, and also giving to these notables (often employed by or protégés of the company) the power to act as courts of appeal in other matters.

The relative porosity also could draw on existing institutional homologies between the colonies and the colonizers. In particular, already in India in the eighteenth century, as Bernard S. Cohn observed (1961), *vakils*—indigenous lay advocates—acted often as agents of powerful groups: "All of the political leaders, great or small, had their wakils [alternative spelling] at major courts and political centers. In addition, zamindars [large landowners] and local figures had their agents to look after their interests in local political centers." The rich and politically powerful had their agents to deal on their behalf with "other rich and powerful persons" (Cohn 1961: 626–27). Similarly, Lev (1972) points out that in Indonesia there was a local lawyerlike role as agent serving the princely houses in Java. In both cases, therefore, there were indigenous practices that could be used to build the role of the lawyer as broker.

The early colonial processes could therefore fit a local model and each could reinforce the other. Mutual reinforcement also came from the merchants' role in the process. In effect, the merchants were playing like judges, and they encouraged indigenous advocates to bring assortments of local practices to them. As Paul noted for India, there were no formal requirements for the individuals who "styled themselves 'solicitors' or 'attorneys'" in the company courts between 1640 and 1727 (Paul 1991: 13). Not surprisingly, the combinations of roles also served to give greater importance to social capital than to legal capital.

This model was more or less the same for the two trading companies. At one point, in fact, there was an earlier evolution by the Dutch toward increased investment in institutions of governance. As we shall see, the two countries' policies then began to diverge. The British transformed their position considerably in favor of law and governance. This first encounter in both settings, however, was characterized by relatively little legal investment on the part of the trading companies in the countries in which they operated. The result was that in each place there were merchant-judges, characterized by relatively little interest in their own law or local norms and practices, and local conflicts were delegated to indigenous notables who tended to be allies and protégés of the trading companies. The focus was on trade and not governance.

Territorial Expansion and Increasing Investment in Governance

The second phase was characterized by territorial expansion and an evolution toward state regulation—initially through taxation policies in order to cover military expenses, then with the development of a cadre of administrative support. This phase was marked by increasing legal investments on the part of the colonizers, which built also on the co-optation of individuals from among more-educated indigenous groups. Since the policies of the two major trading companies began to diverge substantially, we separate them in the following sections.

India: Becoming Britain's Shining Example of Empire

The changes in India are well documented in recent work by Roland Lardinois focusing on the formative period of 1760–1810 (2008). According to Lardinois, in the eighteenth century, with the weakening of the Moghul Empire on the Indian Subcontinent, the East India Company began to take over some of the functions of a state. The various communities behind the East India Company, including bankers, shareholders, the British government, ship owners, and others all had varying interests, but the key division that Lardinois focuses on was between state and commerce. The state side was linked to the military arm of the company, and the trade side centered on the civilian traders. In the beginning, the traders prevailed, insisting, as the ambassador of the company, Thomas Roe, stated in 1615 to a Moghul sovereign, that "war and commerce are incompatible" (Lardinois 2008: 92). Conflict developed as the military began to occupy more land, in particular Bengal in the period 1750–60, justifying the occupation with claims to more taxes, which in turn accelerated conflicts with the Moghuls and led to more occupation.

Both sides of this conflict prospered in India, and they used their profits in part to take their side of the disputes to London—even buying political seats to promote their positions. Their wealth led them already to be labeled nabobs within England. The civilian traders tended to favor the Tories, while the military went with the Whigs (Lardinois 2008: 93) as debates over the power conceded to the company took place in England. The escalation of the costs of empire also brought increased tensions in London. The enlightened elite in London began to publish pamphlets and to criticize the corruption and scandals associated with the imperial policies. They began to call for a government founded more on "justice and humanity" (Lardinois 2008: 95). English ideals—including those identified with the legal profession and virtues of the English rule of law—began to play a larger role in the assessments of empire.

The battle for more humanitarian policies was taken up by Edmund Burke and others. The policies in India were central to British politics in London. Evangelism also began to play a role in India (as it did at the same time in the American colonies). With trade competition accelerating in India and elsewhere, including the impending loss of the American colonies, new groups of traders seeking to open up India began to ally with missionaries. The interests seeking to attack the monopoly of the company grew in strength. As criticism increased further in Britain, the British Crown began to assert more control. One prominent move was the creation of a Supreme Court in India, located in Calcutta and under the authority of the Crown rather than the company. The courts also were reformed in India as part of the same process (Lardinois 2008: 97). Over a thirty-year period, the Supreme Court combined common law and local custom while setting the stage for a legal Raj. The events in Britain and in India thus came together to change the orientation of the empire. As Jennifer Pitts states in her book on British attitudes toward empire, by the end of the 1790s, "Justification of British imperial rule . . . began to rest primarily on arguments that Britain brought (and was alone capable of bringing) good government to India" (2005: 16). The idealistic claims of empire pushed by missionaries and a growing domestic group came to dominate the legitimating rhetoric. Investment in law accordingly picked up and no doubt encouraged more attention to India by lawyers making their careers in Britain.

Henceforth, rather than oppression in terms of corruption and violence, there were "more subtle forms of oppression such as onerous taxation and export polities, policies that were justified as part of a system of improvement in which the benefits of secure property and the rule of law were said to replace despotic indigenous governments" (Pitts 2005: 16). Education became a higher priority for the British in India as part of this shift. As Niall Ferguson stated (2004: 189), "the proponents of modernizing as well as evangelizing India seized on the idea of giving Indians access to Western education." Ferguson further quotes Thomas Babington Macaulay: "We must do our best to form a class who may be interpreters between us and the millions whom we govern; a class of persons, Indian in blood and colour, but English in taste, in opinions, in morals, and in intellect" (2004: 189).

Co-optation and law thus accelerated with the move toward more idealistic views of empire and a heightened focus on governance. Public scandals associated with the company accelerated the move. By the early nineteenth century, the company was controlled by the state, with missionaries and traders on the wane. The company became weaker and weaker, eventually going bankrupt. The Indian Raj was then created in 1858.

Bernard Cohn traces the local involvement in the changing focus on governance (1996). Efforts by the East India Company to collect taxes for its military and other operations made it necessary, according to Cohn, to employ "subtle natives" to aid them—even though the British feared manipulation by the intermediaries. In 1772, the governor general created a core of "collectors" to rationalize the collection and serve as both colonial administrators and justices of the peace. The company encouraged young employees also to study classical languages, in particular Sanskrit, to short-circuit the intermediaries in interpreting "Indian norms."

In researching those norms, in addition, the servants assumed that the Brahmins, given the status almost of law professors with "respect amounting to idolatry," were the key sources (Cohn 1996: 66). They began the task of compiling and translating rules from shastric to Persian and Persian to English. Sir Williams Jones (a Persian scholar, politician, barrister, and judge of the Crown Court of Calcutta) became the "Justinian" of Indian law by following Edmund Burke and others in rejecting the notion that British law should be imposed in India. But the British did not want to be at the mercy of indigenous intermediaries such as the pandits. The task was completed by Jones's successor, Colebrook (son of a banker of the East Indian Company, well educated but not legally trained) (Cohn 1996: 72).

The enterprise of codification then allowed the presentation of a supposedly ancient Indian set of laws. British judges could appropriate it as the legitimate representation of religious and indigenous custom and reinterpret it according to the techniques of the common law. In this task they also drew on the support of the educated Brahmin elite—serving as cultural courtiers.

This process successfully bolstered the authority of the Raj by combining a public strategy of moral authority with a colonial enterprise supported by multiple forms of social, political, and learned capital. It could draw on the bureaucracy of the company as well as the authority of a Justinian-like compilation linked to local elites as professors and oracles of the law. Judges could then interpret the compilations according to common law principles leading toward more utilitarian norms (Stokes 1959).

There was also an element of competition under the new regime that made the courts increasingly important. As noted by Pamela Price,

> as caste organization became increasingly separated from the organization of state activities and the defense of territory, kin conflicts took different turns.... Anglo-Indian courts succeeded, in the course of the nineteenth century, in assuming authority of settlement for conflicts involving large sums of money and substantial areas of land. Institutions of kin-caste governance had evolved in a political landscape of semi-autonomous domains and local units of rule. In an over-arching system of persistent centralization, they could not successfully compete. (1989: 160–61)

Colonial policy in India, therefore, moved more from trade to governance—and more toward idealism—consistent with a changing balance of power in London and a need for a new rationale to justify empire. Accordingly, "justice and community" became more important ingredients. The evolving approach strengthened the Anglo-Indian courts, attracted many locals into the system, and helped establish the courts for major claims regarding land. Indians were participants at all levels, including a Brahmin elite used as cultural courtiers to help codify a so-called Indian body of law. Both sides connected, therefore, setting the stage very nicely for the emergence of a well-positioned and elite legal profession in India.

Indonesia: The Durability of the Trading Colony

There was very little investment by the Dutch in law in Indonesia. One key reason, as Romain Bertrand (2008) shows, was that the Dutch were long ambivalent about this colonial venture. The Dutch government did not have a strong commitment to the imperial project. The Dutch East Indies Company, established in 1602, was a project supported by a new and relatively marginal bourgeois class set apart from the landowning elite and the urban patrician class in the Netherlands (Bertrand 2008:

108). A new group of merchants with strictly commercial ambitions sought to compete effectively with the British East India Company established in 1600. What they found in Java was a group of small states controlled by highly aristocratic sultans. The Javanese aristocrats, moreover, were quite used to external trade given their experience with the Chinese, the Gujarati from India, and others. They in fact had some disdain for trade and were content to let others occupy social positions identified with trade.

The learned Javanese aristocracy, accordingly, was comfortable dealing with foreign traders and with keeping them at a distance. They did not object to the commercial dominance of Dutch traders. The Dutch could insert themselves into a Javanese history that led to a simple division of role. It was not just that the Dutch had relatively little interest in colonial governance in Indonesia. They had no motive to get further involved given the relatively comfortable position they occupied and from which they could reap generous profits without disturbing the Javanese aristocracy.

The dual system of justice was consistent with the division of interests. The matters involving expatriates were handled by a Dutch system, with Dutch lawyers, and with no attention to the indigenous adat. The Dutch asserted the prevailing civil code tenet that "custom does not bind." The colonial bureaucracy was concerned only with the goal of making their exploitation efficient. Before 1850, accordingly, there was no program even to learn indigenous languages. Language familiarity came only later when a few self-taught anthropologists began to interest themselves in local customs. This interest led to a few preliminary efforts to build bridges to local groups. In particular, the Dutch produced a penal code in 1873 specifically for indigenous groups. In fact, however, it was little more than a copy of the European version with some local variations.

The so-called "discovery of adat law," led by Cornelis Van Vollenhoven, helped transform the colonial approach. Van Vollenhoven began his career as private secretary of J. T. Kremer, a colonial leader of industry, political liberal, and Minister of Colonial Affairs. The double system of law in Indonesia began to be questioned at the end of the nineteenth century by Christian political parties and missionaries in part because of the ambiguous legal status of Indonesians converted to Christianity. Kremer and Van Vollenhoven proposed a compilation and codification of the adat law. Late in the century, accordingly, they began what became a flourishing science of adat law. As in India, the move toward a different rationale for colonialism, more attuned to idealism and the missionary project, brought some efforts to take seriously what was considered to be local and customary law.

In 1901, on behalf of a Christian coalition government, Colonel Idenburg launched a new "ethical policy" to elevate the indigenous population in Indonesia. The balance of forces within the Netherlands shifted and pushed the Dutch to make the empire more legitimate. The policy was initially implemented by Dutch lawyers who practiced in Java, but their initial approach was to denounce the supposedly archaic adat in favor of modern Dutch law that was seen to be indispensable for Indonesian progress associated with modernity and good governance. The Dutch Parliament, spurred by Van Vollenhoven, rejected this approach. Local law was seen as part of a more legitimate form of governance. The students of adat under Van Vollenhoven then "obtained important positions in the colonial administration" (Lev 1972: 251). The actual codification of the adat was difficult, however, and Van Vollenhoven himself rejected the task. The result was that much discretion was left in the hands of judges ostensibly charged with implementing the Indonesian customary law. The adat law, therefore, as we shall see in chapter 7, remained in an ambiguous position. For some it was an illegitimate creature of the Dutch, for others the embodiment of legitimate indigenous law, and for others the obstacle to modern law.

The belated effort to work through local custom to make the colonial relationship more legitimate coincided with the effort to invest in local elites to facilitate and legitimate colonial governance. As part of the ethical policy, the first steps toward legal education of the Indonesians began in 1909, and the law faculty at Batavia finally opened in 1924. Legal education was an elite proposition, however. Indeed, Lev wrote, "When legal training was finally made available to Indonesians, it was confined to Javanese priyayi (the traditional aristocracy). Since legal training was seen as preparatory to government service, only the sons of high priyayi . . . were encouraged to study law; the traditional elite was to be modernized, not expanded" (Lev 1972: 256).

Legal training among local elites was therefore late and small scale. The private profession remained small with very few local lawyers. In short, therefore, despite the late efforts associated with the ethical policy, the Dutch legal legacy was clearly quite limited in comparison to the Raj in India. Pressure was slow to develop from within the Netherlands, and the Javanese elites did not in turn make demands to participate in governance. Imperial legal investment in local elites was slow and late in Indonesia.

Contrasts from Japan and China: Legal Professions in the Resistance to Colonial Domination

We now briefly compare the quasi-colonial investment in the law in China and Japan around the same time period. We offer them to show some strong differences and also to set the stage for the Korean story, which depends greatly on the colonial domination of Korea by Japan. In Japan, the era of legal reform began after the Meiji restoration of 1868. Concessions were made in confrontations with the demands of the imperial powers, who insisted in the 1850s "that Japan lacked a legal infrastructure—contract, credit, commercial transactions, a system of courts—that would permit it to conduct trade with the West" (Feeley and Miyazaya 2007: 159). Seeking to learn the techniques from the West, the Meiji government promoted legal education. Some of those who received that education from English- and American-trained teachers began to assert the need for an independent legal profession (Feeley and Miyazaya 2007: 160). In 1895, as a response to the potential of an emerging legal profession, "the government dramatically revised the content and the structure of legal education," moving from Anglo-American law to "German law and legal training, which was thought to be more in line with stronger state control" (Feeley and Miyazaya 2007:161).

The result was a kind of truncated legal importation. Legal resources were put mainly in the service of the central state with only a very small group of private practitioners. The law was used to reinforce the power of the state through state control over the production of legal norms and the judiciary itself. The leading faculties of law such as Todai—the University of Tokyo—were at the heart of this strategy for the reproduction and legitimation of elites, but their learned autonomy was relatively limited through processes of recruitment tied to social and scholarly capital. As Dahrendorf pointed out for Germany, even though legal science was at the core of the law's legitimacy, the privileged students invested very little in it. They instead acquired social capital through such activities as dueling and drinking. They left arcane legal science to less socially endowed or Jewish students (Dahrendorf 1969). There was likely a similar division of labor in Japan. The professors in Japan—the custodians of legal science—were in any event translators and repeaters of an imported knowledge. The law itself tended to play a largely formal or even ornamental role. This instrumentalization of law and its subordination to the authoritarian power of the state then accelerated with the increase in power of the military in the control of the state.

The strategy of fighting fire with fire—importing law but keeping it in a relatively marginal position—helped limit the role of private lawyers. Certainly there were hints of some development on the private side, linked especially to the United States and legal missionaries circulating around the turn of the century (and seen especially in the Philippines, as shown in chaps. 4 and 6).

The Chinese similarly opted for legal reforms largely in order to gain legitimacy from foreign imperial powers (He 2005). The Chinese elites invested in legal training that would serve the state, therefore, following what we saw as the Prussian—and Japanese—model. The relationships to the Western powers, and especially to the United States, however, also helped to develop a private profession emerging partly in opposition to local hierarchies, especially the traditional local cartels. This group was characterized by strong imported investment by foreign missionaries on behalf of the law and saw a rapid increase in the importance of the colonial courts before the entire edifice was toppled. The vehicle for the introduction was the role of Shanghai as an entrepôt.

Shanghai was the point of entry for the colonial powers imposing themselves as traders and investors in China. The business environment was highly risky and unorganized, with both local competition and competition among the imperial powers (T. Lee 1993). The foreign courts, set up, as elsewhere, to decide cases involving foreign traders according to foreign norms, took advantage of a market opportunity and lowered barriers to entry for outsiders, including foreigners and the Chinese. In contrast to the prior models of dual justice, these courts were used more by the Chinese than by the Europeans. From 1914 to 1925, "Chinese suits outnumbered foreign suits by about four to one" (T. Lee 1993: 1349). These courts thus "insinuated themselves into the Shanghai commercial scene" (T. Lee 1993: 1350). Fees were low, and lawyers were not required—although they were frequently used especially as the number of law graduates increased. The foreign courts carved out a pro-plaintiff, pro-business approach in favor of creditors, landlords, landowners, and speculators, and they had enforcement powers not available to the

Chinese courts. Between 1916 and 1935, the number of cases grew rapidly, Chinese judges replaced the foreign judges, and the foreign courts were incorporated into the national judicial system by the regime of Chiang Kai-shek in 1927.

One feature of this imported legal investment was the creation of the Soochow Law School in 1915, which allowed the development of a new elite of Chinese legal professionals. The law school, as described in Allison Conner's splendid study (1994), was founded through the initiative of missionaries and idealists, including Charles Rankin, a lawyer and professor of political science as well as a Protestant fundamentalist. Rankin thus emphasized the "God given opportunity to render an outstanding service to the young republic" (Conner 1994: 5). The Soochow Law School was a night school with teachers recruited from among the lawyers and judges associated with the foreign concessions. The second dean, W. W. Blume, from the University of Michigan Law School, for example, sought to distinguish the students from the "traditional pettifoggers and the bad practice for which they were notorious" (Conner 1994: 17). He emphasized the case method, legal ethics, and preparation for the Shanghai international commercial environment. Law was taught in English. In contrast to other schools, which produced the vast number of law graduates and were oriented toward service to the government, the Soochow Law School produced practitioners who came to represent some twenty percent of the Shanghai Bar and much of its leadership.

The students initially came from Christian families but by the 1920s were drawn increasingly from the commercial and professional families of Shanghai: tea merchants, silk traders, bank directors and managers of foreign hongs, small businessmen, or company clerks. The school emphasized social mobility according to its missionary ideals, but the tuition was relatively high. The family of Soochow Law graduates also reproduced itself. By the end of the 1930s, about a third of the students came from the legal milieu. The link to law abroad was further strengthened by the fact that about fifteen percent of the graduates continued with studies abroad.

Through this institution the expatriate lawyers succeeded in training their successors, but this success was in a relatively closed environment. Soochow trained practitioners. The vast majority of the 1,200 graduates produced over three decades became international practitioners or worked for banks and insurance companies. A small number became judges or professors, but very few went into the government—in contrast to the Chaoyang Law School (10,000 graduates in two decades). There was very little investment in nationalist politics and, of course, even less in the communist movement. This private and Western-oriented legal profession was very small in contrast to the state-led legal investment in legitimating the government. Chinese governments quite naturally protected their role, which was consistent with the more general strategy to bring law as a way to resist a colonial imposition that might threaten the governing state.

While similar in important respects to Japan, the Chinese during the age of colonialism exhibited a stronger genesis of a foreign-oriented private profession linked to foreign trade and business. It also included developments in legal education such as Soochow. But, as in Japan, the strong investment by the state in law in the service of the state was certainly dominant. The circumstances of the origins and the relatively weak position assigned to private lawyers left a relatively marginal legacy for the legal profession.

Concluding Thoughts: Different Paths to Potential Legal Weakness

In all the Asian countries we studied, with Japan and China in a similar position, law was in a position to be denounced as a tool of the colonialists. In India much more than in Indonesia, however, there was a relatively sustained effort and a stronger local connection that together could build the local position of law and lawyers. As we shall see, India is relatively unique in this respect. The stories of Hong Kong, Malaysia, and Singapore, in varying degrees also show relatively weak legal legacies of colonialism. Similarly, the legal profession in South Korea, with Japan as colonizer, had a quite inauspicious beginning, again leaving very little to build on when South Korea became independent from Japan at the close of World War II.

The Philippines, as we shall see, is like India in the relatively high degree of colonial investment in law and lawyers. We turn now to the development of the legal profession in the United States for two purposes. First, the United States replaced the Spanish as the colonial master of the Philippines at the turn of the twentieth century, and it is important to trace the origins of the U.S. approach used ostensibly to turn the

Philippines into a showcase for democracy and the rule of law. Second, and more importantly, we also see in the Philippines the development of the more general U.S. pattern of legal investment—anti-imperial imperialism—that has provided a strong component of U.S. foreign policy since that time.

Lawyers and the Construction of U.S. "Anti-Imperialist" Imperialism and a Foreign Policy Elite

W e turn now to the approach of the United States to empire, which provides a key to understanding many of the recent revivals of law in Asia. Consistent with our effort to understand the role of law by exploring the geneses of law and state, we proceed in two parts. The first, very briefly, draws on recent historical scholarship to shed light on why the legal profession was so central to the U.S. imperial efforts in the Philippines (and elsewhere). The second then explores the construction of moral imperialism in the Philippines itself. Although in a somewhat different way, the Philippines, like India, became a showcase empire in terms of investment in law and legal institutions.

Legal Geneses in the American Colonies

The history of law and the legal profession in the United States is complex, but one obvious theme is that the colonial period saw considerable legal investment take place over a relatively long period of time. One result, as Alexis de Tocqueville famously pointed out in the nineteenth century, was that lawyers could be depicted as a kind of aristocracy in the United States.

To summarize briefly, the European colonization of North America brought a mix of social experiments. They included the Massachusetts Bay Colony and Pennsylvania, both with an early hostility to lawyers and the legal profession; a plantation economy equally hostile, exemplified by the Chesapeake region; and a Dutch-style trading colony represented by New York City (Konig 2008: 157, 162). As we have seen elsewhere, the colonists generally brought and replicated what they had known in England—the justice of the peace system.[1] Writing about Virginia and Massachusetts, David Thomas Konig notes that, "The justices of the peace who controlled the colonial county courts were, like those who controlled the quarter session courts in England, the men of affairs of the county . . . —[a] pattern of rule by a hierarchy of status and wealth" (2008: 159). Furthermore, despite the hostility initially to lawyers in some places, "Legal practitioners abounded in the early colonies, both in number and in variety" (Bilder 2008: 93). Many were trained at the British Inns of Court, some served in governing positions, and others—many of whom may have been self-taught—occupied a variety of notable positions (Bilder 2008: 93–94).

The place of lawyers gained strength. Around 1700, according to William Henretta, "a new legal regime staffed by lawyers was coming into existence in British North America. An important cause was the program of imperial administrative and legal reform undertaken by legal officials in the 1680s" (2008: 564–65). By 1720, there was a "nascent system of common law courts" (Henretta 2008: 569) and a more English style of procedure and advocacy. According to historians, the number of actual lawyers is not clear (Konefsky 2008: 71), but, "The social power and influence of colonial lawyers far exceeded their numbers" (Konefsky 2008: 71). Legal arguments were central to the War for Independence and in the making of the Constitution. Lawyers in the period after the war, not surprisingly, sought to be the "American aristocracy" that Tocqueville identified in the 1830s (see Konefsky 2008: 74).

Lawyers were not of course unchallenged. Their ties to England and the common law did occasion criticism, as did legal links to local elites through business and kinship. The Jacksonian era is usually presented as the high-water period of those attacks (Konefsky 2008: 77). The bar began to grow as restrictions on membership were lifted, but there were still by 1860 "only a few cracks in its façade of social class" (Konefsky 2008: 86). Stratification within the legal profession began in that period

---

1. According to Claire Priest, "Every colony in the British Atlantic Empire established common law courts. The enforcement of debt agreements dominated the business of the courts" (Priest 2008: 412).

to be identified much more with clients as corporate wealth began to build. Railroad attorneys emerged as part of what Konefsky describes as "a segmented and stratified profession . . . reinforced by social kinship and family networks" (2008: 89). Lawyers began to concentrate in cities, to form partnerships, and to specialize in the representation of corporate interests. As the century came toward a close, U.S. industry expanded. The emerging law firms that served them began to occupy a unique social position between business and the state. These developments, as we shall see, reshaped the U.S. legal profession and set the stage for the strong legal role in U.S. foreign policy.

To summarize, the transplantation of the British common law and the leadership role of lawyers in the colonies and in the move to independence paved the way for lawyers and legal legitimacy to become central to the U.S. state. Despite some challenges to their authority, as in the Jacksonian era, lawyers played a very prominent role in the state and the economy in the United States. By the late nineteenth century, in addition, the new breed of corporate lawyers was assuming its position at the top of the legal hierarchy. The U.S. approach to colonialism is very much a product of that emerging legal elite's evolving state strategy.

The United States and Colonialism in the Philippines: The Construction of Moral Imperialism

The colonization of the Philippines provides a key window into the development of the U.S. approach to law, empire, and hegemony.[2] Tony Smith makes the case that in the Philippines the United States found its mission: "the democratization of the Philippines came to be the principal reason the Americans were there; now the United States had a moral purpose to its imperialism and could rest more easily" (1994: 43). The U.S. approach, in addition, was developed with an awareness of the competing European empires and a belief that any U.S. empire was far more benevolent than those of the Europeans (Go 2003: 23). Certainly, as we

2. As Eileen Scully recently noted in her study of international affairs around the turn of the twentieth century, "The underlying logic was that the United States could break from nineteenth-century imperialist interventionism and coercion to 'grow' the rule of law, authentic sovereignty, and democratic capitalism by implanting structures and protocols and cultivating local elites using the 'policy of attraction' that William Howard Taft crafted for the Philippines" (Scully 2008: 640).

have seen, the Europeans in various ways sought to justify their empires on the basis of their civilizing missions, which included investment in law and legal institutions. It is clear in any event that the United States provided a particularly strong place for legal missionaries.

The events surrounding the Spanish-American War in the late nineteenth century were the product of the rise of the new industrial class connected to the railroads, the banks, and the emerging oil industry. That rising class presented great opportunities for lawyers, especially in New York City (Beckert 2001). The rising class also came with the development of the investment banking industry that established New York City as a financial center and became closely tied to the law firms who grew up around them on Wall Street (Rosenberg 2003). The moral imperialism identified with the United States draws on this alliance of the law and the market, concretely embodied in the work of "legal imperialists" and "money doctors" the world over (Drake 1993; Rosenberg 2003).

The profitable opportunities also brought risks to professional legitimacy for the business tycoons and the lawyers and bankers who provided them with financial capital and legitimacy. The so-called robber barons, for example, often used legal hired guns and unscrupulous tactics to defeat their competitors (Galanter and Palay 1991). The lawyers who served the tycoons then became tarnished by identification with the businesses and business tactics they served. The traditional bar, organized more around litigation and small practice settings, saw this emerging corporate profession as a threat to the legitimacy of the profession as a whole. The founding of the City Bar in New York City was in fact largely a reaction to David Dudley Field's notorious representation of Jay Gould (Gordon 1984: 57).

The rising corporate bar in New York City, however, was able to survive the challenge. The strategy adopted by the bar helped provide the structure for the central role of lawyers in U.S. imperialism. The lawyer-statesman role that had been the basis for the self-identity of the legal profession was reinvented and adapted to the world of corporate law. The bar accomplished this transformation by adopting the strategy of building a relative autonomy from their clients in order to make their expertise more valuable and their own roles more legitimate. The Wall Street lawyers invested in the law, including antitrust, and in the relatively porous state through politics in the Progressive Era and beyond. This investment took place at both the local and the international level, involving municipal justice at one level and foreign policy at another (Powell 1988; Gordon 1984; Willrich 2003). Part of the state strategy for the law firms and their clients involved the mobilization of social capital to help civilize the robber barons into philanthropic patrons—led by the Carnegie and Rockefeller foundations (Berman 1983). One example of the close links of these lawyers to the state is Philander Chase Knox, described in the following passages.

Knox was the secretary of state under President William Howard Taft. Appointed in 1909, he was the architect of Taft's dollar diplomacy, according to which investment and commerce were to be the key instruments of U.S. foreign policy. U.S. investment abroad would bring peace and prosperity at the same time it provided outlets for the U.S. banking and industrial giants of the late nineteenth century.

Born in 1853 in western Pennsylvania, Knox came from a well-to-do family. His father was a prominent banker, and Knox attended elite private schools while growing up. While at college in Ohio, he formed a lasting relationship with William McKinley, then the district attorney in an Ohio county and later the President who brought the United States into the Spanish-American War. McKinley encouraged Knox to become a lawyer and helped place him in his first position. In 1877, at the age of twenty-four, Knox joined with James H. Reed to establish the law firm of Knox and Reed, which became the still prominent firm of Reed Smith. Knox's clients with the firm included many of the giants of the late nineteenth century, notably Carnegie, Mellon, and Vanderbilt. Knox was a troubleshooter defending them when they were charged with illegal behavior or were the subject of governmental investigations. In 1899, President McKinley offered him the position of attorney general of the United States. Knox initially declined because he was working to organize a huge trust, U.S. Steel, which brought together the manufacturers of two-thirds of the steel in the United States, including the interests of Carnegie.

After forming that trust, however, he accepted the offer when it was repeated in 1901. As attorney general, Knox was then in charge of antitrust policy. He did bring at least one notable antitrust action, against the Northern Securities Company, but he certainly did not turn against the interests of his former clients. He served as U.S. attorney general under Presidents William McKinley and Theodore Roosevelt from 1901 to 1904. Supported by his former corporate clients, Knox then was appointed to the Senate from Pennsylvania and remained a senator until he became secretary of state under President Taft, serving from 1909 to 1913. As with respect to Elihu Root and other leading corporate lawyers of the era, he actively supported the International Court of Arbitration at The Hague.

One aspect of this elite strategy of corporate lawyers was to invest in legal science—then being developed through the case method pioneered at Harvard. Those who excelled at the case method were invited to join the leading law firms—cementing the relationship between the pure law in the elite schools and the business practice of leading corporate firms.

These strategies required an initial accumulation of symbolic capital—combining social class, elite school ties, meritocratic criteria, political investment, size, and entrepreneurship. The professional firms were able to combine the social capital of the well-bred cosmopolitan elite with the ambition and talent of meritocratic newcomers who were promised a partnership if they could succeed as associates. The Wall Street law firm—often termed the Cravath model—became the institutionalization of this double-agent strategy. The law firms served as buffers and crossroads among academia, business, finance, and the state. This double agency for themselves and their clients can be seen as an institutionalized schizophrenia, according to which the lawyers would alternately seek to find ways for their clients to avoid state regulation and find ways for the state and the law to rein in the clients (Gordon 1984). The practical result, however, as the career of Knox well illustrates, was that the dual role allowed lawyers to construct rules to protect and rationalize the power of their clients, to build the need for their own professional services, and to gain some power in the state and economy. They could in this manner combine virtue and profit in a way that was to define U.S. imperialism.[3]

Elihu Root, who became secretary of war under McKinley in 1899, was one such corporate lawyer. His clients in the late nineteenth century included the famous Sugar Trust, which he helped to survive the challenge of antitrust legislation, and he also invested in good government through the Republican Party. Of particular interest here are his activities in the sphere of foreign affairs, which began under President McKinley. Root became the prototype for the U.S. foreign policy establishment

---

3. The situation for corporate lawyers remained challenged for some time. The establishment of the American Law Institute in 1921 reveals continuing tensions. Built through a large grant from the Carnegie Corporation shepherded by Elihu Root, the corporate bar sought to invest in the American Law Institute to respond to continuing criticisms and join with the academy in the name of relatively unthreatening goals such as better legal certainty (Legemann 1989).

that played a key role in U.S. foreign policy throughout the twentieth century. He was a central figure in deploying abroad the same strategy that built the position of corporate lawyers at home.

One of Root's key tasks as secretary of war was to deal with the continued resistance to the U.S. occupation and colonization of the Philippines that resulted from the Spanish-American War. There had been considerable opposition to the war, and the almost "accidental" taking of the Philippines required a legitimating rationale that could defuse the opposition. McKinley and Root enlisted the help of Judge William Howard Taft, a pillar of good breeding and legal professionalism. Taft at the time was the presiding judge of the Sixth Circuit Court of Appeals and dean of the law school of the University of Cincinnati. Taft accepted the position to lead the effort to build a new government in the Philippines because it was, in his words, "a national obligation, indeed a 'sacred duty,' to create a government adapted to the needs of the Filipinos, one that would help to develop them into a self-governing people" (Minger 1975: 2). Following Root's ideas as well, Taft led "the effort of the United States to transplant its values and institutions in the Philippines" (Karnow 1989: 170).[4] Taft stated simply, "We hold the Philippines for the benefit of the Filipinos" (Karnow 1989: 197).

Along with this idealism came a strategy of winning over the Philippines by befriending the elite—the *ilustrados*, the "rich intelligentsia" emerging under Spanish colonialism (Karnow 1989: 15). The Philippine elites had been given a role in local governance under Spanish colonial rule, and they used elections to maintain their power (Abinales 2003: 151). According to Goh (2008), there were essentially three groups. One part of the elite continued the resistance, led by Emilio Aguinaldo. A second part, which could be characterized as the intelligentsia of the merchant class, decided to cooperate with the U.S. occupation in order to further their own interests. They tended to favor the federal party. And the third included the subaltern bureaucrats of the Spanish colonial state who collaborated in favor of the goal of independence. They tended to be part of the nationalist party (Goh 2008: 66).

---

4. According to Karnow, "Inspired by a sense of moral obligation, they [the U.S.] believed it to be their responsibility to bestow the spiritual and material blessings of their exceptional society on the new possession—as though providence had appointed them to be its savior. So, during its half-century in the archipelago, the United States refused to be labeled a colonial power and even expunged the word *colonial* from its official vocabulary" (1989: 197).

The divisions in the Philippines mirrored political divisions in the United States. The divisions can be described as between progressives seeking to reform the urban political machines and those who operated within machine-based politics. Abinales thus notes that the Americans familiar with machine politics in the United States found that the Philippine responses to occupation "were uncannily familiar" (2003: 153). The intricate politics of local elites and local elections were "analogous to 'the game' that was vintage turn-of-the-century American politics" (Abinales 2003: 153). Taft himself understood the game very well. In his own career, based in Cincinnati, "Taft may have despised machine politics, but 'he rarely fought the Republican bosses, however corrupt'" (Abinales 2003: 154, quoting Pringle 1964, *The Life and Times of William Howard Taft*, 58–59). The tensions between the progressives and those comfortable working with and reinforcing local machine politics are reflected in the policies and personnel who came to the Philippines. Indeed, even though Taft came under the banner of idealism, there was an ambiguity in his mission. The U.S. army in the Philippines was linked more with the progressive and idealistic side, which also meant more aggressive tactics that had been criticized in the United States (Goh 2008: 68).

The strong progressive side of colonial administration ascended again in 1904–5 under Theodore Roosevelt and then again in 1911–13, both seeking to take on corruption associated with the Philippine elites. But the elites regrouped both times. Responding to the second of these political crises, President Woodrow Wilson appointed Francis Harrison, a Tammany Hall machine politician, as governor general of the Philippines. Harrison's main goal was to develop good ties within the Philippine political elite to consolidate the U.S. position there. Policies in the Philippines thus reflect an amalgam of progressive policies—civil service reform, for example—and consolidation of Philippine elite politics. Furthermore, according to Goh, the progressive side remained weak—despite recurring reactions to corruption and oligarchy (2008: 70). The nationalist elites in the Philippines had succeeded in consolidating power within the sphere of U.S. colonial democracy.

The contradictions of the administration of the Philippines were not inconsistent with a legitimacy based on the United States as the vehicle to build Philippine democracy and the rule of law. Some sense of this idealistic role of law can be garnered from testimony of one of the dominant civilizers in the Philippines. George Malcolm was a young law graduate of the University of Michigan who went to the Philippines in order to "see my country initiate a system of ever increasing self-government for the Philippines ... [and] to take a stand in favor of resolute adherence to America's revolutionary anti-colonial policy" (Malcolm 1957: 23).

Through entrepreneurial initiative, Malcolm helped to establish the University of Philippines College of Law in 1911, and he became the first dean. His goal with the law school was "the training of leaders for the country. The students were not alone tutored in abstract law dogmas; they were inculcated with the principles of democracy" (Malcolm 1957: 97). One of the graduates in 1913, who "established the reputation of the new school by topping all candidates in the Bar examination" (Malcolm 1957: 98), was Manual Roxas, who became the first President of the Philippine Republic. The career of Roxas reflects the double strategy of the elite U.S. lawyers. One was to ally with—and even help to produce—their counterparts in the Philippines. The second was to support a moral and legal facade capable of aligning the colonial venture with U.S. values—including the idea of U.S. exceptionalism from the despised world of European colonialism.

Constructing the Foreign Policy Elite in the United States

After World War I and the failure of the United States to join the League of Nations, a group of elite corporate lawyers and others formed the Council on Foreign Relations (CFR) to keep alive the case for active U.S. engagement with the international community. They worked closely with counterparts in Europe representing comparable mixes of social, legal, and state capital (Sacriste and Vauchez 2007). As indicated by the early leadership of Elihu Root and John W. Davis (Silk and Silk 1980: 187), these activists were also leading corporate lawyers. Davis himself was J. P. Morgan's lawyer. He combined his representation of the J. P. Morgan interests with a strong internationalist portfolio including the CFR, which he headed for twelve years, and service as ambassador to the Court of St. James's (Harbaugh 1973). John Foster Dulles, later Eisenhower's Secretary of State, fit the same mold. Dulles joined Sullivan and Cromwell prior to World War I, played a role as a young man in negotiations at Versailles, and went on to a career representing major corporations—including United Fruit—and supporting an internationalist foreign policy. He wrote one of the articles in the first issue of *Foreign Affairs*, the journal of the CFR. Paul Cravath—another pillar of the corporate law firm world—also became a director and vice president of the CFR at the time it was established. In the era of so-called isolationism, the CFR continued to promote interest in international relations: "To oppose isolationism had been the bedrock of the Establishment's policy during its years in the wilderness" (Hodgson 1990: 385).

Henry Stimson is perhaps the best-known representative of the legal elite that dominated the CFR. He combined colonial service in the Philippines with corporate law and government service at home. After Andover, Yale, and Harvard Law School, Stimson in 1890 took advantage of a family friendship to secure a position working for Elihu Root. When Root became McKinley's secretary of war in 1899, he turned over the law practice to his two partners, one of whom was Stimson. The law firm of Winthrop and Stimson thrived by representing the trusts and moving toward specialization in "national and increasingly in international business" (Hodgson 1990: 56). Stimson's personal ties and professional stature led him to be appointed secretary of war by Taft in 1912.

When Stimson returned to the practice of law, he also resumed service on behalf of large corporate interests. He later returned to the government as the governor general of the Philippines in 1927, a year later becoming Herbert Hoover's secretary of state and still later secretary of war for Roosevelt and Truman (1940–45). Individuals close to Stimson, many of whom worked with him during World War II, including Dean Acheson, William and McGeorge Bundy, Cyrus Vance, and Elliot Richardson, were active well into the 1970s. Hodgson makes explicit the role of these individuals in creating the U.S. brand of imperialism: "There was more than a difference of individual style between the raw, assertive nationalism of Theodore Roosevelt and Elihu Root's generation, and Stimson's world view. Stimson shared his mentors' conviction that America was destined for leadership, but he polished it and made it acceptable to a generation of Americans more and more of whom were offended by colonial empires, their own or anyone else's" (1990: 140).

Economic Technocrats, Investment Bankers, and Corporate Lawyer-Statespersons

The Philippines experience, as we have noted, set the stage for U.S. policies that came to be known as dollar diplomacy. These policies were specifically meant to offer an alternative to direct colonial relationships associated with the European powers. Under Theodore Roosevelt, who succeeded McKinley after the latter was assassinated, the recipe came together in the Dominican Republic as a basis for U.S. policy more generally. The United States stepped in ostensibly to prevent European military intervention to collect on state debt. In Emily Rosenberg's words, "The Dominican model became the first major effort to forge the kind of partnership that would continue to be at the heart of dollar diplomacy: a triangular relationship among financial advisers wishing to practice their new profession of fiscal rehabilitation in foreign countries; investment bankers seeking higher interest rates in foreign markets; and activist government officials eager to assert international influence" (Rosenberg 2003: 43). When the U.S. financial adviser in the Dominican Republic needed to find an investment bank to provide the capital to reorganize, Secretary of State Root personally encouraged Kuhn, Loeb, and Company to provide it (Rosenberg 2003: 46). As had happened within the United States, investment bankers and lawyers combined to carry out policies that were in the service of governmental priorities (Rosenberg 2003: 51–52). The relatively weak state that provided the setting for corporate lawyers to play a statelike role gave the same opportunity to investment bankers becoming professionals of business (and state) advising.

Expressly distinguishing the U.S. approach from that of the European colonial empires, Taft as president of the United States sought to open markets for U.S. business as an alternative to military strategies. The aim was to facilitate U.S. prosperity through trade and investment rather than new colonial conquests. Secretary of State Philander Knox, with "close ties to the investment community" (Rosenberg 2003: 63), took the lead in promoting dollar diplomacy. He embraced the assumption that "a strong financial presence would actually decrease the need for military intervention" in countries that the United States sought to maintain in its sphere of influence (Rosenberg 2003: 63). Dollar diplomacy led the way for the policies of Woodrow Wilson, who succeeded Taft as president, and very similar policies were adopted in the 1920s—promoted aggressively by the distinguished secretary of state under Harding, Charles Evans Hughes, who served at the same time as president of the American Society of International Law.

The lawyer-statespersons who guided U.S. foreign policy emerged from the experience of constructing the U.S. imperial role in the Philippines. They sought to develop an approach emphasizing free trade and democracy that would be expansive and profitable without the need for European-style colonies. They were complemented by the so-called money doctors who worked for them around the globe and helped find profitable outlets for New York's growing investment bank industry. These experts began also in the Philippines. Those who began to promote policies favoring the gold standard, central banks, and tax and customs reform in the Philippines were "financial missionaries," according to Emily Rosenberg, who "stimulated the emergence of a new profession of foreign financial advising and a foreign financial policy designed to assist the nation's expanding exportation of goods and investment capital" (2003: 12). Charles C. Conant, a passionate believer in the gold standard and friend to Lyman Gage, the Chicago banker and McKinley's secretary of the treasury, was the first missionary to the Philippines. Again in Rosenberg's words, "Nearly all of the U.S. foreign financial advisers before the Great Depression of the 1930s began their careers in the Philippines administering the system he devised" (2003: 15). Jeremiah Jenks, Conant's friend and fellow apostle of the gold standard, helped build the academic field with appointments at New York University and Cornell in political economy. These economists placed considerable emphasis on mathematics and on economics as an emerging science built around marginal utility curves. To continue the link to the Philippine experience, Jenks recommended his graduate student at Cornell, Edwin Kemmerer, to direct Conant's program of currency reform in the Philippines. Kemmerer thus began a career that saw him become the leading money doctor and first occupant of a chair in International Economics at Princeton that he helped establish in the late 1920s (Rosenberg 2003: 25; Drake 1994).

From Law and Trade to Corporate Lawyer-Statespersons Central to the U.S. Imperial Approach

The approaches of the various colonial powers all contain at certain times and in certain places a strong dose of legal idealism. The idealism is typically connected to demands within the colonies and colonizing countries for more legitimacy, and it coincides also with legal investment in the colonial state—especially by local elites. The strength of the U.S. investment in law at the turn of the twentieth century is quite clear from the literature. In addition, the particular role of corporate lawyers close to the state is also well documented. These features of U.S. governance led to an anti-imperial imperialism associated with open markets and democracy. The Philippines played a major role in producing this approach and in developing the cadre of lawyers and bankers that would take it elsewhere.

Part 2 will contrast the development of law and legal professions in the different colonial settings. The U.S. approach in the Philippines, as we shall see, produced a very different legacy than found in the other colonial regimes.

PART II

Strategies for Constructing Legal Professions and Producing New State Elites

The following three chapters move beyond the periods of colonial geneses to the emerging role of lawyers in the construction of independent Asian states. There are parallel developments that take place in all the countries, which is not surprising given that the colonial powers were competing with each other for legitimacy and influence in the colonies they administered. There was investment within the colonial regimes in the legitimacy associated with the law and in the co-optation of local elites into some kind of delegated administration. On the other side, there was also the investment of local elites in the power that comes from colonial training and the role in state governance. Lawyers gained power as the colonial relationships endured and as elite lawyers helped lead moves to independence.

We organize these chapters by beginning (chap. 5) with the development of the elite legal professions in what can be seen as showcase empires—the British in India after the establishment of the Raj in the mid-nineteenth century, and the United States in the Philippines (chap. 6) after the somewhat reluctant U.S. embrace of colonialism late in the nineteenth century. In different ways, each of these first two chapters illustrates relatively long periods of investment in promoting a legal profession and rule of law that would be legitimate and recognizable in the colonial capitals. The legal professions that developed through colonialism and the move to independence were well fortified with social capital and a set of respected legal institutions. The third chapter in this part (chap. 7) focuses on countries where the investment was relatively weak and late—Indonesia, in particular, but also Malaysia and Singapore. The legal profession that emerged in varying degrees was relatively easily cut off from the social capital necessary for its continued vitality. The chapter sets out the similarly inauspicious beginning of the legal profession in South Korea—where the legal profession was established as part of the Japanese empire. Neither the weak place of law in Japan nor its manifestation in Korea encouraged substantial investment in legal legitimacy.

CHAPTER FIVE

The British Empire and the Indian Raj: A Legal Elite from Colonial Co-optation to State Independence

The merchant beginnings of the British colonial policy in India were consistent with a legitimating ideology that sought to distinguish the British from that of the other colonial powers. There was a "long-held British belief that their empire, unlike those of the Portuguese and Spanish, or even the French and the Dutch, was one of commerce and not conquest" (Pitts 2005: 12). The experience in North America was seen not as a conquest but as the occupation of "essentially vacant land" (Pitts 2005: 12). The developments in South Asia in the second half of the eighteenth century challenged that belief and prompted considerable criticism within Britain. As we have noted, Edmund Burke and others were part of the group increasingly critical of the inconsistency of the British imperial practices with British ideals (Pitts 2005: 117).

By the end of the nineteenth century, the British ideology of empire was very different: "progressive universalism justified European imperial rule as a benefit to backward subjects, authorized the abrogation of sovereignty of many indigenous states, and licensed increasingly interventionist policies in colonized societies' systems of education, law, property, and religion" (Pitts 2005: 21). As was the case for the United States in its later colonial encounter with the Philippines, the legitimating ideology was consistent with investment in legal institutions and the rule of law. As the Rudolphs point out, "For most Englishmen, having established the 'rule of law' on the Indian subcontinent was probably the proudest achievement of the British raj" (Rudolph and Rudolph 1965: 24).

This investment began before the official creation of the Raj in 1859, but it was especially evident after that date. James Mill and John Stuart Mill, both executives of the East Indian Company for most of their careers, were utilitarian proponents of this transformation. Mill was confident that British policies were essentially good for the Indians and benevolent in intent. Mill "greatly mistrusted European colonists and their legislatures," but he "remained confident that British colonial civil servants could rule impartially, knowledgeably, and beneficently over peoples not ready for self-government" (Pitts 2005: 150). As in the United States, the governance of the empire was central to domestic debates at home. This rhetoric favored investment in statelike institutions in India, and the ideology provided opportunities for the emerging local legal profession within India.

From Expatriate Traders to a Local Governing Elite

The first lawyers in India were, as noted above, British-trained fortune seekers who came to India despite initial hostility from the East India Company. They worked in the courts set up by the British to handle disputes involving trade interests, and they began to prosper almost immediately. Advocacy on behalf of business interests was therefore from an early time built into the legal profession in India, and the early indigenous lawyers quite naturally moved into those same advocacy roles.

The progressive opening of high courts in India to participation by Indian advocates in the nineteenth century was, in addition to being part of the legitimation of empire, both a project of professional promotion and a political project for the construction of an aristocracy of compradors. There were several ways to gain access to this role as high-court advocate. The route open to a few individuals was through the internal promotion of a small number of practitioners before indigenous jurisdictions (the vakils, mentioned before in chap. 3, and other Indian pleaders). The vast number of advocates, however, gained their credentials at the English Inns of Court—where essentially only the children of the well-to-do landowning class could attend. Schmitthener notes that, "Few Indians could afford the long [four or five years] expensive training program for barristers that could be had only in England. The earliest candidates were primarily the sons of rich Parsi merchants" (Schmitthener 1968–69: 365).

At the same time, however, the local advocates (termed *vakils*) provided another way to use the law to empower local elites who at the same time bought into English law. In her study of the Madras presidency, for example, Price (1989) explored the particular relationship of the Brahmin elite to the development of the legal profession: "Because of their literacy and social confidence, Brahmins were useful advisers to the new rulers as they developed imperial administration" (1989: 162). The Brahmin elite also turned out to anticipate the changes taking place. Again, as stated by Price, "Brahmin families sent sons, also, to district capitals and to Madras City to become specialists in Western secular learning so that they could be employed in the imperial administration. They also received training in the procedures and rules of the Anglo-Indian court system, where they predominated as lawyers and lower-ranking judges in the course of the [nineteenth] century" (Price 1989: 162).

By the late nineteenth century, these Brahmin lawyers were a recognizable elite: "the profession produced men whose reputations travelled far beyond the city, whose fortunes became more vast, and who demonstrated a brilliance that their contemporaries found awesome. These men replaced merchants as spokesmen in the elite politics of urban areas" (Price 1989: 162). Lawyers were also leaders in the emerging nationalist movement: "Making public speeches, writing in journals and newspapers, lawyers set standards for accommodation with European culture at the same time as they represented to the government complaints of misgovernment and petitions for legislative reform" (Price 1989: 162). Their wealth came from lengthy litigation involving the large estates: "The great fortunes of the 'lions' and 'luminaries' of the Madras Bar were the products of litigation involving the great landholding families of Madras Presidency" (Price 1989: 162–63). By the 1920s, the increase in litigation and in the reputation of the Tamil Brahmins meant that the vakils could match the British-trained specialists in high-court advocacy.

The detour through the metropolis taken by the wealthy sons of merchants was more about prestige than about scholarly necessities. The exam that permitted accession to the Inns of Court was reportedly less difficult than those of the Indian law colleges—not to mention the extremely difficult Indian Civil Service exam. In this manner, the descendents of the well-to-do classes in India were "called to the bar" and returned to India transformed into "English gentlemen" (Schmitthener 1968–69: 369) (although certainly not accepted as such by the English). These lawyers elected also to transplant to India the British tradition of apprenticeship with a senior advocate, which in practice served as another barrier to limit access to the market.

The education of the producers of law in India has always been a family affair. To quote Schmitthener again, "Traditions of the profession were absorbed in the home. The friends and guests who frequented the home were lawyers, judges, and leading men of the community. . . . Without the help of a practicing family member or relative, many a well-trained talented young lawyer had little chance to show what he could do to succeed at the bar" (Schmitthener 1968–69: 375). The role of family helps explain the extraordinary continuity in the recruitment of this professional elite. The importance of family continues today. As one senior advocate noted recently, "It is very difficult actually in India for a young lawyer who does not have lawyers in his family to break into the profession because, unfortunately, there aren't many professional law firms which properly employ young lawyers . . . it's still a very futile profession, in many ways" (Int. India-12).[1] An engineer stated similarly that he was told that "unless your parents are lawyers, you don't become a lawyer" (Int. India-13).

Family support is particularly decisive when securing an apprenticeship in the chambers of a reputable senior. As one senior Indian advocate observed, "you need good chambers" in order to succeed. When a colleague asks "take my son in your chambers," you "can't refuse" (Int. India-12). This apprenticeship stage remains unpaid in the first few years, which adds further, as Abel has noted, to a social selection where family resources count much more than knowledge or personal talent (Abel 1988; Gandhi 1988).

The subsequent career trajectory of Indian advocates only magnifies the importance of the initial difference between the descendants of legal families and those completely new to the profession. Those from the legal families who demonstrate talent are quickly recognized within the elite of the bar, among the high-court judges, and also among the solicitors able to refer to them large business matters—which in turn allow them to further build their reputations in the bar. This process is cumulative and quick: the reputation acquired in the courtroom attracts

1. The authors conducted interviews in each of the countries studied. In order to protect the confidentiality of the interviewees, the interviews are identified only by country and number. The countries are abbreviated as follows: HK, Hong Kong; India; Indon., Indonesia; K, South Korea; M, Malaysia; P, Philippines; and S, Singapore.

not only clients through lucrative referrals but also the attention of senior advocates and judges who control access to the prestigious Supreme
Court bar.

A double selection according to money and family background con-
forms to the logic of high-court justice in India, which is strictly connected to the world of business. The honoraria paid to advocates in the
Indian high courts have long been recognized as exorbitant. In the nineteenth century, it was estimated that they were seven times greater than
those in Great Britain (Schmitthener 1968–69: 346). Barristers who
served in India as expatriates quickly amassed fortunes, but in the colonial context they also tended to spend their fortunes to maintain the
proper appearances. Gentlemen lawyers maintained lifestyles comparable to their rich clients (Schmitthener 1968–69: 348).

The colonial justice system staffed initially by expatriates provided
merchants with a justice well suited to their needs, with practitioners
that were both competent and attentive. The system did not change with
the slow arrival of young Indian advocates predisposed to become gentlemen lawyers. Following the example of their senior expatriates, they
learned to celebrate British traditions of justice. They were also able to
profit from their relative monopoly. At some point, indeed, their acquisition of wealth earned them the title of "Nabobs of law." Thus, in the
1880s, while still in his thirties, Motilal Nehru, the father of Jawarharlal
Nehru, "lived like a prince, had the first cars in Allahabad, and a pala-
tial house" (Schmitthener 1968–69: 370). One reason for the extraordi-
narily prosperity of the Indian legal market was that the number of cases
was huge—2.2 million in 1901. The caseload, more particularly, included
numerous disputes relating to the system of large properties (zamindari),
and the cases lasted indefinitely—often more than a generation.

On the other side, the British had a local political dynamic that made
legal investment in India more important in Britain than in comparable
colonial settings, including what became Malaysia and Singapore. Apprenticeship through law, from the beginning, was a political project—
the construction of a national elite and a source of future leaders. As
Schmitthener stated, "Legal training was regarded as the best possible
preparation for a political career" (Schmitthener 1968–69: 378). Political ambitions were encouraged, even incited among the leaders of social groups such as the Parsi, an elite among the merchant class. As the
profession that drew the elite of the country into its ranks, the legal profession provided the leadership even for philanthropic and educational

institutions (Schmitthener 1968–69: 378). In her study of the Madras presidency, Price notes also that, "The leaders of the nationalist movement in the Presidency, as well as men appointed to high office or elected to new governing bodies, were also, in great part, Brahmin. Lawyers predominated among this new, urban-based elite" (Price 1989: 152).

It may be true, as Weber noted, that the adoption of the British model for the production of justice conformed to a certain market logic, but the Indianization of the model responded also to specific political preoccupations connected to colonial relations. Legal institutions were at the heart of imperial governance, playing a central role in the transmission of colonial power and in the maintenance of both the rules of the market and of social hierarchies. The stability of legal institutions provided a key to an historical pattern of change managed within a story of overall continuity. Continuity is easy to see. The elite Indian lawyers were the principle beneficiaries of a transfer of power that they had programmed and for which they themselves had been programmed. As suggested above, key features for the production of this legal elite remain as they were in colonial Britain.

This long-term political strategy produced significant effects, permitting the bar and its reformist elite to prosper while defending the interests of clients dealing with the colonial bureaucracy. In fact, educated at the colonial schools, these Indian gentlemen were perfectly situated to use the contradictions and ambiguities of the legal system against the colonists. At the same time, that system was perceived to be independent and credible among the Indian population because of the so-called "Vakil Raj," a term the British used to denounce the too easy access of Indians to courts and the lawyers who flourished in them. That easy access was in fact conceived precisely to make colonial domination more legitimate.

The Indian National Congress, founded in 1885, was the principal base for the constitutional and reformist strategy of the Anglicized legal elite. According to the Rudolphs, "Congress began as an organization of anglicized regional elites whose common language, interests, and lifestyle distinguished them from most of the Indians they purported to represent" (1987: 127). Biographers of the Nehru dynasty add that one of the main objectives of the founders of the Congress Party was to gain recognition for the merits of a new class of professionals by an aristocratic empire that ignored them by focusing more on direct relations with Indian royal families (Adams and Whitehead 1997: 25). According to Schmitt-thener, "The leaders with their Western educations and legal training understood parliamentary procedure and constitutional methods. They had confidence in the British system of justice" (1968–69: 378). A biogra-pher of Motilal Nehru, for example, noted that the senior Nehru, then a political moderate with little patience for extremists, "believed that 'able advocacy was as sure to succeed at the bar of British opinion as at the bar of the Allahabad High Court'" (Schmitthener 1968–69: 378). The Con-gress Party learned that it needed more aggressive tactics ultimately to secure independence, but this relatively moderate legal elite with faith in the British legal system helped ensure that independence did not mean radical change in India.

The role of this legal elite is captured well by Price, who provides rich detail on three Brahmin lawyers in the late nineteenth and early twenti-eth centuries. The first, Vembakkem Bhashyam Ayyangar (1844–1908), was part of a family that included "three High Court Judgeships, two Attorney-Generalships and three Small Cause Court Judgeships" (1989: 163). He reportedly was "among the two or three most respected law-yers in south India and for many of these years he was the most wealthy" (1989: 163). His clients included "Nattukkottai Chetti merchant-bankers, whose enterprises extended beyond India to Southeast Asia," and the landowning zamindars (1989: 163). Indeed, "Sir Bhashyam Ayyangar was almost invariably consulted by important men on all occasions of domestic disputes, settlements of property and commercial and other legal transactions" (1989: 164).

The second, C. V. Kumaraswami Sastri (1870–1934), became a high-court judge in 1914. His ancestors included, "a great-grandfather, great-great-grandfather and great-great-great-grandfather" who were notable Sanskrit scholars (1989: 164). His grandfather was on the same career path but he got to know the District Collector, "who encouraged him to study English" (1989: 164). The grandfather became a lawyer and eventually a judge of the Court of Small Causes in Madras. Two of his sons also became lawyers. One, the father of Kumaraswami Sastri, be-came an advocate before the high court of Madras. Kumaraswami Sastri began to practice before the high court in 1894 "and achieved 'brilliant success' with speed which was no doubt accelerated by his succession to his father's extensive practice" (1989: 164). He was not only on "good terms with British barristers who practiced at the Court," but also with such "an impressive bearing that even English observers found in him a dignity and mood which favorably recalled practitioners of their own judiciary" (1989: 165).

The third was V. Krishnaswami Aiyar (1863–1911), "who dominated not only the legal profession of Madras Presidency but the Moderate wing of the Congress movement in south India" (1989: 165). His father, the son of a long line of well-known Brahmins, was very successful with "much landed property" (1989: 165). He was especially known in Tiruvidamarudur for the donation of twelve houses to Brahmins. The family circle included "a number of legal specialists in the Anglo-Indian legal system" (1989: 165). An uncle was a vakil in Madurai. A cousin was a scholar of Brahminical religion, and two of his brothers were lawyers. He began to practice as a vakil at the high court in 1885. He won a famous suit in 1895, which built his reputation. According to Price,

> In the years following, Krishnaswami's palatial residence in the most fashionable Brahmin quarter of Madras and his total earnings of up to seven lakhs of rupees were the fruit, in main, of the litigation of privileged landholders. Following perhaps in a tradition set by his father—and according to Tamil valuation of generosity—Krishnaswami gave away up to half of his fortune to charitable causes, medical, religious, and educational. He also supported the Congress. (1989: 166)

In 1909, in addition, Price writes, "Krishnaswami received an appointment to the High Court Bench. As a Justice, Krishnaswami's Sanskrit scholarship lent authority to his judgments on topics in Hindu Law and he became distinguished on the bench, expanding on his reputation" (1989: 167).

These examples well illustrate the wealth, learned expertise, and political moderation that were behind the Congress Party. Nevertheless, the strategy of political moderation adopted by the Congress Party was not successful enough to prevent major conflicts with the British. The intensification of the struggles led a certain number of the nabobs of the law, including Jawaharlal Nehru, to give up their privileges and follow Gandhi in his strategy of boycotting colonial legal and political institutions. The demands of politics had become such that the comprador elite could no longer accommodate the multiple roles that had facilitated a double game. This "sacrifice" in fact revealed the priority of political ambitions over the pursuit of a career that, in any event, had brought them the financial resources needed to invest in politics and changed their image from Anglicized nabobs to that of ascetics in the service of the Indian collectivity.

The first years of independence represented the apogee of a profession that saw its professional market made even more profitable by the spectacular success of its political investments. The value of legal capital, as we shall see, then began to decline.

British Variations Available for Translation

On the basis of an instructive book on the relationship between law and the railroad industry in England in the nineteenth century (Kostal 1994), we can provide some insights into the relationship among law, business, and the state in England in the late nineteenth century. This world of elite law is what the Indians studying in London found. We cannot say on the basis of existing literature just exactly what impact the British transformations had on attitudes in India, but again the parallels are instructive.

Lawyers played a key role with the railroad industry not only as lawyers but also as brokers and even investors. They created the necessary legal and financial instruments to facilitate the railroad industry (the joint stock company) and guaranteed its value to potential investors (many of them their clients from the moneyed class). They also coached the new entrepreneurs (many of them amateurs or engineers) into this sophisticated new technology, negotiated with the landed aristocracy (also their clients) for the sale of land (at a huge price), and when necessary lobbied in parliament to get a private bill authorizing these railways to operate. Many lawyers were also investors in their own names or even swindlers profiting enormously during the railway financial boom— which ended with a huge crash and an enormous wave of litigation (again to their huge profit). Despite a growing resentment at the size of these enormous legal fees (estimated at over thirty million pounds), particularly after the crash when the small investors lost their investments and the whole industry was financially strangled, most of these lawyers managed to survive the crisis untouched.

What is even more interesting is the hierarchical diversity of treatment. After twenty years, the Parliament imposed a fee limitation on solicitors, but the dozen elite barristers (Queens' Counsel) who had built a cartel to act in front of the parliamentary committees (where they charged between two and ten times more than the normal court fees) managed to continue for decades until the consolidation of the railway industry. Their peers tried timidly to discipline them, but their recommendations were easily bypassed. The only revenge was to exclude these millionaires from the prestigious ladder toward judgeships and political appointments on the pretext that their practice was too specialized and not intellectually challenging enough to qualify them for judicial appointment. Nevertheless, there was a tremendous period of success for these elite lawyers serving the railroads.

The author's explanation for this central and highly profitable role is based on the barristers' strategic position among the landed aristocracy (whose trust they enjoyed since they were frequently second sons or poor cousins), the railroads, and Parliament (where that aristocracy was well represented). The legal construction of this new industry thus served to build a compromise between the new entrepreneurs and the landowners, who relinquished some of their property rights for a huge price (corollary of the huge legal fees)—either directly through the brokering of their family solicitors or after an enormously costly legal battle in the parliamentary committees which were granted power of expropriation. These high legal costs also served as a barrier to entry excluding less wealthy players from the competition. Lawyers thus played a key role mediating between business and the state and the landowning class that dominated the state. As we have seen, the role of the advocates in India at the same time has many parallels. They were closely tied to major landowning families, business, and the ruling government. They built their profits as they served themselves and the interests from which they came.

Conclusion

The British were very successful in establishing a legal elite in India that believed in the Common law and the English legal system. On one side the Brahmins, Parsi, and others positioned themselves to take advantage of what the British sought in order to make their empire more legitimate. And the British were pleased to co-opt local elites in this manner for their own interests. The legal profession became the political elite in preindependence India. State and family capital maintained the high value of legal capital, and the elites reproduced themselves also through law and legal careers. One result was that the leaders of independence echoed the British in claiming that the greatest legacy of colonialism and the one worth preserving was the inherited legal system. The legal system provided legitimacy to them and their social world as well.

The legal legacy of colonialism and independence in India, in short, was therefore quite strong. We turn now to the Philippines (chap. 6), where the legacy of U.S. colonialism and the move to independence was similarly strong. Both these cases can be contrasted with the third chapter in this part (chap. 7), which shows the very different positions of legal elites in Indonesia, Malaysia, Singapore, and South Korea. After examining these contrasting stories, we will then see in part 3 how these different colonial legacies positioned legal elites to survive the challenges posed by developmental states, often led by the military, and by U.S. approaches to law and foreign policy in the cold war.

CHAPTER SIX

The American Empire in the Philippines: Building a State and a Legal Elite in the U.S. Image

The Philippines provides the second example of substantial colonial investment in law and lawyers. However, the U.S. approach differed in major respects from the approach of the British. Drawing on the position of lawyers in the United States at the turn of the twentieth century when the Philippines became a U.S. colony, corporate lawyers rather than barristers were the domestic inspiration for building a colonial legal elite. The initial experience seeking support and legitimacy for the Philippine imperial adventure at home and abroad, as noted in chapter 4, helped put U.S. corporate lawyer–statespersons in charge of Philippine governance and led them to look for their counterparts in occupied Philippines. They found a close match among the *ilustrados*, the educated Philippine elite,[1] and governance in the Philippines came to reflect an amalgam of policies of the United States at the turn of the twentieth century, including civil service reform on one side and the consolidation of Philippine elite politics on the other. The progressive reform side remained relatively weak in this mix of reformism and machine politics,

---

1. As stated by Riedinger, "As had their Spanish predecessors, U.S. colonial administrators . . . relied upon the Filipino landowning elite and their clientelistic networks for social control. The contest for relative power continued between Manila and the localities. U.S. introduction of periodic elections facilitated elite penetration of the state by creating a wide range of elective offices at the local and provincial levels. . . . The clientelistic networks of the landowning elite became the foundation for national political alliances" (Riedinger 1995: 21).

despite recurring reactions to corruption and oligarchy and the hopes of reformers such as George Malcolm (Goh 2008:70).

Suffrage was limited, and the governor of the Philippines, William Howard Taft, "discouraged any sort of popular mobilization that might threaten [the] political dominance of the elite" (Hutchcroft 1998: 289). The lawyer-politicians under the U.S. regime "were quick to discern that the path to power lay in the political sphere—not in the judicial and bureaucratic sphere as during Spanish times" (Hutchcroft 1998: 289). Accordingly, the Taft era in the Philippines succeeded in making the lawyer-politician the "dominant figure in Philippine society" (Hutchcroft 1998: 294). The corollary was that, as in the United States, the locus of political power was in lawyer-politicians-statespersons connected to an elite establishment. The connections were to prominent families and businesses, as in the United States, and in the Philippines also to the Catholic Church and another key source of power—the United States. University of Michigan law graduate George Malcolm played a strong role himself in shaping future leaders from among the elite educated at the University of Philippines Law School, which he established in 1911.

The state constructed in the U.S. image was therefore relatively weak and lacking in autonomy. Power was concentrated in the traditional elites, who fought each other for control over the state. As in the United States, lawyers occupied key roles as power brokers, reformers, and representatives of the elite. The Philippine lawyers also maintained good relationships with their counterparts in the United States. The combination of social and learned capital meant that at different times these individuals could emphasize their legal expertise; the need to implement reforms; their connections to local political, economic, and political power; or their proximity to people, resources, and ideas from the United States.

The prominence of lawyers in the Philippines thus began before the U.S. occupation but was strongly reinforced and transformed by U.S. rule. That prominence continues to the present. Independence from the United States, in fact, was led precisely by the lawyer-politicians who were produced by U.S. colonial policies designed to develop apprentices in U.S.-style democracy. They long played a double game of pushing for independence while cultivating the United States and the power that came from association with U.S. foreign policy elites. As with respect to the Indian legal elite discussed in the previous chapter (chap. 5), independence was led by and was to the advantage of those whose power came from colonially inspired legal training. In contrast to India, however, the Philippine legal elite for the most part was able to maintain its dominance of the state through the 1960s and 1970s and indeed until the present.

A simple way to see continuities through the present situation is to examine the composition of the legislatures. At the time of our research, in particular, roughly forty percent of the members of the House of Representatives were lawyers, down from fifty-seven percent in the early 1990s (Coronel et al. 2004) but still a remarkably high percentage. In addition, ten of the twenty-four senators had law degrees even though they did not all practice law. The general role of the lawyer, more importantly, ensures that, as one Philippine lawyer noted, there is a great overlap among "business, law and politics" (Int. P-1)[2] and that, from another perspective, "professional lawyers are on many sides of social questions." As with respect to corporate lawyers historically in the United States, the lawyers in the Philippines reinforce their power by representing both the side of power and the ideals of reform. As one scholar stated, one of the roles of lawyers in the Philippines is "modeled on the most immoral aspects of American machine politics," while the other emulates "the American moral rhetoric of reform" (Thompson 1995: 30).

The combination of moral rhetoric and machine politics naturally contributes to a literature—often produced from within the elite—detailing the excesses of the so-called Philippine oligarchy. The literature is quite revealing. In particular, a recent book by Sheila Coronel and others from the Philippine Center for Investigative Journalism links the rule by the oligarchy to a long tradition of legal training among the elites (Coronel et al. 2004). This research connects the enduring elite dominance and the traditional political machine tools of "guns, goons, money" to lawyers and the law. Coronel quoted a lawyer-politician who served as governor of Cavite from 1986 to 1988, who stated, "You can't be in politics in Cavite if you don't have goons. Politicians are respected by the number of guns they have. When I was active in politics, I had firearms and a law firm, so I could defend the cases of my men" (Coronel 1995: 13). His major opponent in Cavite, Coronel noted, "had a private army and a law firm as well" (Coronel 1995: 13). Law and violence worked together

2. The authors conducted interviews in each of the countries studied. In order to protect the confidentiality of the interviewees, the interviews are identified only by country and number. The countries are abbreviated as follows: HK, Hong Kong; India; Indon., Indonesia; K, South Korea; M, Malaysia; P, Philippines; and S, Singapore.

as part of the limited but often intense political competition among Philippine elites.

Leading scholars of the Philippines have noted the unusual prominence of legal training in the careers of the Philippine elite and the link of that phenomenon to the U.S. colonial relationship. Alfred McCoy, a leading scholar of the Philippines, made a particular argument about the role of law in the careers of leading Philippine businessmen. According to McCoy, describing several key leaders, "Although he was by all accounts a skilled corporate executive, Eugenio Lopez was educated in law not in business or finance. Similarly, though Ramon Durano, Sr. was a legendary warlord whose taste for violence was legendary in Cebu, he also had a sound legal education that allowed him to translate his political influence into private wealth. . . . Through legal education, politicians learn to manipulate . . . [legal] regulations in their quest for rents. With this introduction to the country's legal culture, even the most virulent warlord has the tools to succeed as a rent-seeking entrepreneur" (McCoy 1993: 25). For McCoy, therefore, this pervasiveness of legal training is a particular feature that requires some explanation.

The puzzle to be explained is that the pervasive legal training among the Philippine elite, as McCoy suggests, goes along with what leading academic commentators have variously called "crony capitalism" (a term invented for the Philippines—Hutchcroft 2000: 208), "booty capitalism" (Hutchcroft 1998), "bossism" (Sidel 1999), and other similar pejoratives. In the words of Hedman and Sidel, two of the most prominent scholars of the Philippines, "throughout the postwar period, a national oligarchy 'essentially recruited from families of long standing economic wealth or political dominance or both' has continued to define the nature of electoral politics. . . ." (Hedman and Sidel 2000: 15). As described by McCoy, the governing elite works locally to build a base, secures national power through elections, takes over the weak state, and then turns state power into economic and political power for allied families and friends (McCoy 1993). This pattern of governance, not surprisingly, is characterized by struggles for power and patronage rather than by technocratic investment in the state. Law is embedded in the political and economic system of the Philippines, but it is not inconsistent with crony capitalism—often thought to be the antithesis of governance by the rule of law.

Law, business, and the state are quite closely connected. According to a prominent business leader, business success is inseparable from political involvement. If a business is able to "reach a certain level of business activity," it "must get into politics"—"all big businesses must do it" (Int. P-2). Businesses gain influence by financing political candidates, or even reaching the stage where they can name "their own cabinet officers" (Int. P-2). One expert in land reform, for example, noted that the end of land reform was quite evident by the fact that the leaders of the sugar industry—dominant landowners—named the person to oversee land reform (Int. P-3). Political power translated into the strongest possible economic protection. These features of the Philippine business-state relationship remain in place today.

From this perspective, the legacy of the U.S. colonial relationship played a strong role for lawyers and at least for the trappings of law, but the state that was produced was far from what legal idealists linked to reform in the Philippines had hoped. Put another way, the Philippines provided the key site for the development of the moral imperialism that became central to U.S. foreign policy, but the moral side in the Philippines did not succeed in building a successful economy or a well-functioning democracy. The Philippines was the prototypical "rent-seeking" economy.

Law, Business, and State Power: The Leading Example of Eugenio Lopez, Sr.

The law degree, as we have noted, has long served as the prime professional credential in the Philippines. It serves individuals who practice law, go into politics, or go into business—or do all at once. Reportedly, only about one-fourth of the law graduates actually practice law (Magallona 2000), with a large number also going into government and many going into business. Probably the most prominent example of the multifaceted legal career, highlighted already in the quotation by Alfred McCoy, is Eugenio Lopez, Sr., the best-known businessman in the Philippines during much of the twentieth century. His story is both illustrative and significant in its own right. Lopez was born to a prominent business and political family in Iloilo in 1901. His father, Benito Lopez, was elected governor of Iloilo in 1906 and assassinated two years later by a nationalist who resented the governor's pro-American position. Eugenio Lopez, Sr., attended the Ateneo de Manila for his BA degree, then took a law degree from the University of Philippines before passing the bar in 1923. He went next to Harvard Law School, where he earned an LLM degree. He returned to the Philippines and practiced law with a man who a biographical account describes as the "renowned and most highly regarded Filipino lawyer at the time" (Abueva 1998: 8). Lopez then moved to business.

With his brother, Fernando, who later went full-time into a political career culminating in two stints as vice president, the second under Marcos, he took over what was then just one plantation and a small printing press in Negros (McCoy 1993: 444). With capital borrowed from wealthy relatives, he revived the family newspaper and moved quickly into transportation and numerous other business ventures. He personified success in Philippine business until his clash with Marcos, subsequent imprisonment, and exile until he reclaimed his empire after the fall of Marcos. Lopez was denounced by Marcos as part of the "oligarchy"—the leader of the "sugar bloc."

Lopez's famous statement, "To succeed in business, one must engage in politics" (McCoy 1993: 448), revealed part of his approach. More generally, as McCoy states, "His enterprises prospered when an ally occupied Malacanang Palace, and they suffered, often badly, under the administration of an enemy" (1993: 448). As a supplement to his relationship with political leaders, Lopez also developed very close relationships with the leaders of the Catholic Church (1993: 447). He also kept up his ties to the United States, gaining honor from Harvard as a distinguished alumnus—the Harvard University Distinguished Service Award, given in recognition of "his accomplishments as business leader, communicator, and champion of sound management in Asia" (Santa Maria 2006). The combination of politics, religion, and U.S. ties naturally worked well with his investment in the law.

As McCoy's description of Eugenio Lopez, Sr., makes clear, Lopez used lawyers and the courts extensively to protect his properties. As we have seen, the legal profession was one of the tools for the various forms of political and internecine warfare in the Philippines. Ambitious young lawyers naturally also found themselves building connections early to people like Lopez. Among the notable lawyers identified with Lopez were Robert Benedicto and Claudio Teehankee, described in more detail below. Jovito Salonga is an especially notable example. As a rising progressive star in politics, he became corporate lawyer to many of the Lopez enterprises as early as 1953 (Salonga 2001: 76). Benedicto introduced him to Lopez (Salonga 2001: 256). Lorenzo Tanada, a partner of Teehankee and another leading progressive politician, was also a lawyer for the Lopez interests. Salonga, Tanada, and, at a much later time,

Teehankee, became known for their opposition to Marcos, who also challenged the Lopez empire.

Jovito Salonga: A Career in Elite Politics and Business

Salonga, a devout Protestant, was the middle-class son of a minister. He attended the University of Philippines, beginning prelaw studies in 1936, and then he enrolled in the College of Law. He was active in debate and in school politics and a member of the Sigma Rho fraternity—a key organization for linking together the legal elites. During the World War II occupation and after the closing of the university, he was arrested by the Japanese for distributing anti-Japanese materials. He was let out after a year and then took the bar exam, tying for first place with Jose Diokno when the results were released in the summer of 1944. After the war he obtained his law degree, began a small law practice, and began also to teach and to build political connections. He sought to study abroad since, "some eminent public figures I admired and a number of my law professors had finished graduate studies abroad" (Salonga 2001: 49). The pattern of elite study in the United States—seen also with Lopez—was established very early indeed. Elite law in the Philippines was closely connected to U.S. schools and contacts.

After a sea voyage on which he met his future wife, from a well-to-do Philippine family, Salonga attended Harvard Law School and received the LLM degree. At Harvard, he met Sotero Laurel, the son of the wartime President, Jose Laurel. He then moved to Yale in 1947 for a JSD, absorbing "the policy-oriented approach of [Yale professors] McDougall and Lasswell" (Salonga 2001: 54) and making important Philippine and international contacts. After completing his dissertation, he returned to Manila, set up a law office with Sotero Laurel, and soon became involved in the unsuccessful presidential campaign of Jose Laurel. With the Laurels and the then Senator Claro Recto, he established a new college and law school in 1952—the Lyceum Law faculty (Salonga 2001: 66). The younger Laurel went to practice with his father, and Salonga continued both to have limited political involvement and to teach—handling the course in corporations at the University of the Philippines and becoming dean in 1954 at the Far Eastern University School of Law. His law practice was then flourishing with some associates recruited through the teaching positions—and with Eugenio Lopez a leading client.

In 1961 Salonga was elected to the Congress as a liberal with the sponsorship of President Diosgado Macagapal. Fueled by the participation of law students from the three schools in which he taught, he was then elected to the Senate despite the election of Marcos to the presidency in 1965. As we shall see in chapter 9, he was a victim of the Marcos era and one of the leaders of the opposition. What is important for present purposes, however, is that his career embodied the U.S.-connected corporate lawyer/professor/politician ideal that Taft identified with and so much admired in the United States. Salonga was in the prime position of the elite in the Philippines with his connections to law, politics, business, the church (although in his case he was in fact a Protestant), and the legal elite of the United States.

Cosmopolitan Power Brokers: Corporate Law Firms in the Philippines

Salonga's career is consistent with the fact that corporate law firms in the Philippines, as in the United States, serve a prominent role in facilitating connections between economic and political power both within the country's boundaries and between the state and foreign interests. The most prominent corporate law firms in the Philippines had expatriate origins typical of those found in other colonies. Around the time Marcos came to power in the mid-1960s, in particular, there were two major corporate firms—Sycip Salazar; and Ponce Enrile, Siguion Reyna, Montecillo and Belo. Sycip Salazar, still one of the top corporate law firms, was at the forefront of the defense of U.S. military personnel in the Philippines in the 1960s, and it also helped restructure U.S. businesses after the amended treaty between the United States and the Philippines forced some change. The Ponce Enrile firm originated as a branch of Coudert Brothers in 1903 and existed as Fisher, Dewitt, Perkins and Brady—a firm largely of expatriates—for some time prior to Philippine independence. It also represented primarily foreign clients, including, for example, Monsanto. It reportedly had about thirty to forty lawyers in 1965 (Int. P- 4).

The specifics of the connections to politics have long varied among the law firms in the Philippines. The overarching theme, however, is the central role of many prominent lawyers and law firms in facilitating and profiting from the close relationship between state power and economic wealth. The rotation of political power has its counterpart in the change and continuity among those lawyers who serve and participate in political and economic change. As summarized by one of the close observers of the Philippine political landscape, "lawyering in the Philippines" has two components in relationship to political power. One can be termed "influence peddling" or "brokering" and the other is "structuring illegal businesses" (Int. P-5). A senior Philippine businessman made a similar observation that "lawyers always make the arrangements" in business for payments of cash as well (Int. P-6). Indeed, according to a prominent lawyer, each administration favors its own set of "fixers and lawyers" (Int. P-7). The ACCRA law firm, which had a very close relationship to Marcos and later to President Estrada, is another superb example that we discuss in chapter 9.

The specific and often very profitable relationship between legal practice and business can be seen also in the career of Felipe Gozon, one of the individuals who became quite wealthy during the Marcos era and beyond. Gozon's father, a lawyer, served in the cabinet of Macapagal in 1960. Felipe Gozon attended the University of Philippines College of Law and then went to Yale Law School for the 1964–65 academic year. He returned and began to work with the Ponce Enrile law firm. No doubt reflecting his family and his educational pedigree, Gozon was given the opportunity to be the head of the legal department of Philippines Airlines in 1972, when he was only thirty years old. He then returned to private practice with a new firm. He was joined by Enrique Belo, a Harvard law degree recipient and former senior partner with the Ponce Enrile firm, and Magdangal Elma, a former appellate judge with a Yale Law School masters degree. After a while, the lawyers "went their separate ways," according to the Martindale Hubbell description of the firm, but they are now together in the firm of Belo, Gozon, Parel, Asuncion, and Lucila. In the meantime, Gozon did very well during the Marcos years and after, as we shall see also in chapter 9.

Chinese Businesses on the Fringe of Law and the State

The close relationship that we have seen among lawyers, business, and the state is made more complicated by the "Chinese" in the Philippines. The ethnic category is somewhat arbitrary, since many of the prominent "Philippine" business people, such as the Cojuanco family of Corazon Aquino, are themselves descendents from the Chinese, but scholars and local observers tend to find important differences in business practices based on status treated as ethnic identity. There are an identifiable number of "Chinese" businesses—for example, there was a Manila stock exchange identified with large Chinese businesses, and there is a history that has tended to produce a particular relationship between the designated Chinese and the state that is rather different from the one just presented. The relationship of the Chinese is of particular interest since they reportedly represent five percent of the population but control roughly sixty percent of the economy.

The Chinese relationship is based in part on the particular history in the Philippines. They were long excluded from "owning land, exploiting natural resources, or operating public utilities" by the Philippine Constitution (Gambe 2000: 26), and it was difficult to become a citizen as well. They could only participate indirectly with the state. The situation began to change in the 1970s, but there are still continuities that reflect this long history.

The history of the Chinese in the Philippines helped promote an approach to law and to the state that was different from that found among those defined as "Philippine." First, relatively few Chinese entered and continue to enter the legal profession, and indeed for historical reasons the Chinese companies themselves relied on non-Chinese lawyers to serve as brokers for them (Int. P-7). The prominent exception of "Chinese" lawyers is Alexander Sycip, one of the founders of the Sycip Salazar law firm, and only one prominent Chinese judge was named by interviewees—Michael Teehankee (and "after him, none even on Court of Appeals" [Int. P-8]). Reportedly the Sycip firm did begin locally with mostly Chinese clients, but it soon gained a strong position with foreign corporations. The law firm rise paralleled the huge success of Washington Sycip, a U.S. citizen and brother of Alexander Sycip, who was Philippine (the third brother was a Chinese citizen who went into commerce). Washington began the accounting firm that is now the dominant accounting firm in the Philippines. In the case of both Alexander Sycip and Teehankee, interestingly, neither reportedly was strongly identified as Chinese from within the Chinese community.

Washington Sycip also was one of the founders of the Asian Institute of Management (AIM), created initially as part of the Ateneo de Manila University in 1966 with a grant from the Ford Foundation and land donated by Eugenio Lopez, Sr. The MBA program of the AIM was modeled after Harvard, and indeed the Harvard School of Business's dean for external affairs, Stephen Fuller, was the first dean. The school is now located in Makati—the business center of Manila—with land given by the Ayala family, one of the leading business families, and the major grants to the business school have come from Sycip and the Lopez family—all seeking to modernize Philippine businesses generally with management technologies imported from abroad.

According to a leading corporate lawyer, describing the current situation, the corporate law firms might be used by the Chinese taipans if a bond issue or IPO was needed, but for their day-to-day matters they would rely on "one well-connected lawyer" (Int. P-7). According to another knowledgeable observer, "once [there is trust,] they keep the lawyer"] (Int. P-9). Accordingly, there are "small firms" of two to three lawyers in Chinatown (Int. P-9). The Chinese, in addition, were not active in "election issues," but rather were "close to all" sides in the government (Int. P-10). As an economist stated, they "bet on everybody" (Int. P-11). Their approach generally was to "not dare rock the boat" (Int. P-8). The effort to maintain a low profile was evident by the well-known unwillingness even to report or use police authorities when Chinese business people or their family members were the victims of kidnappings.

Similarly, a leading expert on the stock exchanges said that the Manila Stock Exchange, which was "mostly Chinese," relied on "word-of-mouth" without being "very particular about the ethics of the industry," with lots of "insider trading" and "no disclosure or transparency." In contrast, the Makati Stock Exchange was more Spanish and "elitist." The government under Ramos, he noted, sought to merge the two stock exchanges, but the merger was like "oil and water" (Int. P-9). As we shall see, there are organizations seeking to bring the Chinese into the Philippine mainstream, including the Makati Business Club, but the starting point is very different than the other groups comprising the elite of the Philippine economy.

The Core of the Law: The Courts and the Law Schools

The character and eminence of the Supreme Court judges made the Supreme Court, according to a book written in 1964, "the most important legitimizing institution" in the Philippines (cited in del Carmen 1973: 1051). In 1957, George Malcolm, the American who served first as dean of the University of the Philippines Faculty of Law and then as a justice on the Supreme Court for nearly thirty years (1917–45), stated that "for the first fifty years of the twentieth century, no national region could lay claim to jurists who outranked the Filipino Justices in the same period in character, probity, and erudition" (1957: 147). They were schooled in the role of the U.S. Supreme Court, as Malcolm also noted about the court. During the period 1954–56, "Nine of the eleven members . . . had been my law students" (1957: 146). Senior lawyers in the Philippines reported that prior to the Marcos era, "lawyers wanted to be judges," and the judges were regarded as "statesmenlike" (Int. P-7). The judges were "insulated from politics" and "independent" (Int. P-7). According to another commentator, there was a "golden age" before the Marcos era, when cases were won "on the merits" (Int. P-11). The high relative stature of the Supreme Court was and remains consistent with the relative weakness of the Philippine state—as in the United States.

The prominence and high status of the courts, however, did not make the judiciary independent from the structures of power. As many commentators have also noted, for example, agrarian reform has failed repeatedly in the Philippines, in contrast to some of the more economically successful developmental states in Asia (e.g., Riedinger 1995). The progressive tradition in the Philippines has long made land reform an issue in Philippine history. Land reform legislation was enacted in 1954, for example, but it did not have much impact (Riedinger 1995: 97–98). Legal tools helped stop reform, with collaborators against reform working from within administrative processes and the courts.

One of the enduring features of the pattern is that, in the words of an experienced participant in the processes, there are "lawyers all the way through" the administrative machinery and ensuing judicial processes (Int. P-3). A legal activist similarly stated that the courts are "generally instruments to slow down land reform" (Int. P-1). Lawyers and the courts were not per se the major enemies of land reform, but they were part of a process that made land reform extremely problematic throughout the history of the Philippines. The law and the courts played major roles that—whatever the prestige and perceived independence of the courts—undermined any change through land reform that threatened the landowning elite.

The high stature of the Supreme Court in the Philippines was not in any event inconsistent with a court very close to the landowning elite. The courts could play a role moderating and setting the rules for the battles among those elites, especially since the courts, as we have seen, were very close to U.S. colonial power. But the relative newness of the Supreme Court and relative weak institutionalization meant that personal connections and alliances among fragments of the elite might still be seen.

Nevertheless, as explained below, the courts and especially the Supreme Court are central to the moral authority of law in legitimating the prevailing structures of power in the Philippines. The courts embody the fragmentation and personalism of the Philippine state but also the moral authority placed in the law. What happens in the courts and with respect to court reform, therefore, precisely parallels what we see in the double role of law in the Philippines more generally.

There are more than sixty law schools in the Philippines. The first school of law, divided into canon law and civil law, was the University of Santo Tomas, established in 1733 by the Spanish. The two most elite law schools today are the University of the Philippines School of Law and the Ateneo de Manila School of Law. The University of the Philippines School of Law was established by George Malcolm in 1911 in order to train political leaders consistent with the U.S. mission of civilizing the Philippines. The University of the Philippines focuses more on full-time faculty and on scholarship than other law schools.

The Ateneo de Manila School of Law was established in 1936 and is now the leading Roman Catholic law school. Most of the law professors are part-time, and it is not uncommon for faculty to be involved in major cases or even politics more generally. The Ateneo, for example, has a faculty that is ninety percent part-time (Int. P-11). Scholarship generally is encouraged more among the faculty than in the past, but scholarly production is still relatively low—consistent with the part-time status of the faculty.

Fraternities play a major role in the University of the Philippines that can be traced to George Malcolm, who brought Masonic ideals to the university. Malcolm was one of the founders of the Acacia fraternity in 1904 at the University of Michigan (and a Manila chapter in 1909 that is still active). Not surprisingly, the Roman Catholic Ateneo School of Law has "outlawed" and "not recognized" the fraternities (Int. P-11), but the fraternities nevertheless exist without the formal approval of the School of Law. According to one former student at the Ateneo, for example, the school was divided in the early 1980s between the "barbarians" and the fraternity members (Int. P-12). Finally, and also not surprisingly, the

Ateneo is composed mainly, as one of its professors noted, of students "from upper class families" (Int. P-11).

The law schools have at various times been very active in politics, but they have served mainly as key producers of the degree of the Philippine elite. Lawyers were active in the competition to take control of the state and gain riches through that control, and lawyers were also linked together through their fraternities and by some respect for the courts, the laws, and the legal imperial connection to the United States. At the time that Marcos took power in 1965, he embodied this alliance. He had strong U.S. allies, was noted for having the leading national score on the bar exam the year he took it, had a degree from the University of the Philippines, close fraternity relationships with his legal peers, and ties especially through marriage to the Philippine elite. The Philippines was hardly a thriving democracy, but as with respect to India and the British, the United States could claim that it left the Philippines with a democratic government and a very strong position for law and lawyers.

Conclusion

The U.S. colonial policy of reinforcing the power of the Philippine elite was quite successful. It included the creation of a relatively weak state and the buttressing of the role of the corporate lawyer as politician, statesperson, academic, and even business leader. The pattern strikingly resembles the one in the United States around the beginning of the twentieth century. One obvious difference is that, while the role of the elite law schools in the Philippines resembles that of the elite schools in the United States, the elite graduates from the Philippines also need to get the extra validation that comes with study at leading law schools in the United States. As with respect to India, but perhaps even more so, the legal capital of elite lawyers was strongly fortified with other forms of capital—in particular, social, economic, political, religious, and foreign capital. Courts and legal legitimacy were central to the Philippine state. That is not to say that the Philippines was a well-functioning democracy or a rapidly expanding economy. It was instead seen as the definition of crony capitalism. But the position of lawyers and law as a legacy of U.S. colonialism was relatively strong, as in India. We now turn to the countries where the colonial legacy left lawyers in a much weaker position— Indonesia, Malaysia, Singapore, and Korea.

CHAPTER SEVEN

Indonesia, Malaysia, and Singapore: Late and Relatively Weak Colonial Legal Investment Converted into State Leadership. Korea as a Different Model of Weakness

This chapter examines a variety of Asian models that contrast with the showcase empires in India and the Philippines. The United States's opportunistic colonial venture in the Philippines was conceived as a way to stake out a position in Asian trade, but investment in state-building came very soon after the colonial enterprise began. India began quite clearly with law in the service of trade, but India's history was also characterized by a gradual nineteenth-century transformation from administration by the East India Company to the Indian Raj. Here we examine the same phenomenon elsewhere in Asia—from lawyers in the service of trade to strategies linked to moral credibility for empires, the co-optation of local elites, and state-building and governance.

Our focus is on narratives of transformation in Indonesia and on the Malay Peninsula—Malaysia and Singapore—where, despite the late investment by lawyers in the state, there was still an important legacy and the development of a legal cohort that used its strategic position and links to the colonial powers to help lead the move to independence. We then focus on South Korea, which requires some further comparative material on Japan and its colonial governance in Korea. The legal legacy in each of these countries, as we shall see, was relatively weak when compared with those in India and the Philippines.

Indonesia: A Late Effort to Legitimate an Exploitive Colonial Relationship

In Indonesia, the lawyers initially involved in facilitating commercial relations were Dutch trained and served both the Dutch and the Chinese trading communities. They were part of a colonial relationship designed essentially to enrich the Dutch. The Dutch elected to invest very little in legitimating colonial administration until relatively late in the colonial period. The investment came because the balance of power within the Netherlands changed in favor of those arguing for a more morally justified form of colonialism. As noted before (chap. 3), the so-called discovery of adat law in the mid- to late nineteenth century preceded a turn within the Netherlands toward a new policy at the beginning of the twentieth century. The dual system of law was questioned but continued to play a major role.

The turning point in colonial policy took place in 1901 when Alexander Willem Frederik Idenburg, on behalf of a Christian coalition government, launched the new "ethical policy" to support and train indigenous populations in Indonesia. At this point, very late in the colonial regime in Indonesia, the Dutch began to invest more in building a colonially trained elite. The first steps toward legal education of the Indonesians only began in 1909, and the law faculty at Batavia only opened in 1924. Members of the Javanese elite, in particular, were trained in Indonesia and in the Netherlands to assume administrative duties.

According to Lev, accordingly, "Most early Indonesian law students were high born Javanese who, from their knowledge of the Dutch language, were already familiar with the national level of colonial authority" (1972: 256). As noted also in chapter 3, legal training was largely confined to the traditional Javanese aristocracy. As Lev stated, "only the sons of high priyayi—often from bupati [local rulers or regents] families—were encouraged to study law." In practice, there was some further expansion: "lower priyayi families also took advantage of legal education" (1972: 256). The expansion of legal education, however, had a limited impact because of the local tradition of the Javanese elite. The priyayi maintained their traditional antipathy to trade and commerce. Social status came from power in bureaucratic positions and not from positions related to trade and commerce.

Private legal practice by local Indonesian lawyers was discouraged both by the Dutch and within the Indonesian social context. One famous graduate of the University of Leiden, Besar Matrokusumo, said, "When I graduated from Leiden . . . I let my family know that I intended to become an advocate. . . . They were very much against this. They couldn't understand or approve such an occupation for a man of my [social and educational] background. It was sinking to a very low level. Government was . . . [acceptable] but certainly not private law practice" (Lev 1972: 262 n. 21). By 1940, there were no more than 350 private non-Dutch advocates in Indonesia, of whom about 175 were located on Java (Lev 1976). These private practitioners, however, tended to be the most politically active, legally trained group on the nationalistic side, since political activity was not allowed for those who were part of the colonial bureaucracy. The private practitioners were also well connected to local and international business. They could therefore draw on connections to local elites, including the Javanese aristocracy from which they came; to Dutch politics and law through their training; and in practice to the businesses that invested in Indonesia.

Not surprisingly, despite their embeddedness in the private world of business, they maintained a strong orientation to the state. As with respect to lawyers in other colonial regimes, this elite foreign-trained group became the source of many of the early leaders of independence. In Lev's words, "The PNI [Indonesian National Party] was . . . significantly a product of the Ethical Policy, which produced the beginnings of a new professional stratum out of the old priyayi class. The founding members of the party were typically new urban professionals" (Lev 1972: 276). There are many examples, including Sukarno, who was an engineering graduate from the technical faculty in Bandung (although he never really pursued the career). Furthermore, according to Lev, of the eight other leading founders, five were advocates (Iskaq, Sartono, Budiarto, Ali Sastroamijoyo, and Sunaryo), another was an engineer (Anwari), and two were doctors (Cipto Mangunkusumo and Samsi Sastrowidagdo) (Lev 1972: 276).

For a time, therefore, "advocates seemed to be very influential in politics" (Lev 1972: 276). They depleted the professional ranks in order to take on positions in the new government: "Sartono was speaker of Parliament, Iskaq a minister of finance, Ali Sastroamijoyo twice prime minister, Besar secretary-general of the Ministry of Justice—two of whose ministers, Lukman Wiriadinata (PSI) and Jody Gondokusumo (PRN, Partai Rakyat Nasional), were advocates—Sunaryo a foreign minister, and so on" (Lev 1972: 276).

Independence in Indonesia, therefore, represented for a time the effective transformation of a foreign-trained legal elite, serving mainly an international clientele, into nationalistic leaders and ultimately state builders. With independence, however, came a separation from the Dutch, paradoxically undermining the position of the nationalistic legal elite. The mainly expatriate lawyers and judges went back to the Netherlands, making the legal community even smaller than it was. The position of lawyers and law at the time of independence was accordingly not very strong. Under Sukarno and then Suharto, as we shall see in chapter 8, it declined even further.

Malaysia: Legitimation through a Strategy of Divide and Conquer

The first efforts to invest in governance in the Malay peninsula came out of a desire to protect the trade that was centered in Penang, Malacca, and Singapore and built on the tin mines worked by Chinese immigrants (Goh 2008: 63). In 1867, according to Goh, riots in Penang initiated a period of instability on the west coast of Malaya. Secret societies of Chinese workers began to form alliances with different groups of sultans to gain control over the tin mines central to British economic exploitation. The British decided to separate economics and politics with an ethnic divide. After 1875, they created a system of indirect administration with the sultans playing the role of local leaders in exchange for political peace. As with respect to Indonesia, there was a certain scientific discourse that fit the approach: "The preservation of the customary authority by the colonial administration coincided with anthropological discourse on the Malays" and what was necessary to "civilize" them (Goh 2008: 63) (associated with Alfred Wallace), but the main goal was to assure the security and viability of the Straits of Malacca.

There were several kinds of Chinese to be managed at that time. One group was linked to the Chinese secret societies that had been opposed to the Qing dynasty. The second group was the Straits Chinese, educated by the British and seeking recognition by the British (Goh 2008: 66). Others were Chinese-speaking modernists typically either on the left or the right politically. The British approach reflected British division between the conservatives and a group of technocrats, both well represented in colonial administration and both with a strong interest in building up the sultans as a bureaucracy and ally of the Europeans.

The British colonial strategy that emerged was essentially to divide, conquer, and co-opt along ethnic and class lines. First, they cultivated the traditional Malay ruling aristocracy and gave to its members a monopoly on political leadership (Hilley 2001). After the turn of the twentieth century, as Hilley notes, "the Malay aristocrats of the younger generation received special education and training . . . and were recruited into the colonial bureaucracy" (2001: 334). Accordingly, by using the strategy of reinforcement and cooptation of a local elite, the result was that, "The prestige and authority conferred by traditional social status were thus re-emphasized by administrative authority derived from the colonial regime" (2001: 334). As with respect to the British in India, the United States in the Philippines, and the Dutch in Indonesia, the colonial strategy was to rule where possible through an existing elite, which also received benefits from the exchange.

Second, the British kept the Malay peasant majority out of the colonial governance arrangement. They justified the exclusion in part by the need to maintain the traditional way of life of the peasants. They therefore also declined to provide them with education in the English language, and the staffing of the clerical and technical positions was left to immigrants from Ceylon, India, and South China. The professional class was therefore imported, providing the basis for a legal profession ethnically different from the political leadership and the bulk of the general population.

Ethnic divisions were reinforced through differential access to education abroad. From the period of British colonialism (1786–1957) until 1962, the solicitors and barristers who practiced in Malaysia were all educated in England (Machado and Said 1981). As was the case in Indonesia, the elite of the profession occupied positions in corporate law firms oriented toward abroad. The traditional law firms connect to the present through the three "S firms," Shearn Delamore & Co., Shook Lin & Bok, and Skrine. All three law firms can be traced to expatriate colonial origins. The three also traditionally focused on litigation—although Shook Lin's stronger Chinese connections reportedly led at one point to substantial conveyancing work (akin to what we shall see enriching the legal profession as land prices rose in the small confines of Hong Kong and Singapore). Shearn Delamore & Co. began operation in 1905. Shook Lin & Bok was initially established in

1918. Skrine, finally, began in 1963 after a split in another firm established by expatriates. These lawyers represented a foreign-educated enclave oriented to the resolution of disputes mainly affecting foreign businesses.

The S firms also provided the bar leadership represented by the Bar Council. In Lev's words, "Ethnic Indians first and then ethnic Chinese, who paid for their own educations, made up the local component of the local bar" (1998). This ethnic make-up meant that, in 1970, the private legal profession had only 38 ethnic Malay lawyers, versus some 364 ethnic Chinese and 251 ethnic Indian (plus 52 who remained and were British) (Lev 1998: 442). The few Malays from the elite who were provided legal education by the British colonists "joined the administration" (Lev 1998: 442) or served as judges rather than going into legal practice. The private bar was almost entirely Indian and Chinese.

Malaysian lawyers began to be produced locally when the Faculty of Law in Singapore began operation in 1959, and the University of Malaya Faculty of Law commenced in 1976. The bar remained close knit and cohesive, however, well into the 1980s. There was a blending of the Malay aristocracy, who were educated to govern, the Indian and Chinese lawyers who served foreign commerce and argued in the courts, and a judiciary that also contained a well-educated Malay group. According to a senior lawyer from one of the traditional S firms, the leaders of the legal profession, including judges who were mainly ethnic Malay, "all studied in London," "met in London," and possessed a "feeling of camaraderie" consistent with their shared experience at the Inns of Court (Int. M-1).[1]

Independence was granted to Malaya by the British in 1957—with Singapore first added to what became Malaysia and then separated in 1965. The leaders of the move to independence came largely from the English-educated milieu of elite professionals and bureaucrats, including the lawyers (Nair 1999: 92). Their legitimacy was based in large part on their ability to manage potential ethnic divisions and by their opposition to the powerful communist movement that characterized what the British termed the Malay Emergency—and sought to quell from 1948

---

1. The authors conducted interviews in each of the countries studied. In order to protect the confidentiality of the interviewees, the interviews are identified only by country and number. The countries are abbreviated as follows: HK, Hong Kong; India; Indon., Indonesia; K, South Korea; M, Malaysia; P, Philippines; and S, Singapore.

until independence. The socialization in and respect for British law helped to sustain the unity and legitimacy of this relatively moderate leadership.

This new government continued the anticommunist focus that the British embedded in the law through colonial legislation enacted in the late 1940s in response to the Malay Emergency—including the Sedition Ordinance, the Printing Presses Ordinance, and the Internal Security Act—all of which became part of an apparatus still used to control expressions of dissent (Annuar 2002: 145). The focus on internal security was part and parcel of the initial elite strategy. According to Nair,

> Official nationalism's initial success in dislodging competing ideas can be explained in part by its discursive construction of an internal enemy after colonial rule ended. The enemy, which was initially the organized left, later included. . . . [students, laborers, intellectuals, and various other political opponents]. The source of the state's legitimacy thus lay in its claims to secure political stability, social order and national security. (1999: 92)

The ingrained respect for British traditions among the elite led to a relatively prominent place for law after the post–World War II transition to independence. According to Lev, "Unlike Indonesia, in Malaysia legal process has been a significant factor in governance, in part because the political elite, many of whom have been lawyers, found it congenial and inexpensive, and because it has been the safest political medium for ethnic relations" (1998: 147) The first three prime ministers of Malaysia came from the legal profession and were educated abroad. As Lev also noted, the English-educated bar was fairly comfortable with the status quo after independence—"membership in the national political and social elites disinclined them either to challenge seriously the decisions of political leaders or to toe the line too respectfully on institutional issues" (2007: 442). They were in a strong local position, prosperous, and still benefiting from their role in state-building. They did not experience the relatively quick decline found in Indonesia.

They nevertheless had some real disadvantages when compared to India and the Philippines. The period of colonial investment in law was relatively short, and it was part of an ethnic divide. The Malay ethnic majority of the population was represented in the judiciary, but it was mostly absent from the private legal profession; and the elite of the profession and the judiciary was very closely tied to trade and to the British legal system.

Singapore: From British Barrister to Leader of Asian Values

The Singapore story of law and the genesis of the state can be seen in the career of Harry Lee Kwan Yew, the founding father of Singapore. He grew up as a leading representative of the British-educated Chinese that comprised one of the groups that emerged during the British colonial period on the Malay Peninsula. Under his leadership, Singapore became a particularly successful example of the classic strategy of converting legal capital into political capital. Lee Kwan Yew's autobiography provides a fascinating account of this process.

The biography of Lee Kwan Yew is almost the paradigmatic example of the generation of colonial lawyers reconverted into leaders of independence. The product of a Chinese family that was highly anglicized, Lee Kwan Yew's first language was English, and he was educated in the institutions reserved for the colonial elite, including Raffles College. This education placed him in a particular milieu in Singapore. As he stated in his autobiography, "When I started my career as a lawyer in the 1950s, therefore, I already had a network of friends and acquaintances in important positions in the government and the professions in Singapore and Malaya" (1999: 43). As he further noted, "It was the easy old-boy network of an elite at the very top of the English-educated group nurtured by the British colonial education system" (1999: 43).

His education was disrupted by the war. He was at one point captured by the Japanese, learning firsthand that he could not count on the British for Singapore's security. After the war he was admitted to Middle Temple and attended Cambridge University. He reported that he was inspired in London by lectures on socialism given by Harold Laski at the London School of Economics. As he stated, socialism was "attractive to students from the colonies" (1999: 105). As happened to many others, the experience of Britain also pushed him in an anticolonial direction: "I had now seen the British in their own country" (1999: 113). Again in his words, "I appeared to have become deeply anti-British" in part because of "my experience of the colour prejudice" (1999: 113). He sought allies for a smooth transition to independence: "I was eager to make contact with political leaders in the Labour Party, especially those who could assist people like me who wanted an early end to colonial rule and an independent Malaya that would include Singapore" (1999: 128). With his education and contacts, he was perfectly positioned to serve as intermediary for British-Singapore relations, whether dealing with commercial matters or with political issues tied to British rule.

Returning with his wife, Kwa Geok Choo, who also was admitted to the bar after excelling in studies at Cambridge, Lee Kwan Yew did his pupilage with a British expatriate solicitor, John Laycock. Laycock was married to a Chinese woman and had been practicing law in Singapore since the 1930s. The colonial bar that Lee Kwan Yew joined was very much the product of Singapore's status as an entrepôt. Asians were a minority within the bar and part of a professional and judicial hierarchy almost exclusively British. The Asian professional group did not possess much local social capital, given that they were cut off from their own ethnic groups both socially and linguistically. The bar was also very small. When Lee Kwan Yew and his wife were called to the bar in Singapore in 1951, the "entire Bar had 140 members" (1999: 142).

The local practitioners described by Lee Kwan Yew tended to be hybrids of the colonial culture and indigenous traditions. They often were married to locals, for example (1999: 134–37). Laycock typified this background. In addition, Lee Kwan Yew described Laycock as the "moving spirit in the main political party, the Progressive Party," whose "nominal chief was another lawyer, C. C. Tan" (1999: 137). The Party's leaders were "mostly returned students who had read law or medicine in Britain in the 30s and were overawed and overwhelmed by English values" (1999: 137). The principal political adversary prior to independence was Chief Minister David Marshall—"A mercurial, flamboyant Sephardic Jew" and the leading criminal lawyer in Singapore (1999: 177). There was also a substantial Indian ethnic group within the bar, such as existed in what became independent Malaysia, and this group included a number of the future ministers of justice—including Kenny Birne, Eddy Barker, and René Eber (1999: 142).

These future leaders of independence did not initially possess very strong local connections. The Chinese merchants, for example, were organized through guilds and clans that controlled Chinese schools and community groups (Yew 1999: 190). They hardly participated in the processes of colonial emancipation, which were led by a very small group with a nucleus among anglicized professionals. One reason was simply linguistic. English was the language of colonial administration and therefore the language also of the moves toward independence. This linguistic exclusion of the great majority of the Chinese community was exploited by the communists in order to stir up hostilities against the colonial regime.

To make a name for himself among a group of better established individuals, both within the professional field and in the emerging political sphere, Lee Kwan Yew understandably adopted the strategy of seeking to gain allies within those dominated or excluded from the political game—as it turned out, workers and Chinese students. This approach led him to a position that was more radical politically than some of his competitors, but he could also reaffirm his legalism as against the communists: "My way of constitutional opposition, working within the law, was in marked contrast to that of the communists, and I got results" (1999: 211).

His first great opportunity came when the British used Gurkas against a picket line in the furtherance of a strike. Lee Kwan Yew was portrayed in the press as "fighting for the downtrodden masses against a heartless bunch of white colonial exploiters," and he succeeded in becoming the negotiator with the British over the matter (Yew 1999: 151). He thus found his political voice as a radical reformer who maintained a distance from communism. In his words,

> The press exposure and publicity enhanced my professional reputation. I was no longer just a brash young lawyer back from Cambridge with academic honours. I had led striking workers, spoken up for them and was trusted by them . . . without frightening the English-educated intelligentsia. My friends and I were now convinced that in the unions we would find the mass base and by extension the political muscle we had been seeking. (1999: 151)

He summed up the experience as follows: "I had established myself as a legal adviser who played by the rules" (1999: 153).

In a later matter involving criminal prosecutions of students, Lee Kwan Yew opted for a more political defense, becoming therefore "famous for championing a left wing cause" (1999: 62). He represented "one of those eccentric Englishmen from the bourgeois class who chose to be more proletarian than the poorest worker while still living the good life" (1999: 162). This tactical choice makes explicit the double game balancing politics and law. In order to invest on the terrain of overtly political advocacy, one must necessarily possess substantial legal authority or links to local social capital. The young Lee Kwan Yew lacked that legal authority at that time and also lacked broad political connections. He had to work carefully to cultivate both his political credibility and his legal reputation.

Indian lawyers in the fight for independence could build their credibility on the basis of a double dose of capital—one side from affiliation with the British bar and the other as notable Indian Brahmins. Ties to major landowners and businesses also characterized the Indian legal elite. In contrast, the lawyer-politicians of Singapore had to try to keep a distance from the colonial power and build up their local capital. They could not seek simply to play on the divide between two groups, foreign and local, that could ignore or even reject one another. This small elite of anglicized practitioners in Singapore instead used their linguistic mastery and their social proximity to imperial institutions to carefully construct the embryo of a local political field in the process of transition. The challenge was daunting. They confronted a population of immigrants, merchants, and workers structured around diverse Chinese and Malay communities with nothing more in common than their weak integration into colonial structures—as confirmed by the lack of facility in the English language. English was not the language used in the institutions that structured their communities—families, clans, and above all the schools patronized by the merchant elite, in which Mandarin was the language of instruction. Lee Kwan Yew recognized the challenge and invested in learning Mandarin and the local popular languages of Malay and Hokkien.

In short, the classic strategy of conversion of legal expertise into political notoriety was not readily available. Both the legal authority and the linguistic ability of this professional elite had value only within colonial circles, which in turn devalued them because of their indigenous origins. This disqualification was not compensated for by the accumulation of local social capital. The result was the opposite of the situation in India where the legal and social capital combined to make Indian lawyers the natural leaders of the movement for independence. These new arrivals in Singapore instead had to nourish and build alliances in both fields, with the risk of being denounced as opportunists or even traitors by both their friends and their opponents.

The brilliant strategy that they adopted combined an effort to become the voice of the disadvantaged at the same time as Lee Kwan Yew and his allies sought to persuade the British that they were the only safe alternative to communism. According to Lee Kwan Yew, they hoped that, in the unions, "We would find the mass base and, by extension, the political muscle" (1999: 194). Without a knowledge of Mandarin, however, it was very hard to link to the "Chinese educated" in Singapore: "But I was also convinced that if I could not harness some of these dynamic young people to our cause, to what my friends and I stood for, we would never succeed. So far, we had links only with the English-educated and the Malays" (1999: 194). He embarked on a linguistic and political strategy to build allies with the Chinese-speaking community who tended to favor the Communist Party. He and the People's Action Party (PAP) initially won an election with the support of the Communist Party (1999: 207). Pushing then for independence, Lee Kwan Yew played a complex game with his British friends. He felt the need for the British to "give us enough room to build a non-communist government," but also "to have the British in a fall-back position if the communists should gain the upper hand" (1999: 229).

He especially made friends therefore with Conservatives in Britain who "were to prove most valuable in the sixties when we had to fight the communists in Singapore" (1999: 234). More generally, his political strategy was to outflank the Communists: "We adopted the proven methods of our communist adversaries" (1999: 327). Thus, after gaining power in an alliance with the communists in 1958, he promised educational reforms and other policies designed to win over the broad populace. As he wrote, "The broad policy . . . was not to be outmaneuvered by the communists" (1999: 349). The culmination of his Asian strategy was a linguistic and political difference from the British: "Speaking in Hokkien and Mandarin, I had convinced the Chinese that I was not a stooge of the British, that I was fighting for their future" (1999: 487). He thus played a leading role first in working with Malaya and then moving to independence from Malaysia when the alliance fell apart in the period 1963–65.

Playing a double-agent role masterfully, Lee Kwan Yew took advantage of his British friends and his familiarity with British colonial institutions. At the same time, however, he could denounce the arrogance of the British and help to mobilize and represent anticolonial sentiment within a general population in Singapore with which he once had very little in common. Certainly the ties and credibility abroad helped him on the path to leadership toward independence. And his legal strategies had helped him build alliances that could be enhanced by substantial linguistic, political, and community investments. Overall, however, relatively little professional authority went into the strategic mix that brought Lee Kwan Yew and his allies to power.

Preliminary Conclusions and the Korean Contrast

The examples in this chapter differ from those in India and the Philippines, where the legacy of colonialism and independence was an elite legal profession strongly fortified with local social capital. We do not see the same legacy in Indonesia, Malaysia, and Singapore, but in each of these cases we still see a legal elite succeeding in making some transition from a colonially trained elite into leadership for independence—with the added local credibility that comes from that leadership.

The Japanese, as noted also in chapter 3, sought to strengthen the state by importing legal institutions from Europe and the United States. Law was above all to be seen as "a branch of public administration," with law graduates going into the Ministry of Justice and staffing the courts and offices of the prosecutors (Feeley and Miyazawa 2007: 160). Despite the activities of a number of lawyers drawing some support from U.S. legal missionaries, however, the bar was quite weak and certainly lacked any ability to resist repression and authoritarianism leading to World War II (2007: 165–66). The bulk of investment in law, as noted before, went into the strong state and its legitimacy. The more Prussian model left relatively little opportunity for the investments undertaken by the small private bar.

South Korea's legal profession suffered from a double weakness, since its creation and legitimacy were tied to the Japanese. The pattern promoted by the Japanese colonial relationship in Korea, which began around the turn of the twentieth century, left a private profession even more marginal to state power than in Japan. According to Seong-Hyun Kim, "Faced with the western world's invasion . . . and with internal demand for the destruction of the feudal system, the Chosun dynasty declared 'fourteen reforms' in 1895," which were in fact forced on Korea by Japan (Kim, forthcoming). Following the Japanese pattern, accordingly, the Legal Training Institute (LTS) was established that year as a means to develop public prosecutors and lawyers. The professors who taught at the LTS were of three kinds of background. One group included

Koreans who had studied law in Japan. The second group had studied French law and was recommended by an advisor, Laurent Crémasy. The last one included Japanese professors who were then "gradually replaced by Korean professors" (Kim, forthcoming). The LTS graduated only 210 individuals before 1909. The graduates' careers, moreover, were initially blocked by the caste system of Chosun society. The *yangban*, which was the dominant class, did not support any increased role for law in Korean life.

Bosung College, a private entity, was established in 1905. Bosung offered a two-year program taught mainly by teachers educated in Japan. The first examinations were held in 1907. Twenty people applied and six candidates were successful. After 1910 and continuing until 1946, Korea was ruled directly by the Japanese. While not a priority for the Japanese, "even under colonial domination, the legal educational institutions continued to develop" (Kim, forthcoming). In particular, the LTS changed its name to Kyong Seong Vocational School in 1911 and again to the Kyong Seong Law College (KLC) in 1916. It moved up in status, while the "Bosung College became the Bosung Private Law and Commerce School (BPLCS)" (Kim, forthcoming).

In 1919, demonstrations for national independence by the Koreans "induced the Japanese government to carry out more appeasing colonial policies." In particular, "The Japanese elevated the Korean education system to the same level as their own" (Kim, forthcoming). There were competing schools of law. Koreans favoring independence promoted Chosun Private School with fund-raising campaigns that began in 1923. The Japanese, however, established a high-level university—Kyong Seong Imperial University (KIU)—the predecessor of the present Seoul National University (SNU). The professors at KIU were Japanese. The first bar examination was held in 1922. From that period until 1942, 181 of the 5,267 examinees passed the examination. There were two lawyers' organizations—the Japanese Lawyers' Association (Kyong Seong no.1) and the Korean Lawyers' Association (Kyong Seong no. 2). Efforts to integrate them failed until, finally, "both sides were integrated into the Kyong Seong Bar Association and it had 230 lawyers as members" (Kim, forthcoming). The very small bar therefore was closely linked to Japan. During World War II, the Japanese integrated the Korean legal system even closer with Japan. As Kim states, at that point "the courts were virtually subordinated to the Vice-regal, and judicial power wasn't independent at all" (Kim, forthcoming).

After the war ended with Japanese defeat and Korean independence, the Koreans created SNU from KIU, Korea University from BPLCS, and Yonsei University from Yonhi College. These schools of law began inauspiciously, however, in part because, "they ran short of professors because the Japanese legal professors returned to their country" (Kim, forthcoming). Also, according to Kim, "The judiciary shortage was so grave that the American Military Government Office even qualified Americans and Koreans who had no experience in the legal profession (Kim, forthcoming). Finally, formal independence from Japan did not bring immediate intellectual independence. As Kim points out, "Until the 1950s, the Korean jurisprudence imitated the Japanese one. Almost all of the legal professors had graduated from KIU or prestigious Japanese universities, and most of the legal manuals were translations of Japanese teaching materials" (Kim, forthcoming).

Not surprisingly, the legal profession in South Korea did not have much to build on. It could not draw on a reputation for leadership and independence. It was too closely identified with the Japanese in terms of laws, procedures, and even direct collaboration. And the Japanese approach, at best, left very little place for a private legal profession to connect to economic and state power. Finally, as Brazinsky notes (2007), the United States made a conscious decision after World War II to resist the Korean left in part by maintaining the central role of the conservative, Japanese-trained civil service in governing the state. The battle against communism, soon to heat up in the Korean War, counseled an alliance with conservatives in many cases tied to the Japanese colonial relationship.

We conclude, therefore, that the legacy of colonialism and independence in Korea was even weaker than in Indonesia, Malaysia, and Singapore. There was a very small private profession. It was linked in many ways to the Japanese. It could not claim any position of leadership in Korea's independence from Japan. And the model of the state implemented in Korea by Japan left very little room for private lawyers in the state or the economy.

Turf Battles of the Cold War: Lawyer-Politicians Challenged by Technocrats as Modernizers

Despite the relatively promising beginnings of legal notables as founding fathers of the new Asian states that are the main focus of our research, the political capital of lawyers declined during the period after World War II and especially that of the Cold War. The chapters in part III explore the patterns of relative decline and the factors that produced them. One general phenomenon was that elite lawyer-politicians who led the moves to independence appeared too linked to large landowning classes, foreign interests, and the foreign legitimacy that had helped to build their stature and wealth. In India in particular, they were too ready to defend those class interests in the guise of protecting political liberties. In the cases where the position of lawyers was relatively weak after independence, exemplified especially by Indonesia and South Korea, elite lawyer-politicians were rapidly eliminated from state power by military or civil dictatorships. Leadership positions in the field of state power were taken by technocrats claiming expertise in the field of economic development. The technocrats were seen to be more useful and more accommodating to the authoritarian and developmental states. This introduction provides the rationale for the structure of the following three chapters and then moves to an elaboration of the context for the pressures and investments that characterized the Cold War period and framed the developments that took place in individual Asian countries. We return to the history of law and state in the United States, which framed the approach taken in U.S. foreign policy in the Cold War and after. We have seen the impact of the Cold War already in shaping the struggles for independence in Malaysia and Singapore. Here we see how the approach so important in the 1960s and 1970s emerged to play such a large role in Asian countries.

The chapters proceed in the reverse order of the preceding part. The preceding part began with the two Asian examples of sustained investment in building a legal elite with some institutional support among law schools, courts, and a legal profession. It began with India and the Philippines and then continued with a chapter on the countries with less sustained legal investment—Indonesia, Malaysia, Singapore and South Korea. We reverse that order here by beginning with the countries where domestic politics and the Cold War led the legal profession to quickly lose whatever position it had (chap. 8)—with Indonesia and South Korea being leading examples. Indonesia's small legal profession was quickly marginalized under Sukarno and was put aside also by Suharto's authoritarian regime. In South Korea, the tiny legal profession played a relatively weak role in the state or economy in the first two decades of the Cold War and South Korea's independence.

Chapter 9 shows two examples, the Philippines and Singapore, involving a relative marginalization of law but strong participation by lawyers in the construction of authoritarian regimes. In very different ways, lawyers helped to sustain relatively unchecked state power, and, as with respect to South Korea and Indonesia in the previous chapter, their actions drew strength from U.S. anticommunist policies in the Cold War. Chapter 10 then provides two examples, India and Malaysia, where lawyers did indeed lose stature and power as states moved toward more authoritarian policies, but the position taken by the legal elite, in contrast to the Philippines and Singapore, turned relatively quickly against those policies and the political actors that generated them.

The chapters in this part highlight the role of economists as competitors with lawyers. One of the features of the period after World War II in Asia (as in Latin America [Dezalay and Garth 2002]) was an increase in the competition between economists and lawyers in the field of state power. We see elements of that same competition within the field of power in the United States, seen especially in the Reagan era of economic deregulation. In terms of U.S. foreign policy toward developing states, there was a division in the relationship between economists and law promoted in the Philippines and in the era of dollar diplomacy. Economics took priority in the Cold War against communism.

This competition between economists and lawyers tended to occur earlier in the outposts of the Cold War than in the United States. As we shall see, Cold War policies responsive to the position of law that U.S. policymakers found abroad helped to create and exacerbate the competition between lawyers and economists. Beginning especially in the 1960s, the legal elite that dominated U.S. foreign policy during the Cold War was more likely to work with the military and to encourage the rise of modernizing economists than it was to promote legal ideals or policies.

The U.S. position, whether promoting law, economics, or military led modernization, reflected the relative strength of the legal elite in the United States as contrasted with the relatively weak position of lawyers in the field of state power in Europe and in countries modeled on Europe. In contrast to the situation in the United States, there was a relative hostility in Europe (and in most other countries) by elite lawyer-politicians to the social state and to state economic interventionism. This hostility helped to produce the relative marginalization of lawyer-politicians from the ruling bureaucracies that presided over economic reconstruction after World War II.

The United States was the only major exception to the more or less dramatic devaluation of the political capital of lawyers in the period before and after World War II. It is true that the corporate bar in New York, with close ties to Wall Street and corporate power, was hostile to the New Deal and its potential threat to its clients (Shamir 1995). But unlike the situation in virtually all other countries, elite U.S. lawyers still managed to adjust through the activities of a fraction of the legal elite who played a central role in the reorganization of the structures of the U.S. federal state. Putting themselves in the service of the Roosevelt administration in order to defend New Deal policies from attacks by leaders of the bar, in particular, a meritocratic group of young Jewish lawyers succeeded, in the words of Jerrold Auerbach, in turning the New Deal in effect into a "lawyers' deal" (Auerbach 1976; Shamir 1995; Irons 1993). The Washington law firms then took their place within the elite of the legal profession, attracting new generations of legal talent anxious to serve private clients as well as the regulatory agencies of the New Deal. The challenge of the New Deal was therefore absorbed, and the position of the legal elite and the corporate law firms transformed and strengthened as part of a more active state.

The strong position of legal elites in the United States shaped the position of the United States in the Cold War and in the period after the Cold

War. As a result, they played a major role in shaping the Asian states during that period. The hegemonic politics orchestrated by the so-called foreign policy establishment, discussed in more detail below, was a strategy to maintain power at home and abroad. As we shall see, it was not inconsistent with supporting authoritarian regimes. For nearly half a century, this club of "wise men" (Isaacson and Thomas 1986) and elder statesmen functioned as what Bourdieu termed the "left hand of the state," or more precisely, as a state authority that transcended partisan politics.

In Wall Street and Washington, D.C., therefore, legal professionals were able to profit fully from investments in the reformist state structures emerging after the Great Depression. In the European countries, in contrast, most legal commentators in the period after World War II lamented a "decline of law," a diminished role of judges, and more generally a devaluation of the role of law and lawyers in the field of state power (Abel-Smith and Stevens 1967). The position of law in the state did not bode well for a strong influence by lawyers in these countries either in their own foreign policies or over foreign legal elites seeking support for their local positions abroad.

The dramatically contrasting evolutions in the different legal fields resulted in part from the geopolitical logic in the period after World War II. The United States was the overall victor in the war. The strong position of the U.S. legal profession, more importantly, also relates to the historical ability of lawyers in the United States to adapt to new social circumstances and challenges. The history of the legal profession in the United States, described briefly in chapter 4, helped to facilitate this kind of adaptation, in contrast to the history of the relationship between law and politics in Europe. The different national histories produced particular hierarchical structures that defined the legal and political division of labor—and therefore the strategies for the accumulation of legal capital through investments in the political field. In this respect, the contrast between the different sides of the Atlantic is quite marked and significant in defining the relative strengths and weaknesses of lawyers with respect both to the social state and the Cold War.

The U.S. legal field has remained relatively open through three centuries of development. It is characterized by a pronounced social and professional diversity, with multiple lines of recruitment ranging from highly selective legal academies and professional occupations to relatively open educations and careers. Furthermore, the lines between legal careers are relatively open in the United States, allowing a circulation among

different positions in the legal field. This mobility permits the most entrepreneurial of lawyers to accumulate quite varied combinations of legal capital and social resources. The internal competition among legal
agents in the United States is also played out on the political field. The
relatively open competition leads to quite diverse yet complementary political strategies that join together to support the extension and renova-
tion of markets for the production of the rule of law, including strategies
through legal clinics or public interest law (Sarat and Scheingold 1998).
This openness was very much evident in the way that entrepreneurial
lawyers took advantage of the New Deal at the same time as much of the
elite bar resisted it.

In contrast, the long political history of the European legal fields has
led to a codification of a quite hierarchical division of labor linked to
pronounced stratification in legal markets (Dezalay 1992). Each of the
segments of the market is protected by rigorous barriers to entry built
through a professional elite that privileges high priests of the law and
deprecates so-called legal merchants—especially those linked to a "vul-
gar" clientele. The various categories of practice in a stratified market
increase the cost and risk of potential conversions of political capital
into legal capital—a situation hardly likely to lead aspiring legal elites,
for example, to invest in radical or militant politics. Furthermore, the
enduring restrictions on entry have long favored a strong family role in
the accumulation and reproduction of legal capital—increasing also the
social homogeneity of the relatively closed circle that makes up the professional elite.

These Malthusian strategies of limited reproduction in Europe go
with a political divide between conservatives and more progressive reformers corresponding to two fractions of the property-holding classes.
The high cost of legal services has made law a privileged instrument for
the defense of large family estates and dominant commercial positions.
Elite lawyers can serve the well-to-do at the same time they invest in politics, but the investments are highly circumscribed. In particular, elite legal practice is not inconsistent with public engagement on behalf of great
causes such as political liberalism or nationalism, since building an appropriate national prominence leads also to prosperous clients. In contrast, however, the social and professional structure of the elite group
tends to preclude work on behalf of activists in the social movements for
which group members have very little affinity.

U.S. lawyers, in contrast to the lawyers in welfare-state Europe, emerged from World War II in a relatively strong position in the field of state power. There were recurring concerns within the legal elite that lawyers needed better training to effectively govern the state, but the legal elite maintained its hold on state power (Garth 2000). By succeeding in establishing the legal elite at the forefront of the Cold War, in addition, the leaders of the major U.S. law firms accumulated important political capital that they could also convert to profit. They could arrogate to themselves the most lucrative legal business from the market in corporate law that they had helped develop and globalize.

This imperial legal strategy of the United States came with some collateral damage to lawyers and their positions elsewhere—in particular, in the dominated legal fields found in the outposts of the Cold War, as well as in Europe. The debacle experienced by the imported legal regimes, which we examine in the following chapters, was therefore further exacerbated by the loss of market position by the Europeans who, with the partial exception of the Philippines, had provided their legal touchstones during the colonial era. The decline in the international influence of European legal approaches was therefore accelerated by the weakness of domestic positions modeled after Europe—with the same Cold War logic at work in each instance.

In Europe, as we have noted, the legal elite was identified with efforts to privilege the protection of the interests of the most affluent classes, neglecting the issues raised by debates focused on "social questions." Indeed, the majority of the legal elites had taken part openly in challenges to the reformist strategies connected to the social state. They not only were losing prestige generally but also were poorly placed to compete in markets of exportation of legal expertise involving new technologies created to be effective "antidotes to communism." The European legal fields were thus doubly affected by the logic of the Cold War. The weakening of their position within the fields of European state power undermined them in the old imperial societies and in peripheral states. The relative power of the U.S. legal profession therefore resulted both from internal developments and from developments within their major imperial competitors.

The relative strength of the legal elite identified with the U.S. foreign policy establishment did not, however, lead to a preoccupation with legal reform. The situation during the Cold War was more complicated. As noted above, the U.S. position was not inconsistent with the support of authoritarian regimes with very little respect for law. To better understand the position of lawyers and law, we now proceed through an examination of the trajectories of some of the major leaders. These elite lawyers remained committed in principle to the basic Wilsonian ideals of free markets and democracy, but the Cold War context made communism the central focus of their attention. Law was but one of the cards that they played in the Cold War in seeking to win friends and extend U.S. influence against communism. Free market—or open door—economics was another. And both were employed flexibly.

The Council on Foreign Relations, as we have noted, was the major institutional connection among the legal elites favoring an activist foreign policy in the aftermath of World War I and until at least the late 1960s. A number of individuals associated with the council kept alive the ideals, and they also served in leadership positions, including in the State Department. World War II then brought the individuals associated with the council to the pinnacle of power, and the Cold War served to maintain and further build that position. Whatever the details of the actual Soviet threat, there is no question that the Cold War represented an opportunity for this internationally oriented elite to promote its brand of leadership. The new political context of opposition to communism was sufficient to overcome "regional divisions in the United States between America First nativism and pro-interdependence globalism" (Silk and Silk 1980: 200). As stated simply by the Silks, "Above all, there was the Communist threat. Resistance to the more humanitarian forms of foreign aid gave way before the ready argument that this was designed to hold off the Russians. Indeed, in many quarters this was the only argument that worked" (Silk and Silk 1980: 200). John J. McCloy noted the particular importance of the Council on Foreign Relations in the 1950s: "Whenever we needed a man, . . . we thumbed through the roll of Council members and put through a call to New York" (Silk and Silk 1980: 202). The elite recruitment policy made sense because of the Cold War.

McCloy, as the emblematic figure of the foreign policy establishment from the 1940s until the 1960s, merits elaboration. John Kenneth Galbraith designated McCloy the Chairman of the Establishment, and it is easy to see how he earned that title. According to Kai Bird, McCloy's biographer,

> His story . . . encompasses the rise of a new national elite, composed largely
> of corporate lawyers and investment bankers, who became stewards of the
> American national-security state. Beginning in the 1920s, these men formed

an identifiable Establishment, a class of individuals who shared the same social and political values and thought of themselves as keepers of the public trust. Unlike the British Establishment, from which the term is borrowed, the American Establishment was dedicated not to preserving the status quo, but to persuading America to shoulder its imperial responsibilities. (Bird 1992: 18)

McCloy began his career at the Cravath firm just after World War I and eventually helped establish another elite or "white shoe" firm, Milbank Tweed, which was the vehicle for his legal representation of the Rockefellers. His career included service as the High Commissioner to occupied Germany after World War II, the President of the World Bank, the Chair of the Ford Foundation, and Chair of the Council on Foreign Relations, to name a few of his positions. He was also, in Bird's words, "legal counsel to all 'Seven Sister' oil companies, a board director for a dozen of America's top corporations, and a private, unofficial advisor to most of the presidents in the twentieth century" (1992: 18–20). Anticommunism under the stewardship of McCloy and his allies at the council was not inconsistent with the global interests of the elite law firms and their clients.

The Kennedy administration brought this group to their peak position in state power. The social profile, professional trajectories, and the political opinions of Kennedy's "action intellectuals" link them closely to the people and approaches that emerged at the time of and through the Philippines occupation. Not all were corporate lawyers. Comparable careers could be made by circulation among the various institutions dominated by the legal elite, including, of course, the related career of investment banker, but the members of this elite group were all cut from the same mold.

The central figure of the Kennedy administration, for example, was McGeorge Bundy, the principal organizer of Kennedy's elite group and later advisor to the President for foreign affairs. Bundy was a direct descendent from a traditional Eastern WASP family, a graduate of Yale, and the son-in-law of Dean Acheson—one of the famous "wise men" of the foreign policy establishment (Bird 1998). He made his name in part by writing a biography of Henry Stimson, a close family friend and key figure in the history of the U.S. relationship with the Philippines. Bundy's cosmopolitan career also included service as a very young dean of the Harvard College of Arts and Sciences, the Council on Foreign

Relations, National Security Advisor, and finally the leadership of the Ford Foundation, which he directed from 1967 to 1979. Unlike his father, Harvey Bundy, and brother, William Bundy, he did not attend law school, but he was nevertheless offered a clerkship by his family friend Felix Frankfurter (Bird 1998: 100). Bundy's generation and close circle of friends also included Cyrus Vance, then in his first government service with the Department of Defense (and whose father figure was his close relative, John W. Davis of Davis Polk); Kingman Brewster, the president of Yale from 1964; Eliot Richardson, secretary of state and of health education and welfare under Nixon; and John Lindsay, mayor of New York City (Kabaservice 2004).

Most general historical accounts of foreign policy during the Cold War recognize the importance of these individuals and their social circle, but they also pay almost no attention to law itself. The neglect is not an oversight. Neither the opening of markets and protection of investments, nor the attention to development in the third world, nor the mobilization of foreign policy against communism, drew very much on law. The academic influences behind the policies of the Cold War were the "realists" represented by scholar/political activists such as George Kennan, Hans Morgenthau, Reinhold Niebuhr, and Arthur Schlesinger, Jr., all of whom built their position by attacking remnants of "Wilsonian idealism," seen as "legalistic" and "moralistic." They scoffed at the idea that international relations might be grounded in international law and legal institutions. Even as late as 1968, for example, Dean Acheson scolded an audience at the American Society of International Law by stating that their focus on international human rights confused what the law is with what they wanted it to be. The rhetorical posture against Wilsonian idealism, however, exaggerated the differences between these individuals and their predecessors.

This relatively weak position of law itself in U.S. foreign policy is not difficult to explain. Elite lawyers, it is true, were quite important as the embodiment of the establishment. These lawyers were at the top of the legal profession despite activities that relied relatively little on the formal law or legal institutions. And they were at the top of the social and political structure because of a combination of activities and connections that placed them above the mundane world of law. A relatively few people could occupy and rotate among a large number of power bases.

These individuals were able to dominate a number of related bases, including the elite campuses, exemplified by McGeorge Bundy's leading position at Harvard (despite only having a BA) and Kingman Brewster's presidency of Yale; the philanthropic foundations, including Ford and Rockefeller; the State Department; the media, especially the leading newspapers exemplified by the *New York Times*; and the role of representing major U.S. corporations and financial institutions. All these individuals were generally united on the goals and tactics of the Cold War, which were of course quite consistent with their vision of the interests of the clients of the elite law firms that provided the glue that linked the other institutions. "Bipartisanship" in foreign policy safeguarded the power of the foreign policy establishment and those they represented.

It also was consistent with a foreign policy built around collaboration with elites in the fight against communism. The approach can be seen in the cultural cold war under the CIA and in the many related programs supported by the Ford Foundation and others. From the perspective of the Ford Foundation, for example, it almost did not matter what kind of economics it supported as long as the programs made friends for the United States (e.g., Chile). Similarly, in the Philippines, as we have seen, one key aspect of U.S. policy was to build friendly leaders—largely from among the traditional Philippine elite—rather than to reform the state or state policies. The primacy of politics over law in the Cold War meant also that the support of elites armed with economic knowledge made perfect sense as a strategy to fight the Cold War and make friends.

The "modernization" theory on the campuses of the elite schools fit this mission perfectly with a scholarly rationalization for the search and support of "modernizing elites." That was also the strategy at home, where this establishment participated strongly in the reformist policies associated with a relatively activist state governed with a large dose of noblesse oblige.

Mainstream economics—whether inspired by John Maynard Keynes or Milton Friedman—was not inconsistent with the methods or approach of the lawyers. Within the Kennedy administration, for example, Walt Rostow's recipe for developmental assistance entitled *The Stages of Economic Growth: An Anti-Communist Manifesto* fit the Cold War strategy perfectly (and the politics of his lawyer-brother, Eugene Rostow, dean of the Yale Law School before joining the government). One of Walt Rostow's collaborators at MIT, Max Millikan, also an economist, was a key leader of the CIA in the 1950s and beyond.

The general consensus survived largely because the Cold War masked potential tensions and conflicts. The legal establishment represented by the Council on Foreign Relations maintained leadership. Indeed, to the extent that the attack on Wilsonian idealism by nonlawyer realists was an attack on law in the name of a new field of international relations in the United States, it could also be absorbed and even used to bolster the position of the legal elite above the law—and therefore relatively unrestrained in the tactics they could promote as part of the Cold War.

Indonesia and South Korea: Marginalizing Legal Elites and Empowering Economists

Indonesia and South Korea are the two countries in this part that emerged after World War II with relatively weakly institutionalized legal professions. We begin with these countries and then turn in the next two chapters to legal professions that had stronger colonial legacies. One of the problems especially evident with Indonesia and South Korea is that they had strongly depended on foreign ties—the Dutch in Indonesia and the Japanese in Korea—severed by independence. Both countries also were high-priority items in the Cold War and therefore particularly affected by U.S. foreign policies and the legal elite sketched in the introduction to this part. The United States fought the Korean War to contain Chinese communism and then invested heavily after the war in the defense of South Korea. Indonesia similarly played a key role in the U.S. effort to contain communism, and, not incidentally, had a particular strategic importance because of its valuable mineral resources (Simpson 2008). In both settings, these factors came together to marginalize the legal profession and promote a competing group of economists as the appropriate leaders of a military-led modernization.

The approach that used the law and was also above the law evolved pragmatically in Asia, partly depending on the country involved and the temperature of the Cold War at the moment. Despite the general bipartisan unity promoted by the Cold War, there were also internal power struggles in the United States that helped shape policies. As seen in the history of the Philippine occupation and in the struggle of the Council on Foreign Relations to gain influence, there was a long-standing tension in the United States between those tending to favor a more hegemonic, internationalist, approach and those promoting a more unilateralist approach that relied more on militaristic strategies (for Korea, see Cumings 1998). The foreign policy establishment agreed on the need to be active abroad, drawing on their expertise, but they had some disagreements on tactics.

The importance of these debates can be taken from a recent book by Brad Simpson on the United States and Indonesia. Simpson documents what he terms, "a bitter debate over Indonesia policy at the outset of the Kennedy administration" (2008: 43). The shift in Cold War strategies that grew out of that debate had important ramifications throughout Asia. For a variety of reasons, Simpson notes, the Kennedy administration began to favor what "was becoming known as 'military modernization' theory, a conceptual and policy turn toward the explicit embrace of military-led regimes as vanguards of political and economic development" (2008: 63). This change once again reversed a relative optimism that had prevailed earlier and had tended to link democratization and development. It also reflected the recognition that the legal profession in most Asian countries, in particular, Indonesia and South Korea, two Cold War strongholds, was not in a position to assert much influence.

The theoretical shift facilitated pragmatic Cold War alliances unclouded by legal ideals. This shift toward the military, even by the less unilateralist factions within the United States, responded in part to the Cuban Revolution, an increase in the Soviet willingness to invest in wars of national liberation, and "the growing political and economic role that armed forces establishments were carving out for themselves throughout the third world" (Simpson 2008: 68). The result, seen in Cold War policies and an emerging academic literature, was a shift to the idea that "democracy ought not to be the goal of modernization and that Washington should side with military-led regimes as a matter of both expediency and principle as the developing nations passed through the turbulent middle phases of economic and political development" (Simpson 2008: 71). What this meant was that the legally dominated leadership in Washington developed a three-prong pragmatic strategy for Indonesia—working with modernizing elites, promoting the role of the military, and seeking to stabilize and open the economy. Law as such played a relatively peripheral role. Similar strategies were quite evident also in South Korea (Brazinsky 2007) and the Philippines in the 1960s and 1970s.

Indonesia: Guided Democracy, the Cold War, and a Small Group of Descendents of the Javanese Aristocracy

The Indonesian legal elite, descended from the Javanese aristocracy, did play an important role in gaining independence from the Dutch and building the institutions of the new state. According to Lev, "during and after the revolution, politically active private lawyers consistently encouraged institutional reforms toward procedural uniformity and legal equality. In positions of authority, they opposed traditional local privileges, eliminated customary (adat) courts, created a nationally unified judiciary, and tried to strengthen courts against executive aggression" (2007: 394). The small number of lawyers and advocates were satisfied more or less by the constitution of 1950. In 1958, however, Sukarno proclaimed a more authoritarian and leftist "Guided Democracy" in reaction to the civil war against him led by regional dissidents and supported by the United States (Lev 2007: 396). At that time, again in Lev's words, the Sukarno regime "razed all the supports professional advocates thought secure" (2007: 397).

By the 1960s, accordingly, the legal profession "had basically collapsed" in Indonesia (Int. Indon.-1).[1] According to one observer of the changes over time, lawyers lost the respect they once had. They were regarded mainly as "scalpers—go-betweens or middlemen, the worst kind of middlemen" (Int. Indon.-1). There was a sense among those with higher ideals that "you don't go into private practice" even "as late as the 1970s" (Int. Indon.-1). Nevertheless, "there continued to be a group of very highly ethical . . . advocates . . . who were—and this dates back into the Sukarno period—trying to maintain the notion of an autonomous legal profession" (Int. Indon.-1). That group became marginalized under Sukarno because, reportedly, "those people were too much Western oriented. And too much [characterized by] Dutch thinking" (Int. Indon.-2).

The lawyers declined also because, as Lev also pointed out, their base in private business declined rapidly in the Guided Democracy period. Lawyers were linked with foreign and domestic businesses that were not

---

1. The authors conducted interviews in each of the countries studied. In order to protect the confidentiality of the interviewees, the interviews are identified only by country and number. The countries are abbreviated as follows: HK, Hong Kong; Indon., Indonesia; K, South Korea; M, Malaysia; P, Philippines; and S, Singapore.

in favor in the Sukarno period. As Lev stated, "Paralyzed and stagnant, the advocacy, then numbering perhaps 250 nationwide, if that, drew scarcely any new recruits" (2007: 397). In 1963 a small elite core created the Indonesian Advocates Association (PERADIN) as an effort to regroup and exert more influence.

The judiciary also declined in the new state. Under colonialism, "the hierarchy of judicial organization had the courts on top, followed by the prosecution and police. But in the independent state . . . the courts were at the bottom" (Lev 1972: 267). Legal institutions were placed increasingly in the service of politics: "law students lost interest in becoming judges in favor of joining the prosecution, where they were likely to become both moderately rich and politically significant" (Lev 1972: 267). Judges educated in the earlier era sought to retain their more independent approach, but the government became increasingly assertive of its right to control even the judiciary in the interests of the Guided Democracy agenda (Pompe 2005). The Supreme Court from what Pompe terms the "Javanese old boy network"—the "traditional Javanese administrative elite"—was increasingly marginalized (Pompe 2005: 389).

The legal elite and their descendants helped energize the student politics that helped promote the end of the Sukarno regime, and they believed that the new Suharto administration would "restore democracy, the rule of law, and human rights" (Int. Indon.-3) in the late 1960s. After a few years, however, neither Suharto nor his Berkeley-trained economist-technocrats (the Berkeley "mafia") discussed below were willing to invest much in law. The "legal euphoria" came to an end. The profession also began to grow and change. Numbering about 250 in 1965, it doubled by 1970 and then began to expand further (Lev 2007: 399). The new lawyers were socially more diverse: "Once the preserve of fairly high-born sons of Javanese aristocrats or well-established families from Sumatra and Sulawesi, as well as ethnic Chinese, the origins of private lawyers now extended downwards into an also changing middle class and outwards to a more diverse array of ethic groups from around the archipelago" (Lev 2007: 400). A new group of "consulting lawyers" emerged with a focus on commercial advising and negotiation. Their offices were larger, as were their incomes, than the traditionally focused advocates. Yet, according to Lev, "they did not join PERADIN, many of whose members refused to recognize them as genuine advocates, which hardly bothered some consulting lawyers" (2007: 400). More generally, within the New Order system (Bresnan 1993), the army gained control over the judiciary in the interests of national security and the patronage system growing up around Suharto and the military that served him.

U.S. governmental policies toward Indonesia began to shift in the latter part of the Sukarno administration. The outright antipathy of the CIA seen in the role of the United States in the civil unrest of 1958 had not worked well. The opposition to communism in Indonesia needed to be retooled. At the level of the U.S. government, Brad Simpson documents the notable change of policy that took place in the early 1960s (2008). The plan of action developed in 1962, in particular, envisioned a "three-part strategy: committing Sukarno to economic stabilization; collaborating with 'those Indonesian civilian leaders who are most interested in modernization and development of Indonesia'; and strengthening the Army's role in 'economic and social development activities'" (Simpson 2008: 29). This policy was consistent with the modernizing plan already underway through the Ford Foundation and recently acclaimed in the foundation's retrospective on Indonesia—*Celebrating Indonesia: Fifty Years with the Ford Foundation 1953–2003* (Mohamad, Harsono, and Hamid 2003).

Paul Hoffman, the president of the Ford Foundation, "had helped to arrange Indonesian independence by cutting off aid funds to Dutch counterinsurgency and by threatening a total cutoff in aid to the Dutch" when he was head of the Marshall Plan in Europe (Ransom 1975). From his perspective at the Ford Foundation, the goal was to make Indonesia a "modernizing country" with an appropriate "modernizing elite." As Frank Sutton of the Ford Foundation noted, "there's no better place to find such an elite than among 'those who stand somewhere in social structures where prestige, leadership, and vested interests matter, as they always do'" (Ransom 1975). And for Hoffman, "Indonesia . . . held a special place for the Foundation, second only to India in importance" (Mohamad, Harsono, and Hamid 2003: 72). It was therefore essential to build such an elite, just as imperial powers had done in the past.

The "Berkeley Mafia": The Promotion of Professors as a State Oligarchy in Indonesia

The American government and the Ford Foundation, as we have seen, both saw an increasingly pressing need to deploy the Cold War strategy of establishing a "modern" professional elite who would be "friends of America." The urgency became especially evident as the Sukarno regime tried to maintain an increasingly precarious balancing act between the Indonesian Army, on the one hand, and a communist party whose support was necessary to stay in power on the other. The Ford Foundation set up a $2.5 million program involving MIT, Cornell, and Berkeley as the major centers of study for Indonesia, combining research and training. According to one of the program's leaders, "Ford felt it was training the guys who would be leading the country when Sukarno got out" (Ransom 1975: 99).

This project of training a new professional elite was especially urgent since the legal aristocratic class trained by the Dutch colonists was pushed out of power by Sukarno. The legal elite, as noted above, had converted to nationalism and played a major role leading to and then governing after independence, but their position in the state was essentially gone by the 1960s. The pioneers of economic expertise were in a perfect position to seize this opportunity, since they had both the social resources and the political motivation to do so.

Sumitro Djojohadikusumo, dean of the Faculty of Economics at Jakarta University, belonged to the Javanese aristocracy protected and educated by the colonial power. After completing his doctorate in Holland, this cosmopolitan nationalist made contact with people in the United States who subsequently supported the independence movement. He was one of the relatively moderate leaders of the socialist party and a member of several governments, in particular serving as finance minister, before being sidelined by the rise of the communists and then entering into open rebellion when Sukarno nationalized Dutch companies. His idea for the role of economists was actually put into action by his assistant Widjojo Nitisastro, who had just completed his PhD in Berkeley.

Although, like most of that generation of economists, Nitisastro also came from a wealthy background, he was less politically aligned than his mentor. He developed a dual strategy: investment in research and the promotion of economic know-how among administrative and military decision-makers. Ford funded the partnership with Berkeley whereby Berkeley sent professors to Indonesia to replace young Indonesian assistant lecturers who continued their theoretical training either by obtaining their PhD in the United States or by working on research programs in close liaison with planning departments (MacDougall 1975: 326).

This external academic investment strategy also made it possible to defend the nascent economics department against criticism from communists and nationalists that had increased in intensity since its founder joined the rebel camp. American doctorates represented not only essential credentials for career advancement but also a form of collective political insurance. Their international scientific qualifications enabled the young economists to market themselves to the upper echelons of government via management-training programs. In particular, they opened doors within the army hierarchy. The best-known professors were invited to give simplified presentations of economic theory in the military academies that turned out the elite officer corps.

These military contacts, which were already very useful in protecting against attacks from those on the left within Sukarno's regime, also proved invaluable after his fall. These contacts eagerly introduced the economists to the new strong man, General Suharto, who made them his advisers as part of the process of defining a new and more international economic policy. Given their cosmopolitan range of skills, they were ideally placed to become key intermediaries in international negotiations with the consortium of countries that wished to contribute to Indonesia's development and to reap the benefits from the opening of its natural resources to foreign investment. After having facilitated the influx of this capital, these academic power brokers were well placed to control both its uses and the resulting profits.

These professors turned technocrats were the principal architects of Suharto's New Order (Bresnan 1993), and they did open up Indonesia to foreign investment. They also helped turn Indonesia into one of the pillars of Asian capitalism. Before sliding into a system of cronyism, Indonesia brought together the capital and technology of the multinationals with Chinese entrepreneurs in pursuit of development managed by state bureaucrats and the army. These latter two groups, in addition, were not content merely to oversee the political stability of this heterogeneous coalition. They also wanted to be actors in the process. They used their positions to develop the enterprises that the state had controlled since Sukarno nationalized all Dutch interests in 1957. They also had no hesitation in taking kickbacks for favors—concessions, loans, or contracts—bestowed on Chinese entrepreneurs.

With time, this blurring of roles and interests resulted in the emergence of an oligarchy of state profiteers, bolstered by family links and networks of patronage. The descendants of these professors-turned-technocrats developed their numerous forms of social capital—aristocratic, cosmopolitan, scientific, and bureaucratic—to gain access to the inner circle of entrepreneurs who were building up the financial conglomerates on the back of this "administrative patrimonialism" (Hutchcroft 1998: 52). Two of Dean Sumitro's sons, for example, became leading entrepreneurs with strong links to the Suharto family, and one of them actually married Suharto's daughter (Robison and Hadiz 2004: 62).

Working alongside the military, the United States with its Cold War strategy, and corporate investors from abroad taking advantage of the newly opened economy, these economics professors found great success in the Indonesian state. The open-door aspect of U.S. foreign policy also met with some success. The situation was different for the legal elite in Indonesia. As we have noted, what lawyers possessed after the Dutch colonial period, even after the "ethical policy" (see chap. 7) began in the twentieth century, was not enough to ensure a continuing role in state governance. The role of lawyers and legal institutions shrank to almost nothing. The economists who worked to build the authoritarian and anticommunist Suharto regime, in contrast, found ways to develop and market their expertise in their own interests and in the interest of legitimating the authoritarian Indonesian state. Nevertheless, taking advantage of the social capital that they did possess, a small number of lawyers found important places in and around the state.

First, even though the focus of the Ford Foundation and U.S. policy more generally was largely on the elite economists as modernizers, there was some legal investment in Indonesia through the law and development movement of the 1970s. In particular, the Ford Foundation–sponsored International Legal Center (ILC) became involved in Indonesia in the 1970s. One program sent individuals to Indonesia (and elsewhere) through a fellowship program that "put principally young American lawyers in positions in the developing world—legal positions" (Int. Indon.-4). According to one participant, "The way in which the program operated in reality was that in most cases the foreign lawyer was working with somebody who was identified as a significant innovator for reform within the legal system of the country concerned" (Int. Indon.-4). Modernizing elites in the law were also desirable. Robert Hornick, for example, who went on to head Coudert Brothers and become the major U.S. expert in Indonesian law, was sent to work with Professor Mochtar Kusamaatmadja (Int. Indon.-5). Many other ILC fellows were also sent to try to upgrade legal instruction in Indonesia (Linnan 1999).

The law and development results in terms of actual legal reforms, however, were minimal at best (Linnan 1999), and the legal profession and legal system continued their decline. The proliferation of law schools accelerated that decline. The Sukarno period began the opening up of the legal profession, and it continued under Suharto. According to one source, in 1992, "around 13,000 new lawyers graduated every year from the more than 200 law schools in Indonesia" (Reksodiputro 1992). The mass of graduates had very little in common with the Dutch-trained advocates or their descendants. The elite group of advocates, indeed, had more in common with the economists and others with similar family backgrounds. The small role the legal elite occupied under Suharto's authoritarian regime did nothing to build the legal system or the credibility of law

Mochtar Kusamaatmadja nevertheless illustrates one role that elite lawyers played in the Suharto regime. He had a legal education that included Harvard, Yale, and the University of Chicago; was a prominent voice for legal reform at that time; an ILC trustee; and the convenor in 1973 of an ILC Workshop on "The Indonesian Legal System" (Linnan 1999). His expertise and international credibility made him ideal for relationships with the United States. He served in a number of capacities—most notably as minister of justice and minister of foreign affairs under Suharto. The other major roles of the legal elite, in corporate law firms and in NGOs, will be discussed in chapter 12. As it turned out, a handful of the descendents of the Dutch-trained legal elite did find a place to prosper and to set the stage for further development after the end of the Suharto regime. They did not have any strong role in the Indonesian state, however.

South Korea: Economists and the Gradual Incorporation of the Liberal Paradigm into State Capitalism

South Korea provides a second example of a very marginal role for law and lawyers at the time of post–World War II independence. Korea's independence from Japan left a legal profession that was closely tied to the Japanese, even linguistically. As Jae Won Kim stated, "After liberation from Japan in 1945, the first generation of Korean legal scholars used Japanese virtually as if it were a mother tongue. The majority of the first generation legal textbooks were therefore no more than Korean translations of Japanese law books" (2007). The law professors sought to disguise their dependency on the Japanese, and in particular they began to go abroad, especially to Germany—the source of much of the Japanese scholarship. The new law schools that replaced or changed the name of those established by the Japanese gradually shifted, therefore, but the shift in orientation still meant that scholarship was very much foreign-based and dependent on foreign legitimacy. Reflecting cold war priorities, in addition, U.S. policy led to the continuation in power of the very conservative bureaucracy that had been aligned with the Japanese and its approach to governance (Brazinsky 2007: 15).

Continuing the Japanese approach, the number of individuals admitted to the bar remained very small. Most of them had relatively little connection to the government in Seoul or Korean family businesses that began to grow in the 1960s in South Korea. Furthermore, as Tom Ginsburg pointed out, the few lawyers who managed to pass the bar "had no incentive to fight for a larger profession because of the monopoly rents they collected" (2007: 47). Private businesses also did not push for reform. Nor did private business much care to push for more lawyers. Accordingly, "The small, cartelised private bar was relatively quiet for most of the post-war period. The organized bar associations were conservative and inactive" (2007: 47). Only one hundred lawyers passed the bar annually, roughly two percent of those taking the examination, and most became prosecutors or judges before moving into the more lucrative position of litigator.

The 1950s did see the development of the first corporate law firms in Korea. The first was the Tae-Hyong Lee and Heung-Han Kim Law Firm, established in 1958 to provide services to foreigners (Kim, forthcoming). Heung-Han Kim modeled the firm after American law firms. His profile shows the trajectory of law firms in Korea. According to Seong-Hyun Kim, Heung-Han Kim went to the United States in 1953 as a judge of the district court and with the support of Il-Young Cheong, the chairman of the diplomatic commission of the Korean National Assembly. Kim obtained MCL and LLM degrees at George Washington University. According to Kim, "He hoped to be an American lawyer but it was impossible for Koreans at the time. Returning to Korea in 1958, he joined with Lee Tae-Hyong to open an American style law firm, Lee & Kim" (Kim, forthcoming). Lee, in addition, "was the first female lawyer in Korean history and the mother-in-law of Kim. She was also Cheong Il-Young's wife. Thus the first law firm in Korea started its history as a family business" (Kim, forthcoming). The combination of social, political, and cosmopolitan capital produced the first successful corporate law firm in Korea.

The military coup in 1961 brought considerable success to the firm, since the new military regime, according to Kim, began to open Korean markets: "Lee & Kim became a unique law firm capable of dealing with foreign clients. Coca-Cola, Kraft Food, Ford, Lockheed Martin and others became Lee & Kim's clients. The firm changed its name to Kim, Chang & Lee (KCL) after Chang Dae-Young's participation" (Kim, forthcoming). As the economy developed, a number of similar firms opened with the aim also of serving the foreign clientele investing in Korea. One in particular, Kim & Chang, "developed legal services in the form of a commercial enterprise. It recruited young lawyers who had just completed the courses of the Judicial Research and Training Institute, and then taught them international affairs. Kim & Chang also offered them overseas training in the US. These methods were rapidly diffused to other firms" (Kim, forthcoming). There was therefore a core of corporate law firms in South Korea, but they handled mainly the affairs of foreign clients. The success of this enclave, however, was not inconsistent with the fact that lawyers in South Korea were for the most part cut off from the domestic economy and state.

The United States, as recently documented by Gregg Brazinsky (2007), had sought to develop a cadre of future leaders who would be sympathetic to the United States and its approach to state and economy. After the Korean War, for example, the United States invested in the development of future political leaders with the Leader Program, which brought promising young individuals to study U.S. political institutions. Future Presidents Young Sam Kim and Dae Jung Kim were among the participants (Brazinsky 2007: 59). Between 1954 and 1967, the U.S. government also spent over twelve million dollars to train almost three thousand students in economic development issues (Brazinsky 2007: 67). The military regime of Chung Hee Park (1961–79) was an opportunity to team the military with a modernizing elite that would be receptive to U.S. ideas and approaches and at the same time hostile to communism (Brazinsky 2007). As in Indonesia, the Kennedy administration embraced the possibilities of the military: "Washington decided to back the junta because its leaders were fiercely determined to promote economic development" (Brazinsky 2007: 10). The United States invested substantially in the development of an elite designed to serve the military state and absorb U.S. values and approaches as well. A priority, which was successful under Park, was to move economists open to economic liberalization—"American-trained technocrats"—into the government to replace nationalists hostile to foreign investment (Brazinsky 2007: 132). Again, as in Indonesia, the economists trained through these programs thrived.

Until the end of the 1990s, as we shall see, economics professors and state technocrats with training in economics had a considerable amount of influence with the military dictatorship that had presided over South Korea's spectacular industrial growth. The economics professors, in fact, possessed significant advantages in the competition for state power. They did not face the same difficulties as lawyers did in reproducing their family capital. The bar examination meant that even those from the best-endowed legal families might not make it through the exam— even if they received admission into the extremely competitive faculties of law. In contrast, the modernizing elites trained abroad had substantial social capital in the form of family ties, knowledge, and a cosmopolitan background.

The economics professors were generally drawn from wealthy, cosmopolitan backgrounds and benefited from an expensive education that gave them access to doctorates from the best American universities. They often went on to postdoctoral studies prior to entering the main South Korean economic research institutes, the Korea Development Institute (KDI) and Korea Institute for Industrial Economics and Trade (KIET). Indeed, these structures had been specifically created to encourage them to return home and to serve as launching pads toward key economic management posts. This international dimension helped entice future generations into a sector of government activity monopolized by a tiny elite of expert economists (Kim 2003: 349). The same tiny group of professors (known as the "School of Seogang"; Kang 1998) held numerous key posts: economic adviser to the President's Office, minister in charge of the Economic Planning Board or minister of finance, foreign trade minister, or even minister of foreign affairs, all of which involved conducting negotiations with foreign investors or creditors.

This aura of expertise was much sought after by the different military regimes that held power for almost thirty years. Thus, the five prime ministers of the Sixth Republic (1987–92) were all economics professors. Military coups saw considerable changes to the inner circle of South Korea's rulers, but they had a much lesser impact on the political mandarins responsible for Korean economic policy. Moreover, they accelerated the normal process of generational renewal and helped to gradually move economic discourse and policy forward with the times. The successes of the economists in providing the leading expertise to legitimate the Cold War governments helped them both to evolve and to contain the pressures of the new economic orthodoxies.

When they stepped into their mentor's shoes, junior economists could gradually import the new monetarist recipes that were steadily replacing the state planning advocated by the pioneers of economic development. These doctrinal debates between state planners and liberals remained relatively muted (Kim 2003: 369) due to the personal relationships that had developed between mentors and their disciples throughout the international apprenticeship process. This theoretical debate over the broad orientation of economic policy fueled a process within the state apparatus which was relatively independent of the wealthy capitalist classes that the military regime had succeeded in bringing to heel with their production deadlines (Chibber 2003; Evans 1995). Thus, Duck-Woo Nam, one of the main forces behind the state planning policies of the Park government, acted as mentor to Jae-Ik Kim, a dyed-in-the-wool monetarist. Following in the footsteps of his predecessor, Kim in turn became one of the main economic advisors to General Chun, who came to power after the assassination of Park. Once in this position, he had to contend with Industry Minister Seok-Jun Seo, one of his old high school friends and a convinced interventionist (Kim 2003: 367). Such theoretical squabbling in no way sullied the symbolic authority of these experts. In fact, they actually reflected the increasing freedom in Korean public debate and paved the way for the more onerous process of steering the chaebols toward the international markets.

Unlike the technocrat professors who were content with working as experts and mostly favored opening up markets and greater monetary discipline, the mandarins in charge of government departments continued to advocate interventionism and big government inasmuch as such policies chimed with the interests of big business whose ranks they yearned to join. They sought to do this either by jumping ship to the private sector or by marrying their daughters to the heirs of the chaebols (Kim 2003: 397).

This coalition of interests between entrepreneurs and top public servants constrained the development of the market for economic expertise. It also illustrates the contradictions of a sphere of expertise whose producers lauded the virtues of the market and free trade but which was rooted in a state that continued to be characterized by its dirigiste origins. The contradiction also meant that, despite the strong presence of U.S.-trained economists in leadership positions, the South Korean economy, paradoxically, did not radically change in response to neoliberal orthodoxies. Those who imported the new recipes were part of a set of structures that managed the pressures for change without fundamentally threatening the power of the South Korean state. To be sure, economists helped keep South Korea open to the United States and other investment (Brazinsky 2007). But the strong Korean state was in a sense protected from too rapid economic liberalization consistent with the emerging orthodoxy of the 1980s.

There was some effort in the 1960s and 1970s to improve the legal profession consistent with the law and development activity elsewhere. Until the late 1960s, "Legal institutions in the ROK [South Korea] had been less subject to American influence than almost any other governmental organ in the country" (Brazinsky 2007: 157). The Asia Foundation did seek to train judges and lawyers through programs of exchange to the United States. But, as in Indonesia, there was not much for the United States to build on and, partly reflecting that finding, U.S. policy in the Cold War focused more on the modernizing elites serving the military. Ties to the United States did mean that every regime needed some veneer of legality to justify its authoritarian actions, even after Park declared martial law in 1972. Law professors also were participants in many of the seminars and debates about modernization and economic growth. Brazinsky (2007) shows, indeed, that key law professors during the Park regime were quite content to lend their legal legitimacy to the regime. Ponggun Kal, for example, a professor of law at Chungang University, justified martial law by rationalizing that it was a time in South Korea for a charismatic leader, not democracy (Brazinsky 2007: 179; see also 182–83 on Pyongjun Ham).

As we shall see in chapter 13, there were a few early forays by lawyers toward the protection of human rights, especially as the Cold War receded and the international human rights movement developed. But lawyers in South Korea were a very small group, were very prosperous, and did not have much to build on out of their colonial past. The change within South Korea only began in the 1980s when the government, for reasons that are not clear, allowed the profession to enlarge somewhat as part of more general educational reform: "In the recruitment of lawyers, the reforms increased the number of successful candidates from 141 in

1980 to 316 in 1981" (Kim, forthcoming). Lawyers at that time were not at all prominent either within or in opposition to Korea's Cold War authoritarian state.

Both in Indonesia and South Korea, therefore, a small group of elite lawyers found ways to prosper despite the fact that law and lawyers were marginalized by the military-led authoritarian states. But economists took the places of lawyers in the field of state power. Lawyers were relatively weak even after independence, and that weakness was exacerbated by the Cold War policies of the United States. At the same time, the policies supported by the economists did provide good business for the few corporate law firms able to serve foreign investors. Modernization theory and pragmatic politics, more generally, led to investment in the military and in economists trained in the United States. U.S.-trained economists, fortified with elite social backgrounds, then provided the tools and legitimacy necessary to give credibility to authoritarian regimes and their economic policies. In both cases, interestingly, the early success of the economists allowed them to manage and control the importation of the new orthodoxies associated with the neoliberalism of the 1980s. Liberalizing took place slowly and in ways that kept the state and its elites in the dominant position. South Korea and Indonesia were therefore examples of places so tied into Cold War policies that, paradoxically, they were able to resist or at least moderate the calls for a new economic orthodoxy in the 1980s and 1990s. Lawyers were relatively weak and economists strong, but that strength did not mean that the recipes coming from the United States were translated into action against the states that these economists occupied and helped to legitimate.

We now turn to two countries, the Philippines and Singapore, where lawyers were not so much set aside by economists and the military but, instead, were key actors in the construction of authoritarian states. Elite lawyers in different ways in the two countries helped to build regimes that marginalized the law and legal institutions. After discussing these examples, the third chapter of this part (chap. 10) will turn to India and Malaysia where, instead of being mostly irrelevant to authoritarian developments as in Indonesia and South Korea, or participating in them, as in the Philippines and Singapore, lawyers were leaders in seeking to resist such developments.

CHAPTER NINE

The Philippines and Singapore: Lawyers and the Construction of Authoritarian Regimes

The Philippines move to authoritarian government and martial law occurred around the same time as the military regimes took over in Indonesia and South Korea, but the role of lawyers was very different. The Philippines occupied a special place in the Cold War akin to South Korea and Indonesia. The strategic position of the Philippines in Southeast Asia was magnified with the Vietnam War and the need to maintain military bases in Philippines. Consistent with the earlier history of U.S. involvement, even after independence was granted, the United States at times—depending on domestic political alignments—sought to improve the legal legitimacy of the Philippine state by encouraging reform in the name of law. Looking to make the government more legitimate, for example, the CIA sought to support a progressive and anticommunist candidate in the 1950s--Ramon Magsaysay. He served as a popular president for four years until he died in a plane crash in 1957.

Another reformist candidate was Diosgado Macapagal, who began his career as a lawyer in a U.S. law firm and later obtained a PhD in economics from a new program began in 1951 at the University of Santo Tomas. He became president in 1961 (and his daughter is the president today). Furthermore, the earlier legacy of investment in legal capital remained very evident in the 1960s, and indeed the legal institutions of the Philippines were considered to be relatively strong despite the essentially oligarchic rule. The pride of George Malcolm in his work as a legal missionary building the law faculty at the University of the Philippines, strengthening the Supreme Court, and training a legal elite suggests this commitment to build up the law in the Philippine state. The exacerbation of the Cold War then took off some of the reformist pressure. U.S. domestic politics favored those who could be counted as allies in the Cold War. As noted before, at that point the military regimes looked more appealing as the key to a modernization consistent with Cold War containment of the left.

Ferdinand Marcos came into power in 1965 well armed with arguments that would appeal to U.S. reformist critics and the business constituency at home. He denounced the oligarchy, called for land reform, and built an initial administration with legal and technocratic legitimacy. Marcos himself graduated from the University of Philippines School of Law and led the nation in the performance on the bar exam. He surrounded himself with notables with a legitimacy that counted abroad. The background of one of his most prominent lawyer allies, Juan Ponce Enrile, now a leading senator, is a particularly striking example. A graduate of Harvard Law School as well as the University of the Philippines, Ponce Enrile was a corporate lawyer from 1954 to 1966 with the law firm of Ponce Enrile, Siguion Reyna, Montecillo and Belo. His father, Don Alfonso Ponce Enrile, was a famous trial lawyer and, in 1936, the first Philippine partner of a U.S.-led firm.[1] He combined achievement with the family connection to achieve prominence as a young lawyer.

Marcos made Ponce Enrile first commissioner of customs and later minister of justice, minister of defense, as well as many other positions of note in the Marcos administration. The relatively technocratic nature of the first cabinet and its U.S. orientation was noted by a member of that cabinet, O. D. Corpuz, who stated that, "During the 1964–5 campaign I worked with my group, Rafael Salas, Johny Ponce [Enrile] and myself—they were my juniors at Harvard—on top strategy" (Hamilton-Paterson 1998: 207 [brackets in original]). The credibility of Harvard and the law were thus well represented in the early career of Marcos. The claims of a reformist agenda, strengthening the state, promoting land reform, relying on a more technocratic set of advisors, and overcoming the oligarchy's resistance to reform, were all consistent also with anticommunist reformist rhetoric throughout Asia. Marcos, in short, was not outside the

---

1. Juan Ponce Enrile was fortunate to be able to draw on his father's prominence. He was born illegitimately and only met his father by seeking him out after secondary school.

mainstream in the Philippines until he took advantage of the Cold War to declare martial law in 1972 as a means to continue in power.

The declaration of martial law gained favor in the United States in part because there was a consistent veneer of legality and in part because it offered the possibility of sustained reform that would overcome corruption and venality. It was consistent with the support of the military in Indonesia and South Korea. At that time, according to Jovito Salonga, the business community, except most notably the Lopez family, whose sugar holdings were under attack, and many others supported martial law. In Salonga's terms, in retrospect, Marcos had appointed U.S.-trained "technocrats, who would be his deodorant" (2001: 210) and "with whom American business interests were comfortable" (2001: 211), and both the United States and the World Bank treated martial law as a way to develop the economy without the influence of special interests. Marcos in fact justified martial law in part on the technocratic need for agrarian reform and the need to overcome the resistance of Philippine elites. But it was the Cold War—and Marcos's shrewd understanding of U.S. strategies—that allowed him to build his power and cut down any countervailing power, including that embedded in legal institutions.

The demise of the courts was relatively slow under Marcos. All the key Marcos decisions—first invoking martial law, then arresting his opponents, and consolidating by enacting a new constitution, for example—were tested by his adversaries in the Supreme Court. The court managed to sustain some of its prior reputation through very pragmatic decisions that did not upset Marcos but suggested some small degree of independence—such as ordering family visitation for some detainees, and allowing the new constitution to go into effect, but refusing to say that it was lawfully enacted. Salonga, one of the lawyers who led the elite political opposition, noted that Marcos craved a "veneer of legality" largely because of "influential figures" in the United States (2001: 235). Therefore, he stated, "As for the Supreme Court, it had been allowed to function, but it could not be considered supreme. . . . Occasionally, one or two dissenting voices would be allowed, for outside consumption, but that was all" (2001: 235).

Legal institutions were therefore demeaned under Marcos. The reputation of the Supreme Court and the judiciary declined over the period of the Marcos regime. Under Marcos, a generation of judges was lost, salaries for judges never increased, and the judiciary lost much of its luster. The judicial branch became one of the least respected among governmental institutions in the Philippines. As we shall see, lawyers were everywhere in the Marcos administration and its policies, but that presence in the context of the Cold War and the Vietnam War did not mean support for legal institutions. U.S. domestic politics reduced the investment in Philippine idealism. Marcos was able not only to continue but also to enhance the pattern of using law and other weapons to enrich oneself and one's cronies through politics and state power (Kang 2002).

Prior to martial law, in fact, the pattern in the Philippines was quite recognizable given its earlier history and political structure. Both sides of the government had much in common with each other. Among the notable lawyers identified with the Lopez empire whom Marcos sought to turn to his advantage were Roberto Benedicto and Claudio Teehankee, described in more detail below (Salonga 2001: 507). Benedicto had introduced Salonga to Lopez (Salonga 2001: 256). Lorenzo Tanada, a partner of Teehankee and another leading progressive politician, was also a lawyer for the Lopez interests. Salonga, Tanada, and, at a much later time, Teehankee, became known for their opposition to Marcos. But all came from the same political structure.

Roberto Benedicto, a descendent from elite landowners in Negroes and a classmate and fraternity brother of Ferdinand Marcos at the University of the Philippines School of Law, was one of Marcos's closest associates (Manapat 1991: 100). In 1965, Benedicto was named by Marcos as chair of the largest state-owned bank, the Philippines National Bank, and he used that base to provide loans to corporations that he or other Marcos associates controlled. He gained further business favors when he served next as Ambassador to Japan. Ultimately, among many other interests, he gained control over sugar exports and used that position to enrich himself and the Marcos family further. His vast holdings included a shipping company, 106 sugar farms, 16 television stations and 17 radio stations (Manapat 1991: 100). The links between law, economic, and political power are quite evident in his career. Benedicto helped build the career of both Marcos and his leading opponents.

The ties among the Philippine elite frayed when Marcos used the Cold War and martial law to maintain power and increase the economic return to him and his cronies. But even after martial law, many of the ties continued. For example, Salonga was a fraternity brother of Ponce Enrile, the minister of defense, and Salonga stated that Ponce Enrile pulled strings to help and even free some of his friends, fraternity brothers, and cofaculty members imprisoned by Marcos when they turned against his government.

At the time of martial law in the Philippines, therefore, there was no real principled opposition to authoritarianism. According to Salonga, "we were only a handful among pre-martial law politicians who refused to compromise with Marcos" (2001: 246). The opposition represented a fragment of an elite out of power that was quickly losing credibility with major parts of the Philippine population organizing and fighting from a far more radical perspective. As Salonga noted with respect to the activists already organized against Marcos, "we did not have a program that would appeal to their idealism, on the one hand, and their desire for meaningful action, on the other" (2001: 246). According to one member of this elite, Manuel Quezon III, dissident voices were few, and "[a]dversity made these leaders [—Aquino, Diokno, Salonga, and Tanada—] men of far higher principle than they were thought to have been previously. Nino Aquino, in particular, transcended his past reputation as a brilliant, but too ambitious and fluid, politician" (Quezon 1996: 5).

One more indication of how Marcos used rather than opposed the system built around the legal elite is his ties to corporate law firms. In particular, one firm was especially close to Marcos and his allies. Around the time Marcos came to power, as noted in chapter 6, there were two major corporate firms—Sycip Salazar and Ponce Enrile, Siguion Reyna, Montecillo and Belo. Both had expatriate origins and served mainly foreign clients (Int. P-4).[2] The Ponce Enrile firm had about forty lawyers in the early 1970s (Int. P-4).

Angara Abello Concepcion Regala & Cruz (ACCRA), the key firm for Marcos, was formed in 1972—just around the time of Marcos's declaration of martial law. The lawyers who started the firm were partners in the Sycip Salazar firm. The founders of ACCRA were also fraternity brothers in the legal fraternity of Sigma Rho. The stated objective of the ACCRA firm at the outset was to link corporate law to domestic clients instead of just "multinationals"—"the emerging Filipino entrepreneurial class also needed such services" (ACCRA 2008). ACCRA, in addition, aspired self-consciously, in the words of one of the pioneers, to be more

---

2. The authors conducted interviews in each of the countries studied. In order to protect the confidentiality of the interviewees, the interviews are identified only by country and number. The countries are abbreviated as follows: HK, Hong Kong; India; Indon., Indonesia; K, South Korea; M, Malaysia; P, Philippines; and S, Singapore.

of an "institutional law firm"—with time sheets, evaluations of lawyer performances, and different departments (Int. P-13). Since a number of Philippine law firms were, like the initial Ponce Enrile firm, descended from U.S. firms and had long histories with U.S. clients, the ACCRA lawyers saw an advantage in serving Philippine businesses. They also innovated by using the emerging word processing programs and computers, for example, and by focusing more effort on systematic recruiting. They borrowed the technologies of U.S. law firms and put them in the service of emerging Philippine businesses.

More particularly, they blended their modern approaches with a willingness to work very closely with Marcos in transforming the business world. ACCRA lawyers from the outset became closely involved in the economic activities of Marcos and his circle. Manapat shows the role of prominent ACCRA lawyers, and even the ACCRA Investments Corporation, in creating the legal vehicles for a variety of transactions connecting state activities and private wealth accumulation (1991). ACCRA lawyers, for example, designed legal entities and served them as board members to allow the shifting of the revenues from the new levy on coconut production into the business activities, especially of Ponce Enrile and Eduardo Cojuanco. The revenues allowed Cojuanco, again using ACCRA lawyers as principals and agents, to take over the San Miguel Corporation—the holder of the beer monopoly in the Philippines.

Among the ACCRA lawyers, the most important was Edgardo Angara, a close friend of Ponce Enrile and in his third term as a Philippine senator at the time of this writing. Angara, from a middle-class family, graduated from the University of the Philippines (1958) and has an LLM degree from the University of Michigan (1964). He was Marcos's choice to be the president of the Integrated Bar of the Philippines (1979) and also to be the president of the University of the Philippines, a position he held from 1981 to 1987. Angara also worked closely later with President Joseph Estrada, becoming his secretary of agriculture and later his executive secretary of the cabinet. Angara in fact played a crucial role also in helping to engineer the resignation of Estrada and the transition to Macapagal Arroyo—the current president. Other appointments held by Angara include chair of the board of the Philippine National Bank. He has gained substantial wealth from his activities (Coronel et al 2004: 13).

The attack on law and legal institutions that went with martial law, the Vietnam War, and Marcos, therefore, was not inconsistent with the continuing rule of major sectors of the elite legal profession in the

Philippines. Marcos and his major advisers and lieutenants were law trained, often with training in the United States, and they maintained just enough of a veneer of legality to let the United States continue to claim the Philippines as an ally in the fight against lawless communism. This position of the legal elite meant that the technocrats supposedly brought in with the Marcos administration did not gain much traction for themselves or their expertise. Economists, as we shall see, did not gain the kind of position that we saw in the authoritarian regimes of South Korea and Indonesia. The lawyers continued to dominate throughout Philippine authoritarianism.

Marcos's Economists: Technocrats Faced with the Cronyism of Lawyer Notables

On the face of it, the process of importing economic theory into the Philippines offers a number of similarities to the situations in South Korea and Indonesia. It involved the same categories of protagonist seeking to develop the relatively marginalized discipline of economics and then trying to use the discipline to provide a cover of legitimacy for new authoritarian regimes born out of the Cold War. It also involved U.S. investment in modernizing elites. The structure of the positions and power relationships at the top of the state apparatus was totally different in the Philippines, however, than in South Korea or Indonesia. In particular, the strong position of the legal elite was maintained under the authoritarian regime led by Marcos. Lawyers were everywhere in his administration and used that position to build economic and political power. The law degree continued to be the key credential for the reproduction of the social elite. The development of economics as a discipline in the Philippines was constrained therefore by a dual handicap. First, it only managed to attract undergraduates with relatively little social and economic capital. Second, and more important, economic rationality was of little relevance in a country where wealth was contingent on political favors instead of entrepreneurial skills.

In this context, as in Indonesia, funding a small group of economics doctoral scholarships was consistent with the reformist strategy of the American philanthropic foundations. For example, under the auspices of a U.S.-supported reformer (Karnow 1989: 349), President Magsaysay, a research and development Institute began operation in 1957 and subsequently became a center of expertise in political economy. These reformist initiatives were interrupted by the accidental death of Magsaysay, but they were put back on track by the election of another U.S. protégé, Diosgado Macapagal. Prior to beginning a career as a lawyer with an American law firm, this son of a poor peasant farmer had benefited from one of the first economics doctoral programs launched in 1951 by the University of Santo Tomas.[3]

It was only with the accession to power of President Marcos in 1965, however, that the first generation of economics professors finally got access to the top jobs. As noted above, Marcos claimed to bring the banner of reform with a U.S.-trained cadre of technocrats. Sicat (PhD 1963, MIT), a pure economist, was named as head of the National Economic and Development Authority. Rather than pure economists, however, business school professors obtained the key political positions including the heads of the departments of finance, the budget, and the central bank. These and other appointments showed that Marcos was shrewd enough to surround himself with a team of American-trained technocrats, suggesting a reformist image, but certainly not ready to give them a strong mandate to follow their theories.

Around the same time, the Ford Foundation and USAID showed some enthusiasm by helping to set up an MBA program in the Philippines at the Asian Institute of Management. The first dean was Stephen Fuller of the Harvard Business School (HBS), and initial funding also came from Eugenio Lopez, Sr., the Harvard Law graduate and businessman described earlier. At the time of the dedication of the building, in 1969, Fuller stated, "This occasion, which marks the dedication of the Asian Institute of Management buildings, can very well be a milestone in the economic development of Asia, for it is our hope that through these halls will pass young men and women of superior intellectual and moral capacity who, fortified by their training here, will exercise strongly beneficial influences in Asian institutions of the future" (http://www .managementparadise.com/forums/archive/index.php/t-49319.html).

This rhetorical commitment to technocracy helped secure the initial support and funding of the U.S. democratic establishment. But this support was short-lived, since it quickly became apparent that Marcos only challenged members of the oligarchy in order to strip them of their perks

3. Mirrored by the path taken by his daughter, the current Philippine President Gloria Macapagal, who is also an economics graduate.

and divert these to his own cronies. Using the fight against communism as an excuse to proclaim martial law enabled him to perpetuate his power by establishing a legal dictatorship. The Marcos years did nothing to build the credibility of economists in the Philippines either as experts providing the legitimacy of recognized economic orthodoxy or as part of the resistance to Marcos. As we shall see, the mass student protests at the core of the "people power" that toppled his regime in 1985 led to the restoration of the old order of elite lawyer-politicians. In an article in which he retraces the national genealogy of his discipline, Professor de Dios observes that the bulk of government positions (i.e., finance, budget, and central bank), which in other countries are systematically entrusted to professional economists, are only exercised "sporadically" by economists in the Philippines (De Dios 1999: 102).

This political devaluation was true also for the general market for economic expertise in the Philippines. The market is characterized by its weakness, duality and dependence. The few positions that actually exist in public research institutes have been doled out under the same system of cronyism that has prevailed in all government agencies. The economics professors who occupied these positions typically graduated from local universities, had only distant links with the wider academic world, and rarely published in international reviews.

Because of this dearth of scientific credibility, politicians have turned to American economists of international repute, such as Paul Krugman or Rudiger Dornbush, or international darlings of the United States such as the Peruvian Hernan De Soto. They are brought in to guide or publicly endorse economic programs. The negligible presence of local economists in the corridors of power has restricted economics professors to lecturing roles, and they rarely get offered the opportunity of more lucrative work as consultants or experts. They also have long faced an international market for economics expertise in which academic publishers have little interest in research that too narrowly focuses on a peripheral nation like the Philippines.

The intake of students in economics departments reflected the low prestige of the discipline, which in turn illustrated the lack of market demand at the national level. Private faculties that drew more of their students from the elite were now focusing on business management. The University of the Philippines, which was obliged by its statutes to recruit its students on a more meritocratic basis, has mainly attracted young people from poor provincial backgrounds. The best these new graduates could hope for, however, were poorly paid bureaucratic positions in accounting firms or even jobs in call centers. Only a tiny number of privileged students managed to avoid such a fate thanks to U.S. doctoral scholarships that provided access to the international academic market. The fragmentation of this professional milieu was also synonymous with the "dollarization" of the academic elite. Its geographical distance from the major academic centers of the discipline as well as its political isolation outside of the corridors of power were mutually reinforcing in creating a sort of vicious circle that prevented the emergence of any real recognized domain of Philippine economic expertise.

Singapore and the Annexation of Law to the State

Lee Kwan Yew and the leaders of the People's Action Party (PAP), as noted in chapter 7, used a Leninist strategy to gain control of the new Singapore state—triumphing not only over the communists but also over other parties whose leaders were lawyer-politicians, most notably David Marshall of the Labour Front Party. Consolidating their power, they put in place an authoritarian and elitist technocracy, characterized by social paternalism designed to appropriate the arguments that had been championed by the communists, their principal adversaries.

The ideology and expertise of lawyers as such had no place in this bureaucratic reconstruction. Instead the PAP gained its legitimacy through a double strategy of social pacification—combining repression and redistribution—and industrial development through collaboration with multinationals using Singapore's disciplined workforce. The strong authority of the government was also supported through external threats to the survival of this very small city-state. Lawyers and legal legitimacy were for the most part not part of this governing approach and its legitimating ideology (see also Tomasic 2003).

Legal capital and institutions had been mobilized in the political struggles to gain power and independence, helping to hold together the various interests. In preparation for independence from the British, in fact, in 1956, Dr. Lionel Astor Sheridan became the first professor of law and head of the law department at the University of Malaya in Singapore. In 1960, the Asia Foundation endowed a constitutional law professorship for Professor Harry E. Groves, the former dean of Texas Southern Law School. In 1962, the school became the University of Singapore with Groves as the first dean. He obtained a grant of $300,000 from the Ford Foundation to help build the law school. Groves, concerned about instability in the tensions that preceded the split between Malaysia and Singapore, returned to the United States in 1963.

The law department continued, but the dominant power that came to the PAP and Lee Kwan Yew came with a devalorization of legal capital in favor of the state technocracy molded pragmatically out of several ingredients. It combined scholarly merit, the welfare state, and the developmental state—before Lee Kwan Yew reinvented Confucianism as one more component of the potpourri. The mix contained admittedly contradictory elements, but they responded well to the specific resources of this colonial entrepôt in the process of conversion into a bastion of the Cold War and an offshore base for multinational corporations seeking to protect their investments in Southeast Asia.

This hybrid strategy made in the image of the founding fathers of Singapore came with social redistribution and paternalism inspired by the welfare state that so many of them were prepared for by their British education, but it also came with a rejection of egalitarianism in favor of elitism defined according to scholarly merit. Scholarly merit was not inconsistent with the general reproduction also of the social and economic elite. In addition, Singapore broke with the orthodox approach of developmental states, which favored import substitution. Instead, the government promoted policies of exportation based on alliances between multinationals and Singapore's disciplined labor force. Cut off from the Malaysian market, Singapore resumed its position as an entrepôt—becoming a champion of free trade in contrast to other developing countries. In this phase of the construction of the Singapore state, the founders in this manner adopted the arguments also of adversaries who had contested the legitimacy of the institutions and discourse of colonial law.

Legal capital tended therefore to lose its value, and the power of the state came to rest more on a double monopoly—the political domination of PAP on one side and the technocratic meritocracy on the other. The two sides reinforced each other as the initial leadership cultivated new generations of carefully selected technocrats educated and then coopted to assure the continuity of the complimentary policies of economic development and social discipline. This state construction in the hands of a meritocratic elite, by definition legitimated through the continuing economic development and social protection, accelerated the political decline of the legal professionals—or at least their marginalization from the field of state power.

The result was a division of labor of domination in which the legal profession occupied a specific place. Lawyers had a monopoly on conveyancing and mortgage work that grew dramatically with the growth of the Singapore middle class and paid handsome dividends in a small city-state where land was scarce. This emphasis on property rights and legalization of property was consistent in fact with the dominant colonial trajectory. The generous return on conveyancing work fit very well with the basic strategy of social pacification followed by Lee Kwan Yew and PAP.

Student activism was limited by the recruitment into the law schools. The numbers were kept relatively small, and the law schools also suffered by the relative devalorization of law in comparison to the meritocracy of state technocrats. The elite state scholarships for the brightest students, for example, were available to only a few law graduates until at least the 1980s (Int. S-1). The recruitment process helps explain why a substantial portion of lawyers long after independence continued to be educated abroad—reportedly some forty percent. This phenomenon further anchored the profession in the colonial order and within the propertied classes since, in the absence of state scholarships, the high cost of study abroad limited access to the less ambitious and talented—and most westernized—among the children of the well-to-do Chinese.

There were also some discrete ties between the administration and the legal profession exemplified most notably by the firm of Lee and Lee, where the wife of Lee Kwan Yew continued to work, but also by law firms staffed mainly by expatriates—Drew & Napier, Allen & Gledhill. These firms were themselves content to enjoy the monopoly profits of conveyancing in particular. A senior lawyer observed:

> Remember that Singapore was still—the GDP was growing 8 percent a year for almost 20 years. There was a lot of construction. There was increased population, a lot of people coming in. A lot of housing. So a lot of conveyancing. And the majority of Singapore lawyers are doing conveyancing. Just like in Hong Kong, the majority of lawyers were doing conveyancing in Hong Kong and they were not interested in the corporate practice. (Int. S-2)

Similarly, describing the work of one of the firms, the same lawyer noted: "Allen and Gledhill had a varied practice. It had one of the largest motor insurance practices in Singapore. In fact, it had the majority of the motor insurance companies. It had a very small banking practice. It had a quite large conveyancing practice. And the rest was just miscellaneous litigation. Rent control, it had a good rent control practice. Now, I can tell you that in 1966, Gledhill Brothers was then acting for, I think at that time was probably the largest bank in the world, you know, Bank of America" (Int. S-2). The practice was built on conveyancing but included litigation and service to key corporations doing business in Singapore.

The expatriate dimension also remained high. According to the same observer with a strong sense of the history, "most of the leading advocates during that period, in the '60s and the '70s, were in fact English advocates. They were the senior partners of the big firms" (Int. S-2). And for the big cases, Queen's Counsel from London were brought in: "there were a lot of cases [where there was a decision to] bring in Queen's counsel." High profile litigation remained in the hands of the British.

In contrast to the monopoly on conveyancing, which linked legal practitioners to the prosperity of the propertied classes, political leaders reserved to themselves the role of serving as intermediary between popular groups and the government. The role of the lawyer as champion of workers, minorities, or other groups was no longer part of the Singapore model of law. Similarly, the leaders discouraged legal clinics or similar social activism within the law schools. The PAP ensured that it occupied the role of spokesperson for the population without competition from lawyers acting as social entrepreneurs. Finally, the PAP strategy also involved giving high positions in the government and economy to a cadre of legal notables who could engineer relations with law and the legal profession domestically and abroad.

Several of the senior partners of Shook Lin & Bok, for example, which was originally a firm in Kuala Lumpur, became key allies of Lee Kwan Yew. One well-known example is Chan Sek Keong, admitted to the Singapore Bar in 1962. He began practicing at the expatriate firm of Braddell Brothers before joining Shook Lin & Bok in 1969. He became the first person appointed as judicial commissioner in 1986 and joined the Supreme Court in 1988. He then served as attorney-general of Singapore from 1992 to 2006 before becoming the chief justice of Singapore.

The role and career of Pung How Yong is especially linked to Lee Kwan Yew. He attended the Victorian Institution in Kuala Lumpur and then Cambridge University in England. At Cambridge he became friends with Lee Kwan Yew and his wife, Kwa Geok Choo. Yong was an outstanding student, graduating in 1949. He was then called to the English Bar in 1951 before returning to Malaya to work in his father's law firm, Shook Lin & Bok. He practiced some criminal law in his early career before moving into tax, real estate, and corporate work. He was a prominent lawyer in Kuala Lumpur before moving to Singapore. He served, for example, as chairman of the Malaysia-Singapore Airlines (1964 and 1969) and as deputy chairman of the Malayan Banking Berhad (Maybank) (1966 and 1971). His move to Singapore stemmed from his desire to have his daughter educated in English and Chinese, not Malay, and he reportedly felt that the situation in Malaysia was becoming difficult for those speaking Chinese and English. He moved initially in 1971, but the relatively small branch of Shook Lin & Bok in Singapore was not thriving, and he decided to accept an offer to join a new investment bank, which he then served as chair and managing director. In 1974, he moved to the Overseas-Chinese Banking Corporation (OCBC), one of the large Singapore banks, and in 1977 became vice chairman. In 1976, according to Lee Kuan Yew's autobiography, Lee "offered to make him a judge of the Supreme Court," but "he declined" (2000: 247).

Pong How Yong did, however, take on other key economic posts and projects for his old Cambridge classmate. He served as a member of the Singapore Securities Industry Council from 1972 to 1981. As one observer of the situation noted, at that time the "government was moving into new things" (Int. S-3). For example, the monetary authority was having some troubles, so the government "sent in a team to decide what to do with it," ultimately deciding to make a corporation and to entrust it to him despite his relative newness to Singapore (Int. S-3). Yong then became the first managing director in 1982 of the Government of Singapore Investment Corporation (GIC), and he also headed the Monetary Authority of Singapore. In 1988, Yong once more was called upon, this time to become the chairman of the Institute of Policy Studies created at that time. Partly because of relatively low governmental salaries, he returned to the OCBC in 1983. He became chairman and chief executive.

At that time, according to an insider, Lee Kuan Yew sent for Yong complaining of "trouble in the courts," including long delays and unproductive judges (Int. S-3). For whatever reason, Lee Kuan Yew had decided to focus on the courts: "he decided he would have it cleaned up." Reportedly, the "backlog was growing," and the prime minister wanted a "world class" judiciary to further encourage foreign investment in

Singapore. In 1990, accordingly, Yong was appointed the chief justice of Singapore. During his first speech at the opening of the legal year, he announced the abolition of the traditional wigs worn by lawyers, as well as the use of such terms as "My Lord" or "Your Lordship." He focused on case management and technology. He also raised judicial salaries to among the highest in the world to eliminate the temptations of corruption and to attract top lawyers to the judiciary. The high salaries and perks of the position no doubt also reinforce loyalty to the Singapore state. The courts have been praised extensively for their efficiency. At the same time, however, human rights activists, especially from outside of Singapore, have been critical of the courts for their unwillingness to take stands against Lee Kuan Yew and his political allies, and for their role in sustaining the libel suits that Lee Kuan Yew has used to challenge and essentially bankrupt his political critics.

A third major player in the legal field for Lee Kwan Yew was Professor S. Jayakumar, a graduate of the Raffles Institution, the University of Singapore, and the Yale Law School, where he received an LLM degree in 1966. He became a lecturer and then dean, in 1974, of the Faculty of Law in the National University of Singapore. He was active diplomatically as well as a scholar, serving as a member of Singapore's delegation to the United Nations Law of the Sea Conference from 1974 to 1979. And then, according to an informed source, "the Prime Minister asked him to join politics and, you know, he was building up a second generation team. And it's difficult to say no" (Int. S-4). He has thus been in politics since 1980. He was elected to parliament in 1980, and in 1981 became the minister of state for law and minister of state for home affairs. Often holding other ministries as well, he served again as minister for law from 1985 until 2008.

Finally, another important legal actor with strong international and U.S. ties is Tommy Koh, a longtime professor of law at the National University of Singapore. He graduated from the University of Malaya in Singapore (1961) and received an LLM degree from Harvard. He has been honored widely for his activities in international arenas. He served among other positions as president of the Third United Nations Conference on the Law of the Sea, 1980–82; chair of the Preparatory Committee of Earth Summit held in 1992; ambassador to the United States; and ambassador at large.

There is a divided literature about the courts in Singapore. There is no question that they operate with some efficiency, and that they have formal independence. But their role has been to support the ruling party in key disputes (Jayasuriya 1998; Silverstein 2008). As stated by Ross Worthington,

> The basis of the extensive criticism of the Singaporean judiciary, which has grown in magnitude over the past twenty years, has not (at least originally) been based on any particular antipathy towards the PAP. It has been based on disbelief that a judicial system can perform so consistently within the principles of English law on most matters, and then seemingly ignore these principles in political cases, as evidenced in recorded judgments. (2001)

This relatively weak position of the courts has been a hallmark of Singapore governance since the beginning of independence (see also Tremewan 1994). Lawyers prospered, the courts ran efficiently, but the story of Singapore has also been the story of a very strong state and a weak role for law and lawyers in the field of state power. The legacy of law after colonialism was weak even if lawyers played the key role in the move to independence and in postcolonial governance.

CHAPTER TEN

India and Malaysia: Resistance of the Legal Elite to Marginalization by Authoritarian Developmental States

The preceding two chapters revealed two different kinds of legal marginalization in the period after World War II, with the Cold War one key aspect of that legal decline. The first, seen in South Korea and Indonesia, was characterized by authoritarian states, the rise of economists within and in support of the legitimacy of those states, and a putting aside of the legal elites constructed through colonialism or as a modernist strategy to resist and absorb colonial pressures. One paradox of this early alliance of economists with the state was that the importation of neoliberal ideas was managed without the dramatic changes associated with, for example, much of Latin America. The second chapter in this part, in contrast, revealed lawyers guiding the path to Cold War authoritarianism. In one case, the Philippines, the government kept technocracy and economic expertise aside, and in the other, Singapore, the governing elite absorbed technocracy into a government founded by lawyers who retained their positions but contributed to a steep devaluation of legal capital in the state.

This chapter focuses on two contrasting former British colonies where the legal elites possessed resources that were mobilized against authoritarian policies associated with the Cold War and economic developmentalism. We begin with India and then move to Malaysia. Lawyers are quite present in these examples at the outset of authoritarian developments.

India: The Bar's Resistance to the Developmental State

The Indian legal elite, as we saw in chapter 5, dominated the Congress Party. Elite lawyers played a major role in the politics of independence from Britain. The legacy of British imperialism was also quite apparent in the institutions of newly independent India. Legal elites embraced the legal legacy of the British Raj, and the common law remained supreme in independent India. In a speech inaugurating the new Supreme Court after independence, the attorney general, Motilal Setalvad, stated that even though the ties to the privy council had been severed, its judgments would still be influential: "This is inevitable, because the roots of our statute law and legal forms are deeply enmeshed in the jurisprudence of England" (Setalvad 1999: 149).

The prime period for lawyers in the new government, however, was relatively short-lived. In the 1960s, the public image of the bar in India began to plummet. In Schmitthener's words from the late 1960s, "The legal profession no longer offers the most honored and profitable work that can be attained in India. It no longer draws the best students, and it no longer dominates the social and political life of the country. The monopoly that it had on the leadership of the country for over a century is now gone" (1968–69: 382).

This relative decline did not come only from the competition of new state knowledge, such as economics, a discipline particularly favored by the politics of development and discussed below with respect to Indian governance. The priority given to developmental politics by the new Indian state—promoted personally by Jawarharlal Nehru—brought to the surface the ambiguities of the accumulation of positions by the lawyer-politicians. As we shall see, lawyers for the large property owners used the courts to oppose the developmental initiatives in support of agrarian reform, but those initiatives were pillars of the strategy of modernization and social progress supported officially by the Congress Party—where the lawyers remained heavily represented. This double role had been very profitable for a time, but eventually it brought risks both to the social credibility of the legal system and to an elite of the bar seeking to embody the national interest.

Recognizing India's prominence in the cold war, the Ford Foundation invested some $275 million in India during the period 1952–92 (Staples 1992), but only a few of the early grants touched law, and experience here as elsewhere discouraged the foundation from legal investment. The history of the grants was recently examined by Jayanth Krishnan in two instructive articles. One effort by the Ford Foundation was in 1958 with a grant to support the library and research facilities of the Indian Law Institute (Krishnan 2005a). The initiative was not very successful.

More ambitious was an initiative focused on legal education, beginning also in the 1950s (Krishnan 2004). The foundation sent a series of notable U.S. legal academics to India to try to develop a policy to improve legal education. The first was Dean Carl Spaeth of Stanford Law School, but Spaeth counseled caution in seeking to push legal education and reform in India. Arthur von Mehren was the next consultant and, building on criticisms within India by the legal profession, he reported that, in Krishnan's terms, "the quality of students was low; law teachers were often incompetent; facilities were shoddy, and so on" (2004: 462). The Ford Foundation then made a notable grant to the Delhi and Banaras Law Faculty beginning in 1964, but a 1971 evaluation concluded that legal education was too resistant to change, that law professors were not of high quality, and that student quality and job prospects were also low. In 1971 the foundation gave up on the project of reforming legal education. According to one of the leaders of the U.S. development program in India in the 1960s, the feeling was that law was a "second rate profession" in India (Int. India-1).[1]

The profession depended largely on fees from property disputes, and it remained divided into two groups. At the top was an elite descended from those trained in Britain to serve British colonialism. The rank and file of the profession, on the other hand, included a mass of lawyers choosing a law career mainly because it was easy to get into and graduate from the faculties of law. Law was not a highly sought-after profession, and the prestigious practitioners at the high courts and the Supreme Court had little in common with the rank and file. The role of the elite in response to the challenges of the developmental state reflects both the challenges and the resources that they had accumulated during the course of colonialism and the struggle for independence.

---

1. The authors conducted interviews in each of the countries studied. In order to protect the confidentiality of the interviewees, the interviews are identified only by country and number. The countries are abbreviated as follows: HK, Hong Kong; India; Indon., Indonesia; K, South Korea; M, Malaysia; P, Philippines; and S, Singapore.

India: Legal Arms and Class Politics

When the Congress Party under the leadership of Nehru embarked on a politics of social and economic transformation, the elite of the bar mobilized to defend the interests of the property-owning classes that they had long defended and to which, in many cases, they belonged. This political fight was relatively easy to orchestrate using the courts, since the large-property owners had already become used to this strategy to resist the colonial bureaucracy and especially its taxation policies. The specific issue was determining the level of compensation for the property-owning (often absentee landlords) zamindars whose property was supposed to be expropriated according to new laws.

The Supreme Court became involved early on the side of the landowners, stating that these expropriation laws violated equal protection of the laws. The government then responded with a constitutional amendment (the first occurring in 1951) according to which the laws for agrarian reform could not be attacked as violations of fundamental rights. That amendment was of course vigorously attacked by the lawyers for the zamindars as inconsistent with the fundamental principles of the constitution. These were the first episodes in a long battle with many legal and political turns. The formulation of this political fight into legal terms conformed perfectly with the interests of the elite of the bar, which found a great opportunity to serve their clients by pursuing legal procedures informed by political knowledge and by using legal knowledge in the political field.

This heavy investment on the terrain of constitutional law brought the Supreme Court rapidly to the center of battle. After a period of relative accommodation to the powerful Congress Party and the strong personality of Nehru, the court affirmed its constitutional authority at the time the Congress Party divided with its first electoral defeats in 1967. The Supreme Court in 1967 (the Golak Nath decision) ruled on the Parliament's ability to amend the constitution, expressly limiting what could be done by the Congress government in the pursuit of reform (Rudolph and Rudolph 1987: 110). In 1973, in an "equally momentous" decision (the Keshavananda Bharati case), the court retreated to allow more activist legislation (Rudolph and Rudolph 1987: 110). According to the Rudolphs, the decisions did not inspire confidence: "[T]he court's reliance on legal solipsism and formal and technical interpretations of the constitution inhibited the efforts of Congress governments to effect social change" (Rudolph and Rudolph 1987: 104).

The next event was another retreat by the Supreme Court when, threatened with the politics of Indira Gandhi, it returned to its more prudent posture to sustain the restrictions on liberty of the declaration of the state of emergency—a policy change denounced by the leaders of the bar. Finally, the last stage of this movement of balancing politics and law came with the reassertion of the constitutional power of the court at the time the Congress Party weakened and governmental coalitions became more fragile. The reaffirmation was strengthened and made easier by the fact that the older generation of lawyer politicians was well represented in the first of the coalitions—Janata—that governed after the administration of Indira Gandhi. The bar and the courts did indeed reassert themselves and regain a good portion of the status and legitimacy that had long been associated with the elite bar. Unlike what we saw in the other Asian settings, the bar and the law in India resisted the attacks of the state.

The vicissitudes of this history have been described often enough that it is not necessary to revisit the details here (Rudolph and Rudolph 1987; Baxi 1980; Dhavan 2002; Kusum and Verma 2000). The prevailing interpretations of this history, however, pose some problems, and indeed the commentators who are closely associated with one side or the other are in fact united by a common perspective. The objective of most is to encourage the activism of the "rights revolution" (Epp 1998). The opposing side underlines the dangers of judicial ventures into politics. In each case, the analysis endorses the idea that the elite justice system is distinct and distant from politics. This view goes also with an image of balancing, with the idea that the courts step in when the political authority is weak.

On the other hand, this evolution can be interpreted as a product of the close connection between politics and law stemming from the double role historically of the great notables of the law. After a period of taking advantage of political opportunities made possible by their participation in the construction of new state institutions, the notables regrouped on the terrain of law as a means to gain a distance from state interventionism and socialism—inconsistent with their professional habitus and hostile to the interests of their clients and political allies. In 1970, for example, the Supreme Court invalidated measures that would have nationalized fourteen of the largest banks, already taken by the government of Indira Gandhi, and which would have eliminated the financial privileges of the princes (the so-called Privy Purse) (Rudolph and Rudolph 1987: 108).

These events represented little more than a rearguard action before the government succeeded in putting its policies in place. But the procedural skirmishes allowed the legal elite to gain time to prepare an ideological counteroffensive, especially important after the conflict had been exacerbated by the state of emergency. Discredited as adversaries of progress and equity, the lawyer politicians rebuilt their reputations for civic virtue as defenders of constitutional freedoms. According to the Rudolphs, "The conflict gradually changed its meaning as the Gandhi government, credited in the sixties with opposing the court because it blocked social change, was accused in the seventies of opposing the court because it restrained the irresponsible exercise of power by a self-serving state" (1987: 104).

The Challenge of the Lawyer Politicians on Judicial Terrain

The representation of this set of events as an opposition between two powers—the political and the judicial—is misleading. In fact, the adversaries mobilized all available resources, whether judicial or political, in the struggle over particular political policies and programs. Two of the principle protagonists of the constitutional debate—Nani Palkhivala and Mohan Kumaramangalam—were learned lawyers representing opposite political poles. Palkhivala was a celebrated commercial and constitutional advocate who was also a director of the Tata industrial group. The Tata business empire, which began in cotton, had been also a key funder of the Congress Party in the struggle for Indian independence. A Parsi, Palkhivala began as an advocate in Bombay in 1944 with a prominent local lawyer and then developed an expertise in taxation and a strong interest in economic issues. He became a vocal opponent of socialism and an advocate against state policies that challenged property rights. According to his profile in a book of his writings,

> Beginning with the Golak Nath case in 1967, he fought a series of historic cases in the Supreme Court to defend the rights of citizens and the sanctity of the Constitution. The cases pertaining to bank nationalization, the Privy Purses, arbitrary restrictions on newspapers, and the rights of minorities

to run educational institutions of their choice, and a number of other well known cases culminating in the Fundamental Rights (Kesavananda Bharati) case, made him a national hero and brought him international fame. (Palkhivala et al. 1999: xxi)

Palkhivala was director of Tata Sons from 1968 to 1999, and he was also chairman of the Associated Cement Companies for many years. He was a leading opponent of the Emergency declared by Indira Gandhi. In 1974, he published a book entitled *Our Constitution Profaned and Defiled.*

Kumaramangalam, a classmate of Indira Gandhi in Great Britain, was one of her closest advisors until his death in 1973. He followed a career in the bar and in politics. As one of the leaders of the socialist wing of the Congress Party, he was one of the architects of the bank nationalization. In addition, in a work on the theory of constitutional law entitled *Constitutional Amendments: The Reason Why* (1971), he justified constitutional amendments 24, 25, and 26 (known as the Kumaramangalam package), which reversed the decision in the Golak Nath case in which the Supreme Court had affirmed its constitutional authority (Rudolph and Rudolph 1987: 111).

The fight was not therefore between the legislature or executive and the courts. The elite of the bar was at the heart of the struggle and played the terrains of politics and law on both sides. The mixing of genres was inevitable. The mobilization of legal resources by the property-owning classes produced a growing politicization of the institutions in the legal field, transformed into an arena of political combat. When the confrontation was exacerbated with the proclamation of the state of emergency, the top leaders of the bar led the movement of opposition. They publicly denounced excesses of state power in the name of the protection of fundamental liberties. The Supreme Court, on the other hand, bent initially toward the exigencies of political power. Indira Gandhi had named five judges who were supposed to be "politically engaged"—and indeed later became the champions of social activism through the Supreme Court–, and she had also bypassed the seniority route to select the chief justice.

Despite the bonds of social homogeneity among the notables of the bar, the violence of these political battles broke the tacit consensus that allowed political investment while preserving the appearance of the neutrality of legal institutions. At the same time, this crisis provided a great opportunity to restore some of the political capital built in the struggles

for independence. They followed the same moral strategy as their predecessors. Indeed, as one interview respondent active in the events noted,
the ideas for a new political party, which became Janata, were forged by
lawyers imprisoned under the Emergency regime (Int. India-2).

The consequences of this resistance from the elite of the bar will be
discussed in more detail in chapter 11, but two career profiles illustrate
the resources available to the legal elite and mobilized both in the battle
against the state of emergency and in the efforts to rehabilitate the Supreme Court after its support of the decree.

As with respect to most prominent Indian lawyers, Ram Jethmalani
came from a family with a strong history in the legal profession. His father and grandfather were advocates, and his great-grandfather was law
trained and served as a district magistrate—the first after the British
conquered the Sindh province of what is now Pakistan. He graduated
from Bombay University in 1941. He practiced law in Karachi until 1948,
when he was forced to leave because of the partition. He moved to Bombay and began a practice with three cases given to him by another young
lawyer. In the three cases, he managed to build a reputation in the Bombay courts as a great jury lawyer. He built the reputation by challenging draconian laws on behalf of refugees in constitutional cases before
the Bombay high court. His practice varied with both civil and criminal
clients. He also was a part-time professor at the Government Law College in Bombay, which was a very prestigious appointment at the time.
In 1964, he was elected to the Bar Counsel for Bombay and within five
years was the chairman of the Indian Bar. He was the chairman at the
time of the Emergency in 1975. He was not involved in politics until the
1970s, except to support some candidates for office.

When the Emergency came, he reportedly "kept attacking Mrs. Gandhi and the party," and the government then sought to arrest him (Int.
India-2). After the warrant was issued, some three hundred lawyers appeared before the Bombay high court and secured an injunction against
the arrest. He then kept speaking around the country. In late April
1976, however, after the Supreme Court backed the Emergency powers, Jethmalani left India for the United States, which granted him political asylum with the support of emerging human rights groups. After
the announcement of elections, he returned to India and decided to run
against Mrs. Gandhi's law minister, H. R. Gokhle, and he won the election. He stayed in Parliament until he lost the election in 1985. At the
same time, he was reportedly "a great supporter of judicial activism,"

in part because he was one of the lawyers who believed that "the judiciary was much cleaner than other branches of the political land" (Int. India-2). Among other cases, he handled the defense of Kehar Singh in the Indira Gandhi assassination case. He was first minister for urban development and then law minister for Prime Minister Atal Bihari Vajpayee, serving from 1998 until 2000, when he was asked to resign reportedly over conflicts with another prominent lawyer, attorney general Soli Sorabjee. He remains active in politics and in law. Now in his eighties, he is often called a "maverick" by the media.

The second career is of V. R. Krishna Iyer, who became one of the most famous activist judges of the Indian Supreme Court and more recently a leading speaker on issues linked to the "antiglobalization" NGOs and human rights. As with respect to Jethmalani, he reportedly had "no inclination for politics, in the sense of gaining power through politics" (Int. India-3). Iyer was born in 1915 in what is now Kerala, India. His father, V. V. Rama Iyer, was a lawyer. After attending Madras Law College, Krishna Iyer began his career as an advocate in 1938. He became very successful representing workers on one side and industrialists on the other. His social justice advocacy led to his detention for a month after Indian independence. He was then persuaded to run for the legislature and won with the Communist Party victory in Kerala in the 1957 elections. Although reportedly never a communist, he became a minister in the government, dealing in different capacities with a variety of topics including law, prisons, and social welfare. He lost his position in a subsequent election and reportedly stated that he would not be a candidate again in an election—that he had no "hunger for power" as an "election politician" (Int. India-3). When nominated as a judge, according to someone close to him, other politicians warned him that he would be too "aloof" and lose his power as "advisor to all the people of the state." Others persuaded him that "judicial power is real power," however, and he decided to become a judge in 1968 (Int. India-3).

He was sympathetic with the Congress Party unhappiness with advocates who stood in the way of progressive reforms. When appointed by Indira Gandhi to the Supreme Court of India in 1973, he proclaimed his support for a judiciary in tune with socialist policies. Soon after he was appointed, however, he ruled against Mrs. Gandhi when she sought a stay of a ruling denying her election. The decision, in fact, gained such attention that Iyer was invited to address the American Bar Association in 1974, where he was praised for his independence. The subsequent state of emergency prompted legal challenges, and this time Iyer was initially on the side of the government. Very soon thereafter, however, Iyer helped to create the public interest litigation used to revive the image of the Supreme Court. He was the great proponent of public interest litigation until his retirement from the judiciary in 1980 (see chap. 12).

Each of these prominent advocates demonstrates a formidable combination of family, legal, learned, political, international, and even economic capital. They were highly successful lawyers descended from other lawyers going back well into the colonial period. They mobilized a renewed commitment to legal virtue when lawyers were attacked on one side, and when the courts lost prestige on the other. As we shall see in chapter 12, their assets and orientation were invaluable when the legal elite sought to retool and regain the credibility that had been lost in the time leading up to the Emergency proclaimed by Indira Gandhi.

From State Planning to the Internationalization of Markets: The Recomposition of Indian Economic Expertise around a Mathematical Approach to Economics

As in South Korea, the pioneering generation of economists in India was drawn from a tiny privileged elite that had accumulated numerous forms of social capital and diverse expertise. Economics also developed very close to state power, also as in South Korea. In India, as we have seen, caste barriers and the colonial legacy reinforced the system of state recruitment from a small elite at the heart of state power—structured around a group of lawyer notables. Notwithstanding a small number of exceptions, the most prestigious jobs for economists as with lawyers remained the preserve of the upper castes, especially the Brahmins. This elite recruitment system characterized not only the genesis of this discipline in India but also its recomposition around new paradigms.

Nothing is more revealing in this sense than the "renaissance figures," as they were termed by their biographer, Terence Byres in "Bengali Enlightenment" (1998), who pioneered in economics. One example is Prasanta Chandra Mahalanobis, a cosmopolitan and charismatic Brahmin trained as a physician before founding the Calcutta Institute of Statistics, one of the main centers of Indian economic thought. He became the "father" of economic planning alongside Nehru, had an abiding interest in cultural pursuits, and loved to display his architectural skills (Byres

1998: 42). He used his international contacts to invite heavyweight economists, especially European economists identified with the political left such as Oscar Lange, Charles Bettelheim, Jean Tinbergen, Nicholas Kaldor, Kenneth Galbraith, and Paul Baran. And he never made any effort to hide his disdain for theoreticians of pure economics (Byres 1998: 45).

His contemporary, Arindam Chaudhuri, described as a "feudal hobo," was an epicurean and dilettante. He cut his teeth in cinema, literature, and philosophic essay writing, before founding a weekly magazine inspired by the *Economist* called the *Economic Weekly*. Nearly fifty years later, it remains the most respected and widely read intellectual publication dealing with economic issues (Byres 1998: 67). Both of these highly charismatic personalities helped shape state policy and intellectual media debate that in India, as elsewhere, represented the two fundamental components of the field of economic thought.

A third representative of the Bengali Enlightenment was C. N. Vakil, who founded the Bombay School of Economics in 1922 along the lines of the London School of Economics. Its graduates headed India's planning agencies, contributed to planning-related political debates, and also branched out to establish new academic institutes, such as the Delhi School of Economics set up in 1948 by V. K. R. V. Rao. Rao had himself studied under Dobbs and Keynes at Cambridge. The 1960s represented the golden age of the school, when it attracted and taught the leading luminaries of Indian economics, including the future Nobel Prize winner Amartya Sen; Jagdish Baghwati, professor at Columbia; and Manmoghan Singh, the current prime minister. Singh came to prominence in the 1980s as a proponent of a more liberal policy inspired by, among others, Baghwati.

The initial development of economic expertise also depended on the privileged access and links that its advocates had to Nehru. Significantly, they were able to bring the entire range of their cultural capital into play, presented as "economic dilettantism," but highly prized in the inner circle of this tiny anglicized Indian elite of which Nehru was the major figure. Thus, the pioneering importers of this expertise were drawn from these elite proponents of heterodoxy, what Bourdieu has termed "hérésiarques" (heresy-sayers) to stress the ambivalence of their position. Instead of going into law like the majority of their peers, these heirs chose a high-risk strategy by opting for little-known or marginal fields like economics or statistics. Furthermore, from a strategic perspective, at a time when right-wing politicians were openly defending the interests of their political base—the large land owners and businessmen—pioneering economists could only bring their expertise to bear on government policy by presenting themselves as the advocates of state interventionism in the name of social development and justice. This ideological stance put them in an awkward position vis-à-vis their own social class. In particular, it limited access to a potential clientele of entrepreneurs that would have enlarged this new market for expertise and made it more profitable.

As elsewhere, in addition, the Ford Foundation was active in India in building the social sciences, especially economics. Indeed, in the early 1950s, the Ford Foundation considered India to be the highest priority among the targets of foundation grants, and again here, as elsewhere, it considered the social sciences much more promising than law. According to the Ford Foundation's retrospective on its work in India, the starting point was a recognition that the economists at the time of independence were mostly British trained (Staples 1992: 45). At the request of the Indian Planning Commission, in 1955, "the Foundation financed grants to introduce specialized training in applied social science research at six institutions," including the Delhi School of Economics and a number of universities (Staples 1992: 45). In 1958, the foundation made grants to many of the same institutions for a program in conjunction with MIT "addressed to planning needs" (Staples 1992: 46; see Rosen 1985). In 1970, the foundation then began a fifteen-year period of investment, totaling some three million dollars, to enhance India's cadre of "skilled social scientists" (Staples 1992: 47). The foundation took some credit for helping to build economics and political science through these grants.

Another key area of the Ford Foundation's early investment in India was management training. In 1959, the foundation "sent a study team to look at the leading business schools in the United States" (Staples 1992: 49). The result was the first two Indian Institutes of Management in 1961, located in Ahmedabad and Calcutta, and then a third in 1975 in Bangalore.

The state of emergency proclaimed by Indira Gandhi in 1975 affected the position of economics as it did law. According to V. V. Bhatt, a leading economist, the Emergency precipitated "considerable public discussion with regard to the negative effects of state controls" (2008: 108). It put the power of the state into some question. The event therefore marked a turning point in the manner in which Indian economic expertise was structured. The climate of authoritarianism bolstered criticisms of state planning initially formulated by Bhagwati and Meghnad Desai and subsequently taken up by T. N. Srinavasan. The criticisms immediately attracted attention insofar as they emanated from young professors at the Institute of Statistics who had previously defended P. C. Mahalanobis's policies favoring the strong state. Similarly, as recently documented by Vivek Chibber (2003), the developmental state in India was never able to impose discipline on the businesses that were the beneficiaries of import substitution. The state thus did not get the leverage necessary to lead in economic growth promotion. Chibber notes that the approach of the Congress Party, which led from above through a paternal strategy rather than mobilizing social groups, such as labor, also made it more difficult to put pressure on the business class.

The turning point in economics was accompanied by a redeployment of resources and a shift in the circuits of internationalization toward the United States. The shift both contributed to and accelerated this ideological and scientific polarization. Sen moved to the London School of Economics, Bhagwati left for the Massachusetts Institute of Technology, and Srinavasan took up an appointment at the World Bank before moving on to Yale. At the same time, the most brilliant mathematics students were turning their backs on European establishments and going instead to the United States, where monetarist orthodoxy based on mathematical modeling was beginning to gain ground. Many students who chose this route, frequently completed by internships in international financial institutions, went on to work closely with Manmoghan Singh when he began to overhaul the elite government corps in the 1980s with the support of Rajiv Gandhi. This shift in the approach of the economic elite led to a gradual opening of the Indian market—which picked up speed in the 1990s. As V. V. Bhatt stated in his autobiography, "The climate for reforms was generated by the studies of eminent [Indian] economists abroad" (2008: 109).

These developments in the sphere of Indian economic thought had a major polarizing impact. In one corner were the standard bearers of this new orthodoxy imported directly from the United States, who were still a minority, albeit an extremely influential one in the upper echelons of the state decision-making apparatus. In the other corner were the majority of the graduates of Indian academic institutes, who had been brought up on a recipe of state intervention but whose influence began to wane with the declining popularity of the European academic institutes that had helped to nurture this tradition. This cleavage, which reflected cultural, ideological, and theoretical differences, was actually perpetuated by being transposed onto the government administrative hierarchy. Graduates of national institutes generally went to work in administrative positions based on the model of the Indian Administrative Service, which had been inherited from the colonial era. However, career bureaucrats eventually came up against a glass ceiling. The most prestigious management or consulting positions were generally reserved for a tiny cosmopolitan elite that frequently combined years of academic achievement in an American university with experience and contacts made in international financial institutions such as the International Monetary Fund or the World Bank.

The contradictions inherent in this genesis of economic expertise within the state sector help account for the turning point reached in the 1970s. The take-up of economic expertise in India depended on the conversion of European know-how into expertise backed up by the authority of the state. However, in order to develop further, the domain would need to be repositioned to enlarge its market beyond the state. As such, this theoretical and political reconversion may appear to be the beginning of a process of normalization initiated by the most highly qualified of the new producers. They were able to present themselves as both successors and innovators.

In addition to making the most of the institutional and scientific opportunities created for them by their predecessors, these new generations of economists began to delve into new areas more suited to the new larger market for their expertise. They used their mathematical skills to reposition Indian economic thought from an international perspective. It tended to move away from its European and essentially British roots towards the U.S. influences now dominant in economics, and to open up new markets in both the private and public sector to economic expertise. Elite economics therefore joined elite law as it retooled more toward U.S. approaches and expertise. We shall explore in chapter 11 the process of retooling Indian law in the period after the Emergency, but it is interesting to see how similar elite economists and lawyers remained.

A key leader of public interest litigation as a justice on the Supreme Court—along with Krishna Iyer—was P. N. Bhagwati. Jagdish Bhagwati, his younger brother, is one of the leading U.S.-trained economists from India and was critical to the switch in orientation of the profession. The younger Bhagwati, whose academic career began in India and then continued in the United States, remains highly influential. Interestingly, according to the economist Bhagwati, he "turned to economics even though I came from a family of distinguished judges—my father was on the Indian Supreme Court, and my eldest brother went on to become India's chief justice—and was persuaded to keep term at Lincoln's Inn to possibly become a lawyer. I was saved from that cruel fate because I was seduced into economics by the great economists in Cambridge instead. That was the reason I abandoned the study of law" (Bhagwati 2002). The role of the Bhagwatis is an apt illustration of the relationship between the elite economists and their lawyer counterparts, and of the family capital so important in both fields.

Both groups served to reorient the technologies of governance at the same time they found ways to maintain their elite status. Drawing on their family and social capital and on the new technologies of governance from the United States, the elite economists reoriented economic policy away from the state-led economic policies that dominated the first forty years of Indian independence. As we shall see in chapter 12, we see the same process in the rebuilding of legal credibility through educational reform and public interest litigation, both connected to reformist ideas and approaches coming out of the United States.

Malaysia: The Corporate Bar and Elite Judiciary Offer Some Resistance

Malaysia provides the second example of the elite bar taking a strong stand against authoritarian policies. The confrontations that produced this resistance began when Mahathir Mohamad became prime minister in 1981. Mahathir was a strong supporter of the policies of Malaysia's New Economic Plan, designed to build the strength of the Malay population in the economy. Mathathir was the first non-English–trained chief executive in Malaysia and also the first not to be law trained. He was educated to be a physician and came from the ordinary middle class. He was not offered the education abroad shared by his predecessors. According to Hilley, he also shared some of a Margaret Thatcher–like enmity to the more traditional ruling elites: "one can observe in Mahathir's relationship to traditional elites a hybrid tone of qualified respect and latent resentment" (2001: 84). That resentment was especially evident in his policies with respect to the sultans who had been propped up by British colonial policies. He quickly stripped them of many of their privileges.

The law and the legal profession were not the focus of Mahathir in his early years in office. The elite of the profession, as noted in chapter 7, occupied positions in corporate law firms oriented toward the British and founded by expatriates. The three so-called S firms, Shearn Delamore & Co., Shook Lin & Bok, and Skrine, dominated the Bar Council and focused mainly on litigation. The courts were imbued with the British tradition of judicial independence, and that attitude was not inconsistent with a reluctance to quarrel with executive power. In contrast to the practicing bar, those in the judiciary were prominently of Malay ethnicity. According to Crouch, "the judiciary was mainly a Malay institution despite the overwhelming preponderance of non-Malays in the legal profession as a whole" (Crouch 1996: 118). The attitude was basically conservative: "On the whole, the judges shared the broad conservative outlook of the rest of the Malay elite" (Crouch 1996: 119).

Furthermore, as Andrew Harding states with respect to the period before the mid-1980s, "The character of their decisions resembled that of the English judiciary more than it resembled any other" (1990: 72). Indeed, according to Harding, the courts were criticized for being somewhat too deferential to the executive: "Generally lawyers and academics have criticized decisions from a standpoint of 'constitutionalism,' while reform groups have criticized from the rather different standpoint of 'public interest' or development'" (1990: 73n43). The courts were relatively conservative even as proponents of law and development began to look for a more aggressive role (e.g., Machado and Said 1981). As one of the leading lawyers noted, "our courts are very reluctant to interfere. . . . [T]hey were coming from the English school, Dicey, where Parliament is supreme" (Int. M-2). This lawyer complained that even in 2002, "the lawyers of Malaysia don't appreciate that we are living in a constitutional system" (Int. M-2). According to Harding, writing in 1990, in "32 years of independence only seven statutory provisions have been struck down by the courts as unconstitutional" including three "since the abolition of the appeal to the Privy Council" (1990: 71).

The legal profession began to expand with the establishment of the University of Malaya and other law schools that required majorities from the Bumiputra population (reportedly seventy of the one hundred places in the University of Malaya law class are reserved to Bumiputras) (Int. M-1). The profession went from three hundred in 1960 to five hundred in 1968 (Burn 1968) to seventeen hundred qualified lawyers (one thousand practicing) in 1975. As of that date, furthermore, the bar was quite prosperous consistent with the small size. A survey in 1975 showed that new lawyers quickly gained economic success—defined by the study as reaching the top one and one-half percent of Malaysian income within a few years of starting practice (Machado and Said 1981: 253). According to Machado and Said, as of 1974, "[l]ess than one fifth of Kuala Lumpur lawyers, but between half and two thirds of lawyers in the other regions of Malaysia, primarily serve individual clients" (1981: 260). The bar in the capital thrived by representing foreign and some Chinese ethnic businesses.

Mahathir's Attack on the Courts

There was a steady erosion of legal capital after Mahathir came to power, accelerated by a crisis that occurred in the late 1980s after the Malaysian Supreme Court began to test the limits of executive power. The bench and the elite bar began to become more assertive in the late 1970s, resisting some of the policies enacted in the name of development. The bar leadership initially expressed concern over the use of preventive detention justified by the Internal Security Act. According to one of the leaders, the bar was the "only organization that was vocal in criticism of legislation" and the Internal Security Act (Int. M-1). Still, as one activist noted, in the period prior to 1987, Mahathir did "not see lawyers as a threat" (Int. M-2). He paid little attention to lawyers and judges who, to that point, had posed no danger to his policies. His approach then changed.

The reasons for Mahathir's change stem both from the new position taken by the courts and internal politics in Malaysia. First, the courts began to take more initiative. The Supreme Court in 1985, following the abolition of appeals to the Privy Council, decided to "chart a new course" (Abas and Mohamed 1989: 49). They sought to step into the position that the Privy Council had purported to occupy as a guarantor of the rule of law English style. According to the then President of the Supreme Court, "For us English law remains a model where the decisions of the English Courts are constantly cited with great respect and approval" (Abas and Mohamed 1989: 49). As one leading advocate observed, at that point the relationship between bench and bar was also very solid: "It was very good, I mean, in the sense that I think the judiciary would consult the bar on judicial appointments. Because most of them—the members of the judiciary and the lawyers—had all studied at that point in time in London" (Int. M-1). British colonial legal capital tied the legal system together.

The changing attitude of the courts may have also been influenced by economic policies favoring the Malay ethnic group, the Bumiputras, and the state. The president of the Supreme Court at the time, for example, noted the tension in the role of the judiciary between a focus on protecting "individuals" versus "economic and social developments" (Abas and Mohamed 1989: 6). During the period after 1985, the Malaysian courts began for the first time to clash explicitly with Mahathir's administration. Summarizing the decisions of that period, Harding notes that "A number of the decisions had gone in favour of opposition groups and the legal profession, which has often voiced opposition to the present government" (1990: 76). One case reinstated an employment pass to a foreign correspondent because he had not been given a hearing (Harding 1990: 74). Another overturned a law that sought to control Muslim radicals. And another allowed an opposition leader, Lim Kit Siang, to assert standing to challenge a highway project on grounds of corruption. Karpal Singh, another opposition leader, was also granted various habeas corpus rights when he was detained under the Internal Security Act (Harding 1990: 75).

These developments were rooted in emerging applications of English administrative law. There was also some influence that came from the Indian judicial activism of the 1980s, discussed in chapter 12. But unlike the situation in India, where the Supreme Court was at that time developing public interest law, Malaysia lacked any local tradition of constitutional law. As one of the bar leaders noted, it still is not possible to name twenty or thirty advocates who do constitutional law in Malaysia (Int. M-2).

The new assertiveness of the courts in Malaysia came to a head because they intersected with developments within the ruling party and government. The economic crisis of the early to mid 1980s—the increase in debt, a decline in oil prices, and declines in prices of other commodities including tin and rubber—created pressures for economic change. Mahathir began to voice the concern that the economy needed to move away from excessive state control and toward more entrepreneurialism. He drew support from the neoliberal ideas emerging internationally to the effect that entrepreneurial initiative could be achieved by privatization (Hilley 2001: 58). In the words of Hilley, Mahathir used "privatization to assuage foreign investors and transform Malay rentiers into an internationally competitive business group" (2001: 61). Working through Daim Zainuddin, the finance minister from 1984 to 1991, Mahathir followed a strategy of privatization to strategic Bumiputra elites—also allowing the Chinese to regain a stronger role in the Malaysian economy through participation in privatization (Gomez and Jomo 1999; see Likosky 2005).

The career trajectory of Daim Zainuddin illustrates the ethnic division that divided law and the state. Zainuddin, a highly successful businessman who served as finance minister in the period 1984–91, was one of the very few ethnic Malays to have been called to the bar in England. Daim began his legal career with a prominent foreign-established law firm, Allen & Gledhill, moved to solo practice, and then left the practice of law. He reported that a client said to him in 1969, when he left the practice, that "there was no way a Malay lawyer could go up. This was true simply because there was no Malay business then" (Sui and Amin 1995:13). The prominent law firms—staffed almost entirely with ethnic Indian litigators and Chinese transactional lawyers—served the Chinese businesses and foreign investors who together dominated the economy.

Daim went on to participate and profit from the transformation of ethnic Malay—"Bumiputra"—political power into economic wealth through the so-called New Economic Plan and after. He quickly amassed considerable wealth as "the first Malay property developer" (Sui and Amin 1995:13) and, more generally, by going into "areas that were new to Bumiputras" (Sui and Amin 1995: 18). Once in the government, he then presided over privatization policies in the mid to late 1980s that solidified the growing position of Malay ethnic business (Gomez 1999: 133–34, 149–50). As Daim illustrates, part of the story of Malaysia is the misfit between the legal establishment built to serve British colonial interests and the growing Bumiputra business clout.

The external strategy followed by Mahathir, as noted by Hilley, was at the same time an internal one: "By appearing to transfer the burden of state services to the private sector—a process facilitated by the absence of any open tender system—UMNO [United Malays National Organization] had brought all the key public-sector assets under closer party control" (Hilley 2001: 62). The deregulation and redistribution precipitated a "hegemonic crisis" within UMNO. Tengku Razaleigh Hamzah sought the post of party president on the basis of an anti-corruption stance which went along with a base of support among small and medium businesses and a civil service unhappy with Mahathir's deregulatory policies (Hilley 2001: 88). The flow of patronage had gone to new elites.

Razaleigh and his so-called Team B filed a lawsuit at that point. They lost at the high court level. Then the Supreme Court president decided to convene a special panel of nine to hear the appeal (instead of the usual three). The political divide also went to the courts in other ways, for example, through arrests of dissenting academics and intellectuals under the Internal Security Act. The status of the election, the privatizations, and the handling of dissent were all finding their way to the Supreme Court. According to the then-President of the Supreme Court, speeches and remarks of judges "coupled with the independent attitude of the Supreme Court must have distressed the Prime Minister as could be seen from his reaction" (Abas and Mohamed 1989:14). One early reaction by the government in March 1988 was a constitutional amendment seeking to curb judicial power, which further raised the stakes.

The speeches escalated on both sides, culminating in a letter written by judges late in March seeking to go over the head of the prime minister to the king and other Malay rulers. The letter then precipitated the dismissals of the president of the Supreme Court and others by Mahathir. One indication of the stance of this English-educated judiciary is that, when summoned to see the prime minister, the initial attitude of the lord president of the Supreme Court was that "the Prime Minister can come see me" (Int. M-3). In Hilley's words, "the legal impasse now offered an expedient moment to confront the judiciary itself" (2001: 89). After some complex and highly suspect legal actions, Mahathir dismissed Supreme Court President Tun Salleh Abas effective August 1988. He also dismissed two others and at one time had suspended six members of the court.

The key judicial decisions after suspensions—all favorable to Mahathir—were made by a suspect majority including three relatively junior high court judges. According to one of the Supreme Court judges, "Ranks were ignored and apparently bypassed with scant respect for justice" (Seah 2004). The compliant judges then moved later to the Supreme Court (see generally Harding 1990). The courts' brief period of assertiveness therefore ended quickly. In Harding's words, "The judges, one might say, had broken the unwritten rules of judicial behaviour. The executive's action was designed to restore the status quo ante" (1990: 78). Mahathir's attack was also one related to social class. As Crouch states, the difference between Mahathir and his predecessors was that, "earlier prime ministers had similar social backgrounds to the Malay judges and mixed with them socially" (1996: 139). Mahathir simultaneously took on the Indian bar and the weakened Malay elite in the judiciary.

At that point the judiciary and the critics within the elite bar and what remained of the elite judiciary represented what Andrew Harding, visiting Malaysia at the end of the 1980s, characterized as a "split in the establishment" (Harding 1992: 234). Harding optimistically forecast that, "The middle classes are on the move, lawyers are in the vanguard, and [there is] the universal though recent interest in the constitution and the law as an institution" (1992: 234). In fact, however, Mahathir increasingly turned the courts into instruments of his political power. The resistance fell short.

The traditional Malay elite, which had been closely linked to British colonialism, lacked the resources to assert a strong judicial role. As illustrated by the trajectory of Daim, the new Malay generation took advantage of the state-led transformation of the economy, investing relatively little in law and legal institutions except as instruments of state power. The judicial crisis, however, helped to redefine the role of the Malaysian bar, which was another ethnic enclave fostered by British colonial policies. As we shall see in chapter 12, the corporate bar, which traditionally had been characterized by great economic success coupled with political apathy, became identified strongly with the activist role of political champions against state authoritarianism. In contrast to the elite bar in India, however, the Malaysian bar did not possess substantial familial, political, and state capital in relation to the state led by Mahathir. Furthermore, as we shall also see, their relative weakness came through their orientation to the British, who could offer very little to sustain them. The next part will compare how the legal elites in the different countries were able to rebuild credibility, retool their approach to align more with the approach coming from the United States, and strengthen their positions in the field of state power. Malaysia, we shall see, provides an example of a relative lack of success in that venture.

PART IV

Merchants of Law as Moral Entrepreneurs

We now examine the position of the legal profession as it takes shape today in the different Asian countries. That position relates to a variety of historical factors, including colonial geneses, the place of the country in hegemonic political struggles, and the palace wars that take place within particular countries and within the dominant power in the post–World War II period—the United States. In each country, as we shall see, there has been an opportunity to rebuild or revamp the profession beginning in the 1980s and extending to the present.

The symbolic imperialism associated with the rule of law, which can also be seen as a globalization of domestic hegemonic fights, takes place at the intersection of law and politics. The initial stage of this process, explored in the previous part, came in the context of the Cold War, and it helped produce—with notable variations—a relative marginalization of law in relation to economists and the military in so-called developmental states. The symbolic imperialism explored in this part again results in large part from the exportation of U.S. palace wars now centered on a revamped moral imperialism. This new symbolic imperialism, which in part represented a return to power of the foreign policy establishment through policies of human rights, democracy, transparency, judicial reform, and anticorruption, contributes to a restructuring of the fields of state power in Asia (and elsewhere).

This part therefore begins with a return to the political and legal history of the United States in order to understand both the elitist origins and then the more general institutionalization of the practices of legal and judicial reform. The exportation of these policies is in one sense top down, with U.S. global actors such as the Ford Foundation and the Asia Foundation ever present in promoting and funding reforms. From another perspective, however, the relative success of the exportation comes from the ability to link to local strategies that suit locally embedded actors. In this introduction we examine the forces that led to the particular top-down approaches that ascended in the late twentieth century. The subsequent chapters will examine how they intersected with local strategies.

The U.S.-style reforms, we shall see, are also most recognizable in the places where the Cold War investment and U.S. influence was strongest, in particular India, Indonesia, South Korea, and the former U.S. colony of the Philippines; and where the position of legal elites was weakest, exemplified especially by Indonesia and South Korea. Where the position of legal elites was weakest, there was also more of a need to draw on foreign capital as a source of legitimacy and support. We also see the role of lawyers as social justice entrepreneurs or cause lawyers emerging more dramatically in these countries of relative weakness than in the others, even if always within a locally embedded context that provides the specific characteristics of the activities.

There is less of a dramatic influence in the legal fields that had managed to conserve enough of their social and political capital, epitomized by India and the Philippines, even though their strong ties to the United States and the U.S. legal field lead to practices that certainly take the pattern of social justice entrepreneurs. We see still less influence in places where the legal profession has retained a minimum of autonomy centered on relatively limited but prosperous markets—for example, Hong Kong, Japan, Malaysia, and Singapore. This position provides at least a base on which legal elites could build the classic model of the bar as the defender of civil and political liberties threatened by state authoritarianism. The construction of this role also tends to link to the highly prosperous international corporate bar, which increasingly becomes the touchstone and international point of contact for legal reform activities.

Political Strategies for the Promotion of the Rule of Law

The "comeback of law" in recent decades has been promoted through a "rights revolution" linked to the revamping of law in the United States.

As we noted above, the U.S. legal profession had a number of advantages in the market for legal exports and imports. Lawyers were in a very strong position in the United States after World War II, much in contrast to the legal profession in European countries. The Cold War, led by a legal elite associated with the Council on Foreign Relations, involved many marriages of convenience with military governments identified with anticommunism. But there was always some part of the U.S. foreign policy that drew on law and the ideals of the rule of law.

The Cold War, for example, brought CIA investment in the establishment of the International Commission of Jurists in the 1950s, which then led to Amnesty International. And even when the United States was for the most part training economists as the key modernizing elites to govern developmental states as part of the Cold War, there remained some attention to law. The Law and Development Movement of the 1960s and 1970s showed that there was still a place, even if a subordinate one, for law in Cold War development strategies. We have already seen examples in India, Indonesia, the Philippines, and South Korea. The antistate economics that came in with the Reagan era of neoliberalism was associated with a more severe depreciation of the importance of lawyers and law in foreign policy. But, as related elsewhere, the role of law and lawyers in the field of state power in the United States and in foreign policy revived through the human rights movement, which was as much an effort to regain power against President Reagan as an effort to transform states elsewhere (Dezalay and Garth 2006; 2008).

The role of lawyers advanced with the advent of globalization, bringing much more open economies, increased foreign investment, and the proliferation of non-U.S. lawyers operating—increasingly with advanced law degrees from the United States—on the model of the corporate law firms pioneered on Wall Street. Democracy promotion and the rule of law by the end of the 1980s became hallmarks of American foreign policy, institutionalized in the philanthropic foundations, the teachings and programs of elite law schools, the policies of USAID, the World Bank, and European organizations joining the effort to build law and legal institutions abroad. As we have noted elsewhere (Dezalay and Garth 2008), the power of individuals associated with the foreign policy establishment declined, but the approaches associated with the alliance of Wall Street law firms and investment banks, philanthropic foundations, and elite law schools regained a strong position in the field of state power. The situation in the United States made scholars and policymakers anxious to find, promote, and sustain a "rights revolution" abroad (Epp 1998; see generally Dezalay and Garth 2002).

This rights revolution merits the name in two senses—a revolution in political practices led by law and also a revolution in the mode of production of law. The two aspects are strictly connected: the transformation in the political usages of law proceeds by calling into question the hierarchical structures that determine the political choices of the agents of law. The importance of this change in incentives and hierarchies will be elaborated on below.

The legal discourse on the recent politics of exportation of the rule of law tends to present it as a revival of the entrepreneurial efforts in the 1960s and 1970s to promote law and development through the exportation of U.S. legal conceptions. Certainly one finds a great number of similar projects, for example, those seeking to modernize legal instruction on the U.S. model—more rigorous selection of students, teaching by full-time law professors, more priority to practical courses, and of course reliance on the case method of instruction. This programmatic continuity is essentially tactical. Learned competence is one of the most legitimate exports, and it also helps support the role of the law schools and the professional identity that sustains the U.S. approach. The U.S.-oriented law schools also provide places that recognize and sustain the importance of local elites educated in the United States or practicing in corporate law firms tied to U.S. legal practices.

Despite the tactical continuities represented by similar legal projects, the history of the export of the rule of law is also marked by significant interruptions and reorientations. There has been a constant sense of failure augmented by the self-criticism of the missionaries of law and development (Trubek and Galanter 1974; Gardner 1980; Carothers 1998). Toward the end of the 1970s, the emerging criticism coincided with the ascendancy of neoliberal economists who highlighted the lack of effectiveness of developmental assistance, including the law projects, and basically abandoned the legal component.

The hiatus in law and development programs, however, was rather short-lived, as legal assistance returned in the 1990s in a quite favorable ideological and political context—that of the politics of structural adjustment aligned with the so-called Washington Consensus (Dezalay and Garth 1998). Legal expertise was no longer marketed as a technology supporting national developmentalist bureaucracies but became an object in itself. Consistent with the comeback of law in state power within the United States, law was deemed central abroad to govern the new commercial order, to protect against overreaching state bureaucracies, and to position countries to participate in expanding global markets in goods and services.

The modernization and reform of legal institutions became one of the key priorities of developmental assistance generally, promoted in particular by the World Bank and, in Asia, the Asian Developmental Bank. The first round of legal assistance projects in the new era had relatively limited impacts, focusing mainly on technical and financial support to modernize overburdened and long-criticized approaches to the administration of justice—largely ignored by the bureaucracies of authoritarian governments focused on development.

Limited successes in these endeavors did not discourage the development funding agencies, however. They moved toward more ambitious reforms seeking to give legal voice to the burgeoning "civil society" (linked also to the major financers of developmental assistance). Improvement in the administration and operation of the judicial system was increasingly seen as one of the key levers favoring the acceleration of liberalization and democratization against the corruption characteristic of "clientelistic states." Even when seemingly imposed from the outside in conformance with the new ideological hegemony associated with the opening of markets and the liberalization of the state, this new political order could at the same time appear as if it was simply the product of local initiatives. Activist NGOs called for judicial reform in the name of civil society.

The operation of the courts became a key political stake in a number of countries because courts were among the most easily challenged—and most fragile—of state institutions. The critics could use great principles of justice to challenge the operation of the courts. And the criticisms were all the more telling because the courts often had lost whatever credibility they had through decades of disinvestment by the authoritarian regimes. The disqualification and obsolescence of legal capital made the task of the external critics even easier since they could count on the discrete support of a small group of legal professionals eager to arrest the local legal decline. Local lawyers invested in international resources to try to arrest the self-reinforcing cycle of disinvestment and devaluation.

The effort to restore the value of legal capital relied on coalitions that may appear a priori paradoxical since they rely on providers of international funds and on professionals who represent quite different modes of imported legal excellence—academic, activist, and entrepreneurial. But these different groups have also come together under the (not necessarily valid) title of "people's power" in various national and historical settings—including notably the periods leading to the fall of Ferdinand Marcos in the Philippines and of Suharto in Indonesia. Similar coalitions can be seen in varying degrees in movements found in South Korea, Hong Kong, Malaysia, and elsewhere.

These coalitions are characterized in varying degrees by a discrete but central role of entrepreneurs from corporate law firms. These lawyers possess important and diversified resources for this role, predisposing them to serve as courtiers and mediators between the different groups of agents and institutions engaged in strategies of political mobilization through and around the law. They use their international credibility and connections to serve as both sponsors and disqualifiers of local NGOs and their activists, both with respect to the foreign entities that finance them and the foreign media outlets that are central to the effectiveness of their local campaigns. They decide which groups are respectable and worthy of philanthropic or other support. In this manner, the themes that are privileged in these campaigns are emblematic of a particular coalition of interests oriented toward the fight against the corruption of the justice system and its subordination to political power—and in support of more transparency and less clientelism in the selection and promotion of judges.

This mobilization of public opinion is then also a mobilization of law, since it demands respect for legal rules by those institutions charged with that very task. This objective is perfectly consistent with the agenda of the international organizations, but it also corresponds to the interests and resources of these notables of law that benefit from a kind of double authority: their expertise in transnational law, attested to by their clientele of multinationals, and the capital of local legal authority they possess in most of the countries as direct descendants of the families of the colonial lawyers who furnished the initial leadership in producing the law and in governing newly independent states.

These elite lawyers in fact tend to be the only locals able to embody legitimate legal capital, especially in places where decades of military leadership weakened the institutional structures—the courts, the faculties of law, and the bar—in which they had once invested in order to reproduce legal capital. The poor health of the institutions fundamental to the legal field of peripheral states helps explain another paradoxical situation. The descendants of the outdated colonial legal elite after three or four decades can convert into the vanguard of an enterprise promoting law based on a completely different hegemonic model.

The accumulated capital of legal families descending from the traditional colonial elite is in effect able to halt—at least temporarily—this dismantling of the structures of legal fields assailed by military regimes and the Cold War. The most enterprising or luckiest among the descendants also are able to take advantage of their cosmopolitan resources to effect a double conversion—both conceptual and geopolitical. They supplement their legal learning acquired from European faculties of law with an apprenticeship in the techniques (as well as professional ideology) transmitted in the U.S. law schools. In this way some of the descendants of the lawyer-constructors of the nation state succeed and even prosper by becoming courtiers of the new international legal regime. They acted to represent multinationals seeking to protect their investments and also their reputations as they did business with often-suspect governmental bureaucracies. Local corporate lawyers with ties to the old elite could thus help minimize the risks of doing business in peripheral markets where legal rules counted for very little in comparison to exchanges of favor within networks of clientele—formed by those who dealt with the authoritarian bureaucracies and family oligarchies who control what are often characterized as patrimonial states.

Variations in these patterns are explored in the following chapters. The processes of retooling and reorienting are first explored in the Philippines and India (chap. 11), where the elite legal profession began with the most substantial resources to build credibility through resistance to authoritarianism. We then turn to Malaysia, Singapore, and Hong Kong, providing examples where that resistance has been relatively unsuccessful (chap. 12). The chapter (chap. 13) that immediately precedes the conclusion (chap. 14) then shows the emergence in varying degrees of U.S.-oriented strategies linking corporate lawyers and social entrepreneurs in two countries where the colonial heritage was very strong, the Philippines and India, and very weak, Indonesia and South Korea.

CHAPTER ELEVEN

Lawyers as Political Champions against Authoritarianism: Relative Successes Exemplified by the Philippines and India

French advocates in the eighteenth century, as we described in chapter 2, developed the strategy of gaining power in the state and potentially profitable legal notoriety by championing excluded groups against authoritarian governmental activities. We have seen this enduring legal and political strategy adopted by aspiring elites in a number of Asian countries, including Lee Kwan Yew in Singapore prior to his ascendency into political power. This strategy is a characteristically European one, with strong roots in Britain and France and in countries with legal professions built along European lines. Within the United States, of course, this strategy has also long been present. It is a strategy that helped place lawyers in a strong role in moves to independence. We next explore the relatively successful adoption of this strategy in two countries—the Philippines and India. The revamping of the legal field in the Philippines after the period of martial law under Marcos and in India after the Emergency proclaimed by Indira Gandhi in each instance reveals the relatively strong initial position of the legal elite.

Philippines: Revamping the Legal Elite and Maintaining the Oligarchy

The process of revamping the legal field in the Philippines draws substantially on the relatively strong initial position. We can see the connections and the deployment of legal, familial, religious, and international capital by following the careers of those who became the leaders of the resistance to Marcos and the brokers of the transition to the post-Marcos era. Many of the same figures—with similar strategies—were instrumental in the impeachment of President Estrada and the transition to the current president, Gloria Macapagal.

Jovito Salonga and a very few others, most notably Jose Diokno and Lorenzo Tanada, were the leading elite opponents to Marcos. Their resistance to Marcos was noted in chapter 9. Salonga, as noted before, was a devout Protestant from a middle-class background and a graduate of the University of Philippines Faculty of Law in the late 1930s, where he was active in debate and in school politics and a member of the Sigma Rho fraternity. He went abroad after the war to attend Harvard Law School, where he received an LLM, and Yale, where he earned a JSD. Typical of those of his generation, he was active in politics, represented major businesses, and taught law. With Tanada (who had supported Marcos in 1965) and a few others, Salonga participated in legal attacks on martial law—declared in 1972—and in the defense of leaders of the opposition, including Diokno and Aquino. He noted that, "Where the imprisonment was unjust or dubious, we did not hesitate to bring the facts and surrounding circumstances to the attention of martial law authorities, particularly Minister Enrile, a fraternity brother" (Salonga 2001: 241). That combination led to the release of ninety prisoners in the mid-1970s—until Ponce Enrile lost the power to release prisoners.

At that point, according to Salonga, "we were only a handful among pre-martial law politicians who refused to compromise with Marcos" (2001: 246). Furthermore, with respect to the activists organized against Marcos, "we did not have a program that would appeal to their idealism, on the one hand, and their desire for meaningful action, on the other" (2001: 246). In late 1976, Salonga began meeting with a "small group of social democrats" led by two Jesuit priests, a businessman, and a few others. They began working on a "third way." According to Salonga, "I shared the view that neither the CPP-NPA [the communist left]—with its dogmatic reliance on armed struggle to achieve its ends regardless of the means—nor the Marcos dictatorship, with its greed and repressiveness, provided the answer" (2001: 251). Salonga then agreed to head the Kabaka, an acronym for the People's Alliance for Freedom.

Around the same time, after his release from prison in 1974, Jose Diokno founded the Free Legal Assistance Group (FLAG)—modeled after the Legal Aid Institute in Jakarta—to provide lawyers to help detainees. The organization was initially funded by the Ford Foundation. The idea, according to a lawyer close to the organization, was to try all tactics "short of illegal" to resist authoritarianism (Int. P-14).[1] Part of its authority came from the fact that the lawyers were "respected in their own communities," including a certain deference even from Marcos (Int. P-14). Its mission was not only to help detainees, but more broadly to provide "developmental legal aid" (Golub 2000: 203)—such that "lawyers should attack injustice in ways that address underlying issues and reach beyond individual cases" (Golub 2000: 203).[2]

From the beginning, FLAG was close to another organization—the Task Force Detainees of the Philippines (TFDP) established in 1974 by the Association of Major Religious Superiors in the Philippines (Clarke 1998: 165). The TFDP was close to but emphatically "independent" from the united front institutions of the Philippine left. The first head was an American Jesuit, and his successor after a short time was Sister Mariani Dimaranan (Clarke 1998: 168). She met with Diokno when he was in prison, helped provide funding for FLAG, and introduced FLAG to Novib (a Dutch developmental agency now called Oxfam Novib to reflect its long affiliation with Oxfam). From her perspective, the organizations were "brother and sister" (Clarke 1998: 168). According to Diokno, the TFDP was one of the key institutions for awakening attention in the United States to the human rights abuses in the Philippines (Clarke 1998:

---

1. The authors conducted interviews in each of the countries studied. In order to protect the confidentiality of the interviewees, the interviews are identified only by country and number. The countries are abbreviated as follows: HK, Hong Kong; India; Indon., Indonesia; K, South Korea; M, Malaysia; P, Philippines; and S, Singapore.

2. FLAG and its offspring have moved from civil and political rights to economic, social, and cultural rights. The leading senator concerned with legal and judicial reform, Francis Pangilinan, worked with FLAG as a student activist in the 1980s. Another very prominent senator, Joker Arroyo, was a corporate lawyer whose work with FLAG helped him to political prominence, including taking the lead in the impeachment of President Estrada. Along with FLAG, many of the same individuals founded MABINI (Movement of Attorneys for Brotherhood, Integrity, Nationalism).

173). More than any other NGO, according to Clarke, it "undermined
the Marcos dictatorship" because it was able to crystallize "Church concern for human rights" (Clarke 1998: 187).

At this point in the Philippines—the late 1970s—human rights were
gaining a stronger place on the international agenda. Salonga began to
speak about human rights internationally, encouraged to do so first by
a leading Indonesian human rights lawyer, Yap Thiam Hen, at a meeting of the World Council of Churches in Britain (Salonga 2001: 253).
Through connections to Philippine activists in exile in the United States,
Salonga then met Congressman Donald Fraser and others "deeply dis-
turbed about the situation in the Philippines" (Salonga 2001: 254). With
the Carter administration's emphasis on human rights, Patricia Derian,
assistant secretary of state for human rights, visited Manila early in
1978, meeting and encouraging the opposition, including the still-jailed
Aquino.

Some of the official U.S. outside support for dissent then waned. A
rigged election in the Philippines and a decision by the Carter administration that human rights in the Philippines had to "yield to overrid-
ing U.S. security considerations" (Salonga 2001: 275) set the opposition
back in its quest for a third way. Salonga still sought a legal means to resist. Pleading continuing physical weakness from a bombing that nearly
killed him, Salonga declined an invitation to assume leadership of the
resistance "in the hills" (2001: 284). Later, in late 1980, he was arrested
again. A flood of international petitions and the coincidence of a meeting of Asian Jurists in Manila prompted Marcos to order his release
(2001: 316). International connections kept his oppositional voice out of
prison.

Building on his alliance with human rights activists abroad, Salonga
then accepted an invitation to be a visiting scholar at Yale Law School.
From there, he and his wife settled in Los Angeles for almost three years,
ending in January 1985. During the time in Los Angeles many of the opposition leaders met with Salonga. The Reagan administration had reem-
braced the Marcos regime, making it difficult to get a sympathetic hearing
from Washington, D.C., but matters finally changed with the assassination of Aquino upon his return from the United States late in 1983.

U.S. pressure for a new election then mounted (Salonga 2001: 369).
The opposition, including Salonga's allies, agreed to participate in the
election held in 1986, and they made Corazon Aquino the presidential
candidate. After a notably fraudulent vote count, mass demonstrations

began in EDSA (Epifanio de los Santos Avenue) at the same time that two key members of the Marcos administration, Juan Ponce Enrile and General Fidel Ramos, defected and stated their readiness to help negotiate the transition to a new administration. The Catholic Church, led by Jaime Cardinal Sin, supported the mass nonviolent demonstrations after warning Marcos to reconcile with the nonviolent opposition (Thompson 1995: 118). A group termed the "Convenor Group"—including Father Joaquin Bernas of the Ateneo Law School, Senator Lorenzo Tanada and others, as well as Salonga—urged a clean break rather than a contest of the election. When the Reagan administration refused to back Marcos, he had no choice but to step down. "People power" had been mobilized and sparked political change.

Aquino was sworn in early in 1986 by two existing justices of the Supreme Court who had started out pro-Marcos but moved into opposition—Claudio Teehankee and Abad Santos. Teehankee, mentioned earlier, had also been a law partner of Tanada, and Santos had been the dean of the University of Philippines School of Law. The new government included Ponce Enrile as minister of national defense (for a short time only) and Ramos as chief of staff of the armed forces. Salonga was then elected to the Senate, as were Ponce Enrile and Edgardo Angara, both of whom were close to, and enriched by, the Marcos regime.

Salonga's story provides an elite perspective of an opposition relatively slow to galvanize. The Catholic Church was also relatively slow, only beginning to move after martial law. Jaime Cardinal Sin "was not a firebrand," but "he would change" (Quezon 1996: 4) and become the leading figure in the overthrow. As Manuel Quezon III noted in the passage quoted earlier, "Adversity made these leaders [–Aquino, Diokno, Salonga, and Tanada–] men of far higher principle than they were thought to have been previously" (Quezon 1996: 5). This group and those close to them managed the transformation while preserving the institutions of the government, relegitimating the Supreme Court, and controlling the left which, at one point, "felt increasingly assured of its premier role in anti-dictatorship efforts" (Quezon 1996: 9). Salonga's deep involvement in protestant religion served in the Philippines also to connect him to the moral leadership of the Catholic Church. In particular, he worked closely with Jaime Cardinal Sin and Father Joaquin Bernas in the downfall of Marcos.

The role of Father Bernas, a Jesuit with law degrees from the Ateneo de Manila School of Law, Fordham, and New York University, has been especially important in connecting the Catholic Church and the Ateneo to the movement to refurbish Philippine law. Indeed, the Ateneo represents a kind of elite base for the Catholic Church in law to compete with the University of the Philippines—more radical and more tied to the ideals of the freemasons. His service as dean of the Ateneo School of Law in the period 1975–77, as president of the university until 1992, and then as law dean again, helped to infuse Catholic legal activism into the anti-Marcos struggle. His role as a key member of the Constitutional Convention after Marcos, then again in the impeachment of Estrada and the defense against the impeachment of Chief Justice Hilario Davide, and as the leading Philippine constitutional law scholar, has given him great prominence and stature. He has lent his influence to many reform movements connected to the Ateneo, including the Human Rights Center established in 1986 and the Alternative Law Group, both of which are discussed in chapter 13.

The group that came to power thus brought back the legal establishment to restore order and their position. Never too far from power even though threatened and persecuted by Marcos and his allies, they invested more in legal virtue than their earlier careers would have predicted. Hedman and Sidel, in their book on political developments in the Philippines (2000), draw on the concept of *trasformismo* from Gramsci, which they define as a counteroffensive mobilizing one fraction of power elites and facilitating a reactualization of hegemony through the reappropriation of the rhetoric of contestation. More succinctly, "Trasformismo involves a political process whereby radical pressures are gradually absorbed and inverted by conservative forces, until they serve the opposite of their original ends" (2000: 13). They use this concept to analyze the recuperation of the anti-Marcos movement by the religious hierarchy in alliance with the more virtuous fraction of the Philippine establishment. In their words, "Viewed in this light, the People Power Revolution appears less as an example of the spontaneous resurgence of civil society in the process of transition from authoritarian rule and more as the climax in a cycle of recurring crisis and temporary 'resolutions' stemming from deep rooted tensions" related to issues of "political citizenship and social class" (2000: 29, 14).

One way to see the story of continuity is to examine the role of some key lawyers and law firms both during and after the Marcos regime. As noted above, Juan Ponce Enrile turned against Marcos at the last minute and helped engineer the final stages of his removal from power. Earlier, in addition, Ponce Enrile had worked to help his fraternity brother Jo-vito Salonga secure the release of some political prisoners in the period of martial law. Ponce Enrile was still one of the wealthiest individuals in the Philippines and the president of the Senate as of 2008. Salonga, the key figure in revamping legal virtue in the Philippines, showed some reciprocity when he was the chair of Corazon Aquino's Presidential Commission on Good Government. Salonga conducted an investigation and determined that there was "no evidence" that "would warrant" an investigation of Ponce Enrile (Manapat 1991: 198). Elite ties counseled more informal sanctions. As reported in his autobiography, Salonga also gave a speech in 1987 on the "Role of Lawyers in the Concealment of the Ill-Gotten Wealth," and he hoped that some of his "friends in the legal profession" "felt the sting of his speech" (2001: 240). Whatever the "sting," the lack of any formal sanctions helps show the ties among the elite serving law, business, and the state.

The Supreme Court, restored to power after the end of martial law and even strengthened in the new constitution, played by the same rules. One of Marcos's closest cronies was Eduardo Cojuanco, who became a billionaire under Marcos through license fees and monopolies. All his legal work was done by ACCRA, whose lawyers were major figures in the Marcos regime and occupied positions on the boards of shadow companies set up as vehicles for Cojuanco's accumulation of wealth. Cojuanco left the Philippines when Marcos fell from power but later returned and regained his position as a central figure in business and politics. His reemergence was not without some controversy.

Along with Roberto Benedicto, Cojuanco was a principal target of the Philippines government's effort to recover some of the wealth acquired by Marcos and his cronies. The effort was not very successful, and the courts played a role in thwarting the investigation. In particular, in 1996, the Supreme Court of the Philippines helped both ACCRA and Cojuanco by holding that ACCRA partners could invoke the lawyer-client privilege to decline to disclose the name of the clients for whom they set up the wealth-plundering corporations during the Marcos era (*Teodoro R. Regala et al. vs. The Hon. Sandiganbayan et al.*, G.R. no. 105938, September 21, 1996). Drawing on U.S. legal sources but reaching a result that would have surprised U.S. lawyers, they effectively put an end to the investigation of the law firm. ACCRA remains one of the most important corporate law firms in Manila, and, as noted, Edgardo Angara is a powerful senator.

The legal elite, in short, took advantage of their social capital to commandeer the resistance to Marcos in the name of a third way between the left and the right. They reinvented themselves as defenders of democracy against authoritarianism, staved off more radical movements, and regained their position of strength in the field of state power. The elite leaders of the resistance to Marcos are now prominent politicians with strong constituencies abroad. They succeeded in toppling the Marcos government, but only after the United States finally turned on Marcos when Aquino was assassinated. But when the elite lawyers playing the strategy of virtue came to power, they also helped to maintain the position of their friends and fraternity brothers who had committed themselves to Marcos and received handsome rewards for that commitment. The corporate lawyers closest to Marcos similarly maintained their strong position as brokers in the field of state power and also as respected counsel to multinationals. The *Legal 500* for 2008 states that, "The same full-service players maintain their positions at the top end of the market. Sycip Salazar Hernandez & Gatmaitan and Angara Abello Concepcion Regala & Cruz (ACCRALAW) remain at the top of the tree, with over 100 lawyers apiece" (see http://www.legal500.com/c/ philippines).

India: The Emergence of Public Interest Litigation and the Retooling of the Legal Elite

The Indian bar came through the attacks culminating in the Emergency declared by Indira Gandhi in 1975 with substantial resources. The elite bar, produced through colonial history and the Congress Party's long campaign for independence, occupied a very strong position linked by family capital and led by the Supreme Court bar. The increasingly numerous faculties of law—approaching five hundred by the late 1980s— were relatively weak and dominated by numerous law students and a relatively low-prestige faculty, despite early efforts by U.S. reformers and the Ford Foundation to improve the position of legal education. The electoral defeat of Indira Gandhi in 1977 allowed the old notables of law who had resisted her rule to regain further prominence in the political field.

This first attempt at a restoration to political leadership, however, was quite short-lived. The diverse coalition that came together under the Janata Party banner to oppose the Congress Party divided once they gained political power. The older lawyer politicians, in addition, were quick to resort to the courts, and both sides accused the other of corruption. Still, the model of notable politicians did not disappear. Even today, lawyer politicians are found in leadership positions in the Congress Party and in the various coalitions that have governed since the late 1980s. The lawyers have no doubt lost their quasi-monopoly on political power secured in the first days of the Indian republic, but they still tend to hold nearly a third of the seats in the legislature with numbers that increase as one climbs the political hierarchy: fifty percent of the cabinet positions and sixty-seven percent of the ministers in 1985 (Gandhi 1988: 381).[3]

Today, the leaders of the Supreme Court bar continue to serve governments as populist coalitions continue to seek the capital of the elder statesmen of the bar. At the same time, however, these elite lawyers are no longer the leading popular politicians that they once were. As one of the elite lawyers tellingly put it to explain the decline in the power of his group, "you see, the universal franchise will not draw the best people. And particularly when there are so many diverse sites, . . . religious, communal, caste. . . . Every group would like to have its own share in political positions. And that was when the standard came down" (Int. India-4). Another very prominent lawyer notes that "this proportion in Parliament has been steadily decreasing, in complete proportion to their declining social acceptance" (Int. India-2).

The resistance to authoritarianism, as we noted, allowed the elite bar to renew some ties with the centers of political power. The bar leaders took the opportunity also to refurbish their tarnished reputation in specific ways that reinforced the value of elite legal capital. Some actions were directly related to the period in which they returned to governing power. Under the influence of the elite bar, for example, the Janata government sought to restore the independence of the judiciary and its authority in constitutional matters. Internal political divisions, however, prevented the enactment of a number of other desired changes.

3. There is in part a generational effect, since the ministers in the cabinet tended to belong to the older generation involved in the fights for independence, but the percentages remain remarkable. The means of access to state careers and politics have multiplied while the number of offerings from the elite bar remains limited by the elite and familial mode of reproduction. Also, the political careers are less rewarding due to the fragility of coalitions and the frequent turnover of government personnel.

More importantly, even though Indira Gandhi returned to power in 1980, the Supreme Court backed away from the concessions to authoritarianism made during the Emergency. It then began a period of paternalistic activism in favor of the underprivileged and the victims of police violence, using a new procedure to encourage very liberal standing at the court on behalf of public interest litigation (PIL).

Most commentators saw this activity as part of a "populist quest for legitimacy" (Epp 1998: 85). What is missing from those analyses, however, is the nature of the political resources mobilized in order to permit the success in the restoration of judicial authority. Two of the principle protagonists of this judicial activism, Krishna Iyer and P. N. Bhagwati, were judges named to the Supreme Court by Indira Gandhi, then advised by Mohan Kumaramangalam, because of their political engagement. They publicly announced their beliefs and political allegiance to Indira Gandhi.[4] After the strong political reaction against the Emergency, however, these judges skillfully maneuvered to rebuild the public image of the Supreme Court and to affirm—prudently—its authority, thereby avoiding the risk of political retaliation. As S. P. Sathe notes, "The post-emergency judicial activism was probably inspired by the Court's realization that its elitist social image would not make it strong enough to withstand the future onslaught of a powerful political establishment" (202: 107).

For the government, furthermore, this activism was not particularly threatening, since it tended to denounce abuses of power perpetuated by the lower echelons of the state bureaucracy—police and prison guards— who encountered the lower castes.[5] Finally, by the time of the period of judicial activism, social justice was no longer the priority of the govern-

4. The Rudolphs (1987: 108) note two public declarations published by the journal *Statesman* in April 1980, shortly after the return to power of Indira Gandhi. For Iyer, "Even after 30 years of independence, . . . the Indian judicial system followed the Anglo-Saxon legacy left behind by the British. The law, framed by the British to reflect their class interests, has no relevance to the present Indian social conditions." With respect to Bhagwati, the future chief justice expressed in striking terms his complete faith in the "iron will and firm determination" of Prime Minister Indira Gandhi.

5. According to the Rudolphs, "Because the court's PIL version of judicial activism suited Indira Gandhi's (1980–4) and Rajiv Gandhi's (1985–9) populist agendas, the two Congress prime ministers did not perceive PIL as a threat to their governments' claim to parliamentary sovereignty" (2001: 134).

ing regime, now marked by the anticommunism of Sanjay Gandhi and seeking a politics of economic opening and deregulation more in accord with the neoliberal tenets of the 1980s and their embrace by Indian economists. While neutralizing the potential hostility to their power, these radical judges formed alliances with the new urban groups and professionals who, after becoming mobilized for the protection of civil rights during the Emergency, reconverted into social activism in the form of NGOs (Cunningham 1987). The elite bar thus enlarged the domain for legal intervention and the social base of the courts outside of the small circle of elite descendants, while also building links with the most enterprising of the new meritocratic professionals just beginning to get recognition by the establishment.

The PIL strategy adopted by the Supreme Court and the advocates around it connected to the rise of public interest law abroad, especially in the United States, with the support of the Ford Foundation. Marc Galanter, from the University of Wisconsin, came to India a number of times in the early 1980s, "at a time when public interest programs were expanding elsewhere" (Int. India-7). The Ford Foundation reportedly was "looking for groups who gave legal representation to people excluded or outside the system" (Int. India-6). The model the foundation had in mind was California Rural Legal Assistance, an activist organization serving California's rural poor, but the "top-down" Indian legal aid program did not fit the bill, and other potential Indian grantees did not go for the U.S. model. Indeed, many activists still would not accept money from the Ford Foundation because of alleged ties to the CIA. Nevertheless, one major Ford Foundation initiative emerged in favor of this new emphasis on grassroots activism.

The Ford Foundation gave a grant to the Public Interest Legal Support and Research Center (PILSARC), which was set up in 1987 and led by Rajeev Djavan, a prominent Indian legal academic in Britain who returned to India to become a Supreme Court advocate. Rather than a public interest law firm, however, PILSARC was designed to coordinate and support public interest advocacy by regular advocates. As we shall see, the difference was important.

From the perspective of the Ford Foundation, as stated by a former official, it had made a "big bet" on PILSARC, but the "really big hopes" did not pan out (Int. India-8). The criticism from the donor perspective was that PILSARC was unable to help build "institutions on the ground" or "take risks" (Int. India-8). It did not build a grassroots legal advocacy group. It also did not provide a place to build a new generation of public interest lawyers outside of the elite—and highly Brahmin—Supreme Court bar (Epp 1998). As a former official of the Ford Foundation stated, there remain very few public interest law firms in India. Instead, there are "individuals with practices who will do public interest law" (Int. India-8).

This "failure" from the point of view of the Ford Foundation was a success for the image and position of the elite Indian bar. Public interest litigation in India reinforced the position of the sector that also serves the largest business clients—domestic and foreign. It built closer ties between the U.S. legal establishment—with other grants as well—and the elite of the bar, and it helped in at least a small way to maintain the prominence and position of that elite—which served the United States very well, for example, in the Bhopal litigation. A group of the Indian legal elite was able to secure its own position with the help of a program that ostensibly had been designed to accomplish something else—promote grassroots legal advocacy. According to Upendra Baxi, "Eminent 'public interest' lawyers see no role-conflict in appearing one day vigorously arguing for transparency in governance and the next day indulging in spectacular forensic displays aimed at the protection of the rights of people in high places charged with corruption!" (Baxi 2000: 159; for a discussion of the highly stratified public interest bar and the relationship to prestige, see also Krishnan 2005b).

The public interest bar's role was further noted by one of the advocates serving in a major environmental case. According to the lawyer, his involvement came very late in the game:

> for a long time, they were just advocating on the ground before the governments . . . and they decided not to approach the courts. . . . [T]his issue was a highly contentious one [within the organization]. . . . [T]here was a perception among them [in the mid-1980s] that the courts are also instruments of the ruling establishment of this country. . . . Well, yeah, it was partly my persuasion [after a year of discussion]. I told them that, "look, we have a very good case." (Int.-India 9)

The elite lawyers still are not involved extensively with grassroots social movements. They keep their distance until they find a good legal case.

Conclusion: Relatively Successful Strategies of Elite Lawyers as Political Champions Opposing Authoritarianism

The examples of the Philippines and India illustrate the reconversion of relatively elite lawyers serving leading multinational and national businesses into political champions against authoritarianism. Elite lawyers in the two countries came from very different histories and possessed different resources, but key fractions in each country of the most elite lawyers helped rebuild the power of law and lawyers by assuming this classic role developed long ago in Europe. In each case, notably, the relative success came from the close links historically and at the time between opposition lawyers and powerful fractions of the elite more generally. In the Philippines, in particular, ties were to businesses that had lost their property, such as the Lopez family; to the Catholic Church; to leading elite families; and to the academy. In India, elite lawyers had similar ties to major businesses, notably the Tata family holdings through their lawyer Nani Palkhivala; the courts, which remained staffed by leading elite advocates; and wealthy families opposed to the populist policies of Indira Gandhi. In both cases, in addition, the relative success depended on connections outside the Philippines and India, most notably connections to legal elites in the United States quick to side with and sustain the antiauthoritarian lawyers. Foundation funding from the United States also came quickly to bolster the human rights and antiauthoritarian agenda of local legal elites.

At the same time, as we shall see, these relative successes could be seen as glasses that are half-empty rather than half-full. In India, the return of elite lawyers and high courts did not transform the general pattern of a highly stratified, family-dominated legal profession able to command huge fees representing businesses in the courts. The Ford Foundation, as noted above, lamented its inability to build a cadre of lawyers dedicated to helping the poor and promoting the public interest. The elite of a very divided profession gained more credibility, but it did not change significantly.

In the Philippines the revival of law meant a return to power of a group very similar to what it replaced. Indeed, replaced is the wrong word for the Philippines, since many members of the old legal elite that sustained Marcos returned to power after Marcos fell. Lawyers for a brief period of time regained the mantle of antiauthoritarian statespersons, but the general scholarly conclusion is that the "people power" led by this elite did not end up substantially changing the pattern of crony capitalism that it ostensibly opposed.

There are two sides to the refurbishing that are closely related. The strength of the capital embedded in the law enhances the possibility to resist authoritarianism. As in the United States, the embeddedness of what can be called the "establishment" in law makes it easier for lawyers to retool and stage a comeback in periods when the image of law and lawyers is tarnished. But that means the comeback brings back that same establishment embedded in the law.

The accounts of Malaysia, Singapore, and Hong Kong in the next chapter (chap. 12) describe what happens when legal capital does not have the same degree of social capital embedded in the law. Legal resistance to authoritarianism is correspondingly much weaker.

CHAPTER TWELVE

Lawyers as Political Champions against Authoritarianism: Relative Failures in Malaysia, Singapore, and Hong Kong

The same strategy of serving as political champions against authoritarianism is evident elsewhere in Asia, but with relatively poor results. The legal elites who were armed mainly with legal capital fared poorly, succeeding at best in delaying authoritarian policies. The example of Malaysia's corporate bar is especially instructive, since it documents the erosion of connections to the state and the economy and the concomitant loss in the position of lawyers and the law. We follow the discussion of Malaysia with shorter accounts of comparable situations in Singapore and Hong Kong. In both of the latter cases, although in different ways, the role also remains very marginal. The strategy that at least some lawyers in Singapore and Hong Kong sought to pursue did not significantly build their position in the field of state power. There has been some impact of the activities in Hong Kong, but lawyers investing in state power in Singapore have so far found no traction.

Malaysia: Leading a Charge on the Basis of an Established but Marginal Position

Most of the elite bar in Malaysia, as noted in chapter 10, had been pretty content with the status quo after independence. The bar was heavily of Indian and Chinese descent, but the elite of the bar had a good relationship with the judiciary and the state cemented by common educational bonds abroad. The Malaysian Bar Council in the 1970s began to take stronger positions against the government of Mahathir Mohammed, clashing over issues of preventive detention, for example. The key incident in the revival of legal activism against authoritarianism came in the late 1980s, as noted in chapter 10. The attack by Mahathir on the judiciary brought a number of these lawyers into a political role.

During the judicial crisis of 1988 and the confrontation with Mahathir, the defenders of the Supreme Court were the senior lawyers of the corporate law firms known as the S law firms and descended from expatriate firms. Leaders of the defense included Cyrus Das, Tommy Thomas, and Cecil Abraham, all of who are still among the leading litigators of Malaysia; and reportedly one S firm had a team of some twenty lawyers working on the dismissals of the Supreme Court justices. After this affront to their ideals for the judiciary and to the Malay judicial elite with whom they had bonded at the London Inns of Court, the bar council refused to have "any relationship with the new Lord President" (International Bar Association 2000: 19) and moved to a position very much like that of an opposition NGO.

In the late 1970s and 1980s, environmental and human rights NGOs developed in Malaysia as they did elsewhere (Nair 1999: 94). Among the most notable were the Consumers Association of Penang (CAP), ALIRAN, the Third World Network, and SUARAM. These groups, however, tended to be relatively small, with a relatively elitist membership including "doctors, lecturers, journalists, engineers, lawyers, and teachers" (Nair 1999: 96). Many of the groups also developed in Panang, which "has long regarded itself as the intellectual heartland of Malaysia, at least for the English-educated, non-Muslim, middle class intelligentsia" (Harding 1992: 231. According to one activist (Int. M-4),[1] Panang has a more "autonomous middle class not so close to the state" as those in Kuala Lumpur, and it has an "English educated middle class." The lack of mass organization comes in part because, as with respect to politics generally in Malaysia, "few leaders transcend the ethnic divide."

The elite bar was able to transcend that divide in the early period af-

1. The authors conducted interviews in each of the countries studied. In order to protect the confidentiality of the interviewees, the interviews are identified only by country and number. The countries are abbreviated as follows: HK, Hong Kong; India; Indon., Indonesia; K, South Korea; M, Malaysia; P, Philippines; and S, Singapore.

ter independence, but its ability to manage the contradictions of ethnic politics in Malaysia declined with the policy favoring Bumiputra economic power and with Mahathir's decision to take charge of the courts, rather than let them get in the way of his general economic and political decisions. More generally, the weakness of the bar and the NGOs meant that pressures for change eased fairly quickly. Mahathir won the next election after the '88 crisis, and his version of UMNO (United Malays National Organization) rebuilt itself as economic prosperity returned.

This clash with Malaysian judges asserting British administrative law, in addition, fed into Mahathir's participation in the development of the so-called Asian challenge to the human rights movement then flourishing in much of the world (Bauer and Bell 1999). Mahathir joined with Lee Kwan Yew in opposition to Western notions of human rights. The so-called Bangkok Declaration of an Asian position was issued just prior to the Vienna Convention on Human Rights in 1993. Mahathir later noted that the attack was "defensive" in nature, designed to resist Western efforts to pressure Asian countries.

The very lawyers defending the judges under attack, in contrast, were quite active in the mainstream international human rights arena. Param Cumaraswamy, another prominent S lawyer and the chair of the Malaysian Bar Council from 1986 to 1988, served also as chair of the Human Rights Committee of the International Bar Association and as a commissioner of the International Commission of Jurists from 1990 to May 2000. In the period 1994–2003, he served as the United Nations Special Rapporteur on the Independence of Judges and Lawyers under the auspices of the United Nations Commission on Human Rights. He has frequently been honored for his human rights activities. Tommy Thomas is also well known in the international human rights community.

The bar's increased activism and international visibility did not succeed in having a positive impact on the judiciary. According to one leading litigator, the "appointments that were made to the judiciary [after 1988] leave much to be desired. I don't think a lot of members of the Bar were keen on becoming judges after that—the good ones anyway" (Int. M-1). In the words of another bar leader, "the judiciary, they say, never recovered its independence" (Int. M-3). The legal low point in Malaysia perhaps came with the tenure of the chief justice of the Supreme Court, Tun Eusoff Chin, who served from 1994 to 2000 despite charges of corruption and great hostility among the bar. Mahathir, in short, enhanced his control further in the years after 1988 (Hector 2003:8).

The bar nevertheless kept a strong position against the trends in the judiciary. According to a bar leader, for example, a "resolution of the bar call[ed] . . . for the removal of the Chief Justice. . . . The bar was very strong. . . . We had armbands and we had badges in support of judicial independence." (Int. M-3). The bar was virtually unanimous at that point but, again, it did not have any notable impact on the judiciary or the executive.

Mahathir, in fact, had sufficient control over the courts to use them instrumentally in the late 1990s to remove his chief rival for political power, Anwar Ibrahim, the former deputy prime minister. The Asian economic crisis of late 1997 had again stepped up international and national pressure on Mahathir. Anwar Ibrahim was the favored successor by many groups locally and by those in the United States looking for a more liberal successor to Mahathir. According to Hilley, "the West by this point saw Anwar, Habibie [for Indonesia] and Estrada [for the Philippines], three close intimates, as the 'new generation' for this region" (2001: 75). Anwar was seen to be "'sponsored' by the IMF-Washington network as the man to do business with" (Hilley 2001: 75). In Indonesia, indeed, the Reformasi movement precipitated by the economic crisis led Habibie to power in May 1998.

Reformasi took a different turn in Malaysia. Two days after Mahathir imposed new capital controls in response to the economic crisis, he expelled Anwar from UMNO (Gomez and Jomo 1999: 199). Anwar was then dismissed as deputy prime minister, arrested, held, and charged with the crimes of corruption and sodomy. The defense, led by a former president of the Malaysian Bar Council, again failed despite widespread belief in the innocence of Anwar. After a long trial in front of the most junior judge, a number of obstacles in the way of the defense, and public statements by Mahathir that Anwar was guilty as charged, the trial judge found Anwar guilty and ultimately sentenced him to fifteen years' imprisonment (International Bar Association 2000: 45–48). The highly suspect decision did provoke demonstrations and talk of a Malaysian Reformasi movement, but the political significance once again was relatively short-lived.

While Mahathir remained in power, the Federal Court (as the Supreme Court was renamed in 1994) upheld the corruption findings against Anwar. Finally, on September 2, 2004, after Mahathir stepped down, Anwar was freed from prison when his sodomy conviction was overturned two-to-one by the Federal Court. The corruption charge, however, was left standing, making Anwar free of prison but banned from politics until 2008. The Anwar saga continues with new charges emerging in 2008, but the charges did not derail electoral success for him in his comeback. The Malaysian Bar, led by the bar council and the corporate law firms historically active in that council, has continued to stake out a position as collective advocate for democracy and the rule of law, but again its impact has been quite limited.

Corporate Lawyer Activists and the Evolving Structure of the Malaysian Bar

The problems with the sustainability and ultimate impact of the activist role of the traditional corporate bar merit a closer look at the legal profession in Malaysia. The traditional bar, as we have noted, was represented by the bar leadership and the three colonially based S law firms. This mostly English-educated elite has provided the core of the activism since the bar began to confront the authoritarian policies of the Malaysian state in the 1970s and especially in the 1980s.

The traditional corporate bar's role relates to the fact that it became increasingly divorced from local economic power with the rise of the Bumiputra economic elite linked to the state. In the 1970s, according to one leading S firm lawyer, "we used to represent a lot of government agencies . . . and it is not so now . . . and the government now has gotten even longer feelers, you know, because they set up corporations and things like that" (Int. M-5). Another leader in an S firm, however, suggested that the law firms were not much affected by the policies in favor of Malay nationals and the state. Government work was never dominant. In the words of the elite lawyer, "we tended . . . to act for multinationals . . . the government work . . . would already go to the Malay firms" even before the late 1980s (Int. M-1). The S law firms tended to concentrate on litigation, employment, banking, and on the representation of branches of foreign corporations.

In the words of another prominent lawyer from an S firm, we were "careful to play it straight with little government work. . . . [We did not want to] play intermediary" (Int. M-3). Accordingly, "We decided that we will concentrate on our core business, which is litigation, employment law, intellectual property, corporate work, and real estate and banking. . . . [T]here are a lot of foreign banks" (Int. M-1). Shook Lin, which "used to have a large Chinese clientele" (Int. M-1) and conveyancing practice, is now the same as the other S firms (Int. M-5). The close connection to foreign clients provided external support for these elite lawyers. As one leader stated, "I think they looked at it slightly differently, you know, here was a firm with a certain integrity, and it was prepared to stand up. . . . So I think in the long run we benefited; short term, people were worried" (Int. M-5). The elite values—honed in many cases at the Inns of Court—helped sustain the reputation of the firms abroad. At the same time, however, it meant that the lawyers did not develop ties to the growing Malaysian state.

A characteristic that also made it more difficult for the S firms to broaden their identities was the difficulty they had—and attitude toward—bringing in Bumiputra lawyers. According to one insider,

> The three S's don't want to take in persons who are merely what the Americans would call, you know, rainmakers or door greeters. You know, we want working partners who are there on their merit. . . . And there's always a danger that when you bring in a person because of the so-called Bumiputra profile, he might not be a working partner. . . . we have difficulty in bringing in persons because of their connections. (Int. M-6)

Furthermore, "on the litigation side, we find that many of them are a little impatient" (Int. M-6). One Bumiputra lawyer stated that, "the typical makeup of Bumiputra lawyers is rather . . . [as a] platform to some other thing. . . . [Y]ou become less and less a lawyer" (Int. M-7). In addition, according to one S lawyer, "I think large firms have a particular problem in attracting Bumiputras who will stay with you, who—and who are good Bumiputras, 'cause they expect . . . special treatment and shortcuts, you know, to the top. And if you can't give it to them, then they go elsewhere" (Int. M-5). "[T]here aren't so many Bumiputra lawyers, I think, who will stay on in practice. . . . Halfway through, they might find, you know, they can get more money" (Int. M-5). Reportedly they tend to "prefer politics or business" (Int. M-5).

For various reasons, therefore, the S firms still tend to be dominated by non-Bumiputra lawyers, which tends also to mean lawyers with much less connection to state and economic power. The Shook Lin & Bok firm in 2008 appears to have only one Bumiputra partner from its Web site.

The lawyers also tend to have been educated abroad where the English tradition is reinforced. The firm appears from its Web site to have some thirty-two partners, with seventeen educated in Singapore, seventeen in England, two in Australia and one in the United States. Skrine had some thirty-five partners with perhaps two or three Bumiputra partners. The educational background is sixteen educated in England, eight Singapore, seven Australia, one New Zealand, and two Malaysia only. Shearn, with twenty-one partners, may have one Bumiputra partner. The Web site also showed sixteen educated in England, two Australia, one New Zealand, and two Malaysia only. The bar is still very English in orientation.

From the Bumiputra side there are also issues. The Bumiputra law firms have strong connections to the state and to the businesses connected to the state. But they have not to date joined forces with the traditional bar elite to sustain law and legal institutions. One reason is the traditional Malaysian bar appears too conservative. A leader of a Bumiputra-led firm stated that the bar council "opposes too many things" and focuses too much on litigation (Int. M-5). They note the S's "inherent conservatism" (Int. M-7). An S leader acknowledges that "They feel that the Bar Council is rather archaic" in its hostility to advertising even though, "We certainly disagree" (Int. M-8). The bar council would not hesitate to discipline a firm seeking to promote its track record, for example. A group led by Bumiputra-dominated firms, in particular Zaid Ibrahim and Co., campaigned for the Bar Council on a liberalization platform in 2001. According to an article in the *New Straits Times*, they wanted "the removal of fixed fees for property transactions, to be allowed to have truthful advertising including websites, contingency fees and for a more open reception to liberalization" (*New Straits Times* 2001). Reflecting some growth in the power of the Bumiputra firms and their more entrepreneurial approach, there was in fact some liberalization in advertising in 2001.

The Zaid Ibrahim firm is currently the largest law firm in Malaysia by some distance with about forty partners and one hundred thirty lawyers. It appears that eight to ten partners are Bumiputra, and the educational backgrounds are not provided on the Web site. Another prominent firm is Zul Rafique. Zul Rafique is also led by Bumiputra lawyers, but again only five of the twenty-three partners appear to be Bumiputra. Education was also dominated by England with twenty of twenty-three English educated, one Australia, and two Malaysia. Founded only in 1999, the firm is "headed by Mr. Zulkifly Rafique, the brother of Malaysia's Federal Territories Minister, Zulhasnan Rafique, a fast-rising politician with close ties to Prime Minister Abdullah Ahmad Madawi" (Lopez 2007).

The rise of the Bumiputra-controlled firms is directly related to the state and the Bumiputra-focused economy. A Legal 500 article on Malaysia posted in 2008 makes this point quite clearly:

> A number of law firms dominate the Malaysian legal market. Known locally as the three S's, Skrine, Shearn Delamore & Co and Shook Lin & Bok are long-established and widely-respected historic Malaysian firms. However, they are not necessarily the biggest, and players such as Lee Hishammuddin Allen Gledhill, Zaid Ibrahim & Co, Kadir, Andri & Partners, Raja, Darryl & Loh and Wong & Partners are hot on the heels of the leading group. Bumiputra policies remain part of the legal landscape. This means that firms with a strong Bumiputra contingent will often have especially good links to government bodies which will can lead to mandates. (http://www.legal500.com/c/malaysia)

This success with the state, as the paragraph suggests, also translated into better success in gaining clients from multinationals seeking to work with the state. According to one lawyer close to the Zaid Ibrahim firm, an "open line to ministries" and a "track record" bring multinational clients (Int. M-5). Reportedly, Zaid's success even made Mahathir proud as a "local boy taking on giant" (Int. M-5). Zaid sought to be the largest firm in Malaysia and specifically articulated an identity as a more U.S.-style than British-style firm. The firm affiliated with Andersen Legal in 1998 and retained the affiliation until April 2002 and the collapse of Andersen—reaching at one point the size of 140 lawyers. The affiliation was controversial, but, according to the knowledgeable observer, Zaid was sufficiently "prominent" that the "Bar couldn't crush him" (Int. M-5).

The perspective of the lawyers at the S firms on the rise of the Zaid Ibrahim firm is somewhat different. The problem of turnover among the Bumiputra lawyers is said not to exist only, for example, because Zaid is "not bothered about people leaving them" (Int. M-5). The size of the Zaid firm is criticized in part as the result of "many mediocre" partners who could not gain partnerships elsewhere—notably the S firms. A prominent lawyer lamented the fact that many multinationals do "not come for honest lawyers, want connections to power, same as Indonesia" and that "A lot of work is not given on pure merit—nothing to do with merit. It's political connections. So a lot of project finance work goes to firms with political connections" (Int. M-1).

Describing the period after the 1980s more generally, another lawyer stated that "more and more investments were coming into the country and lawyers became "sucked in" with the government (Int. M-3). Furthermore, "They became aligned with the government. And in order to get some of the very juicy, lucrative legal work, where the government, you know, was investing, the government, the multinationals, they always looked for lawyers and law firms who are plugged in with the government . . . One particular firm flourished . . . is the largest today . . . with that kind of backing from the government [Zaid Ibrahim & Co.]" (Int. M-3). From this perspective, the elite of the bar as found in the S firms became further cut off from political and economic power—even the power of multinationals teaming up with government-connected companies. They became even more defensive of their role apart from the new Bumiputra elite and the strong state built in the Mahathir era.

To summarize the developments in Malaysia, the Bumiputra power that resides in the ethnic coalition behind UMNO did not respond to the kinds of foreign pressure to increase investment in law and legal autonomy seen elsewhere. The pressures were blocked in Malaysia. Periods of economic crisis and strong international focus have not resulted in any particular strengthening of the position of law in Malaysia. Indeed, the opposite has occurred. Furthermore, the Cold War and then the War on Terror provided international reinforcement of the position of national security as a trump for individual rights. When the United States began to use preventive detention after the events of September 11, 2001, for example, according to one representative of the United States in Malaysia, Mahathir's people said the United States was using a "page out of our book" to control terrorism (Int. M-9). Mahathir again took advantage of international developments to enhance his space of operation at home.

It is indicative that Rais Datim, a lawyer in the government whose doctoral dissertation in London in the 1990s—after falling out of favor with the government—focused critically on the Internal Security Act, changed his tune once back in the cabinet (FAC News 2002). He reportedly made an about-turn . . . by saying that the Malaysian Bar Council is being "unmindful of the country's national security and public order" in making the call for the Government to immediately release the National Justice Party (Keadilan) leaders and Reformasi activists held under the Internal Security Act.

The state apparatus, including the law, remains well oriented toward the control of ethnic-based dissent and not ready to embrace the tenets of the rights activists.

Furthermore, as we have also seen, Bumiputra investment in legal legitimacy has further been diminished by the structure of the law firms. They remain conservative and dominated by foreign-educated lawyers from Indian or Chinese ethnic backgrounds. Entrepreneurial and well-connected lawyers from Malay ethnic backgrounds, moreover, might begin their careers in the establishment firms, but the legal platform tends to open up opportunities to make money quickly given the strong economic policies in favor of the Bumiputras. Bumiputra investment has therefore tended to flow away from law and into business and politics.

This pattern is consistent with higher percentages of Bumiputra lawyers in the judiciary, which does not translate to autonomy from the state. The judiciary increasingly comes from those who are not educated abroad. As mentioned above, there is now a fairly large legal profession, numbering some twelve thousand, but the vast majority of lawyers have very little in common with the corporate bar dominated by those educated in England, Australia, or Singapore. The active investment in professional values and judicial autonomy still comes mainly from this relatively small sector cut off from the state and the local economy.

Finally, the Chinese ethnicity of much of the elite bar has not translated into special relationships to Chinese in business, despite the fact that ethnic Chinese still represent the dominant private economic power in Malaysia. Shook Lin & Bok, one of the S firms, may at one time have had relatively strong relationships with Chinese businesses, but the Chinese now either link up to the Bumiputra economic elites (see Gomez and Jomo 1999) or continue to focus on connections to other Chinese in different parts of Asia. According to Wee and Wah, "Malaysian citizens of Chinese descent have felt pushed by their marginalized conditions of citizenship to explore transnational possibilities elsewhere. The results are evident in the large numbers of Malaysian Chinese, with deployable capital, in Singapore, Hong Kong, Taiwan, Australia, Britain, and elsewhere" (2006: 339). According to one prominent corporate lawyer, "if it's a smaller company, they would be more comfortable going to—quite often going to a smaller [law] firm, Chinese maybe. . . . But with a larger—with these public companies, then it—they possibly. . . . I don't think race matters so much then" (Int. M-5). The companies need personal connections that do not depend on law to work with the state.

The particular colonial origins of the Malaysian state, and especially the ethnically fragmented bar built on the British model, has limited the amount and the impact of investment in legal institutions. The capital represented by the S firms and their allies sustains a strong foreign-oriented voice with relatively little domestic influence. Malaysian legal elites are very active internationally, where the capital is more highly valued, but the domestic impact is relatively weak. Recent examples include Param Cumaraswamy, who was already mentioned, and Tunku Abdul Aziz, who founded Malaysia's branch of Transparency International and became the special adviser on the Establishment of the Ethics Office of the United Nations. The growing role of international commercial arbitration in Kuala Lumpur is also consistent with this international investment. Many of the judges who resisted the executive pressure on the judiciary beginning in the late 1980s went into arbitration: "Because of the judicial crisis, . . . there has been a gravitation towards arbitration. A lot of ex-judges who retired now have become arbitrators" (Int. M-10). Well-known lawyers from the elite group, including Cecil Abraham in particular, are also prominent in international commercial arbitration.

The Malaysian elite's efforts to become political champions against authoritarianism were therefore relatively unsuccessful. They gained attention, especially from abroad, and in particular crises came close to gaining more local political influence, but ultimately the bar by itself lacked the resources to arrest a steady decline in legal autonomy and legal institutions. There are, however, some places where greater investment in the law and legal institutions may emerge in the future.

One possibility is that the relatively new firms with Bumiputra leadership and strong representation of Indian and Chinese lawyers will promote more legal credibility. Very recently, for example, Zaid Ibrahim published an article calling for the reform of the judiciary, in particular for the creation of an "independent judicial commission" to put some distance between judicial appointments and executive power. According to Zaid Ibrahim, the plan is urgently needed to "restore public confidence in the judiciary." The proposal has not gained support, but it suggests some focus on the credibility of the legal system (*New Straits Times [Malaysia]* 2007). The purported U.S. style of the Zaid Ibrahim law firm might imply some greater commitment to judicial power, but so far this effort—added to the weight of the traditional bar—has had little impact.

A related development is the reported movement of leading S lawyers into law firms close to the Malaysian state in the post-Mahathir period. The notable recent example is the move of Cecil Abraham, one of the leading litigators and leaders of the bar, from Shearn Delamore & Co. to Zul Rafique—"a fast-growing and politically well-connected law firm where his younger brother Wilfred is a senior partner." According to the press account, the change was a response by Cecil Abraham to "tensions . . . when Mr. Abraham proposed plans aimed at expanding the firm's client base. While Shearn Delamore was successful in attracting business from foreign multinational companies, it was never successful in attracting work from government or government-linked companies, which dominate Malaysia's private sector" (Lopez 2007a; Lopez 2007b). Evidently Abraham had proposed a merger with the firm that was rejected by his more conservative partners (Lopez 2007a). The move by Abraham in 2007 may have promoted a countermove by Shearn. According to another recent story, "One of Malaysia's most established law firms is set to draft the younger brother of Deputy Premier Najib Razak into the partnership in a bid to fill the vacuum created by the resignation of managing partner Cecil Abraham." Johari Razak will reportedly return as a senior partner—assuming a position he held before "leaving in the mid-1990s to pursue business interests" (Lopez 2007b). The article reported that "'Johari isn't the top litigator that Cecil is,' says a senior Kuala Lumpur lawyer who knows both men well. 'But he will bring other strengths to the partnership, such as networking and helping market" (Lopez 2007b).

Finally, legal investment may come from some of the old Malay elite returning to political power relying in part on their legal legitimacy. Again, it is difficult to ascertain the impact of the return of many who split with Mahathir, but the examples are worth following. One that is already evident is the return to power of the family of the founder of UMNO, Dato' Sir Onn Bin Ja'afar. His son was Tun Hussein Onn, the third Prime Minister of Malaysia (just prior to Mahathir), a British-trained barrister and at one time a partner at Skrine. He split with Mahathir, supporting Team B along with Tunku Abdul Rahman, and he became a vocal critic of the

Mahathir administration. The grandson of the founder of UMNO is Hishammuddin Hussein, born in 1961 and currently the minister of education in the Malaysian Cabinet. He obtained his law degree from the University of Wales in 1984 and an LLM in commercial and corporate law from the London School of Economics in 1988. He also practiced law for a time with Skrine (and then also with Lee Hishammuddin Allen & Gledhill). His wife reportedly is a princess from the State of Pahang in Malaysia (http://en.wikipedia.org/wiki/Hishammuddin_Hussein).

The question for the future is whether any of these developments outside the traditional corporate bar or in alliance with it will lead to renewed legal investment in the state, building on the stance of the traditional bar. The traditional corporate lawyers continue to prosper and gain international recognition and business in part through their strong stand against authoritarian state policies, but they remain marginal in the field of state power. The relative failure of their strategy is especially notable given that they at one time controlled the organized bar, the most prosperous and prestigious practice settings, and the courts (in alliance with a traditional Malay elite). Their history and the policies of the Malaysian state, however, cut them off from the ties essential to the fortification of legal capital. They only had legal capital, and that is not enough to resist state authoritarian power. We see similar problems in Singapore and Hong Kong.

Singapore: A Few Elite Dissenters Pushed to the Economic and Political Margins

A few English-educated elite lawyers in Singapore did seek to speak on behalf of civil liberties against the dominance of Lee Kwan Yew and the People's Action Party (PAP). Chris Lydgate's book on *Lee's Law: How Singapore Crushes Dissent* (2003) details the story of Joshua Benjamin Jeyaretnam, "Singapore's perpetual loser" (2003: xi). Jeyaretnam, a graduate of University College in London, began his legal career in 1952 in Singapore. He served as a judge, prosecutor, and private lawyer, and he was elected in 1981 to Parliament as a representative of the Workers' Party, the first opposition candidate to win election in Singapore. Brought down by libel suits instigated by Lee Kwan Yew and criminal prosecutions that caused him to be imprisoned for a month in 1986, he was stripped of his right to practice law even though the Privy Council in London took jurisdiction and ruled in his behalf. He remained active until his death late in 2008. There was even some support by the Singapore courts for the rights of dissidents arrested in the late 1980s, as Silverstein shows (2008). He suggests that there were some signs of courts "ready to follow a familiar pattern of judicial empowerment" (2008: 80). In fact, however, the PAP amended the constitution and took away whatever room had been there "for judges to assert their authority to exercise this sort of judicial review" (2008: 80).

The story of Francis Seow, whose autobiography is *To Catch a Tartar: A Dissident in Lee Kuan Yew's Prison* (1994), makes clear the enduring limits of the political strategy of challenging authoritarian policies. A British-trained barrister, he became the solicitor general of Singapore and then was elected to be chair of the Law Society in 1986. In his words, "I had plans for a more assertive and caring bar, that the Law Society should be consulted on the selection and appointment of Supreme Court judges, and be heard on the appointments, promotions, and transfers of subordinate judicial and legal officers" (1994: 56). He also thought the Law Society should speak on issues of legislation, and he immediately got in trouble with respect to a law that allowed the restriction of the circulation of foreign periodicals in Singapore (1994: 58). The Law Society was then criticized as a "political pressure group" (1994: 8).

According to Seow's account, in addition, it appears that there was a small group of lawyers around the same time who were persecuted as communists, including another leader of the Law Society. They were embracing the cause of human rights and supporting Jeyaretnam. Seeing them as a potential political opposition, Lee Kwan Yew sought to "nip them in the bud" (1994: 79). In 1988, when there was a judicial proceeding involving one of the detainees represented by Seow, Harvard Professor Jerome Cohen, representing Asia Watch, came along with representatives of Amnesty International and the International Commission of Jurists and dined with Seow (1994: 100). The next day Seow was arrested under the Internal Security Act for "his American connection" (1994: 119). The idea, according to Seow, was that the U.S. friends he had met were "backing my entry into national politics" (1994: 127). He was pressured financially and his taxes scrutinized leading to a prosecution for tax evasion. He ran for political office without success and then was convicted in absentia. He remains in Boston as a university fellow at Harvard and is now a U.S. citizen.

In neither case did these dissidents succeed in gaining a real foothold

either within the public at large or within the legal profession. According to a local corporate lawyer, "Well, I think by and large the life in the
legal fraternity or in the business world goes on. And it tends to be apolitical. There are people who will get involved with politics. And it tends
to get really, really fiery in that sense because the People's Action Party,
the government of the day, tends to take a very hard line. . . . You know,
if you want to get into the kitchen, then you must be prepared to take
the heat" (Int. S-5). The PAP has succeeded in preventing the development of lawyers seeking to take the political path that, in an earlier day,
helped to bring Lee Kwan Yew to power.

The Top-Down Reinvention and Instrumentalization of Law in the Service of Promoting an International Financial Center

The successful marginalization of the legal field by the political leaders
in Singapore, combined with the growth of Singapore as a financial center in the 1970s, was a great benefit to imported lawyers from the major
international law firms. The separation of the legal profession from the
core of political power not only diminished the prestige and authority of
local practitioners but also made legal technology in Singapore increasingly obsolete. The most ambitious and best-connected students chose
other careers. The new state elite—and the government scholars that fed
it—militated against the choice of a legal education.

The transformation of the corporate sector has been quite pronounced. From the perspective of one observer of the changes, "I started
out in litigation [in the 1980s]. We actually knew every single lawyer at
that time. Where now it's not the same anymore. And at that time, I
would say if you asked me how many lawyers were seriously in the corporate financial services field, I would say less than a dozen at that time. . . .
If you asked me today how many people are seriously in the corporate
financial services, I would say easily anything between 500 to 1,000" (Int.
S-5). According to one of the leaders in the top-down transformation of
the profession,

> I think beginning in that period [the late 1980s], we began, we means not just
> the Law Ministry but the government, began to more seriously address the
> role of law, legal institutions, and legal framework, within the broader context
> of competitiveness of Singapore economic growth. I mean, everybody knows

that, you know, you need these good institutions to support the country. But we began to get feedback from financial institutions and multinationals that although there were large numbers of lawyers here, there were not enough firms with the requisite skills to put together certain very complicated—or to advise people to put together complicated—deals, you know, the syndicated loans or whatever. And from then you find by different ways that we began to tackle several things, both numbers of lawyers, the quality of lawyers, the evolving of offshore law firms, and the whole evolution of the joint ventures and other alliances. So it has been an incremental step. And the common denominator of all this is that the legal side has to be geared up to support these overall economic systems. (Int. S-6)

Lee Kwan Yew himself initiated a series of measures initially focused on the courts. As in other activities, he maintained control of the institutions and personnel that would take on this project. The first track was simply to upgrade and modernize the courts, and the task was entrusted to one of his Cambridge comrades, Pung How Yong. Described in chapter 9, Pung How Yong parachuted from business activities into the position of chief justice of the Supreme Court in 1990. Part of the reason for the appointment may have been to ensure that the courts would continue to back Lee Kwan Yew when he used legal tools to take on potential political challengers such as Francis Seow, but there is no evidence that the judiciary's loyalty was ever in any doubt. One clear goal was to make judicial institutions more effective in meeting the needs of offshore investors in Singapore and more generally Southeast Asia.

A major emphasis on computerization of the judiciary both helped the legal system in its role of maintaining public order and enhanced the international legitimacy of the courts. This focus on legitimacy was opportune and coincided with Lee Kwan Yew's effort to minimize attention to human rights issues in Singapore—also through the promotion of Asian values as an alternative to the West. Singapore's reputation as a no nonsense and honest place to do business was consistent with court efficiency that could then be trumpeted as a reason to invest in Singapore. Citing a survey conducted by the 1993 World Competitiveness Report, published by the Geneva-based World Economic Forum, for example, the *Straits Times* headlined in October 1993 that "Singapore's legal system rated best in world: Full confidence that justice will be fast and fair" (cited in Seow 1997).

The focus on the judiciary did not immediately mean any state interest in building up the Singapore legal profession. Following a speech by Lee Kwan Yew in 1992, a blue-chip *Report on the Legal Profession* (1993) concluded that the growth of the profession actually should be slowed and standards made more exacting to enter the bar. Citing the speech, the report notes that the strongest reason for the restrictions is that, "Singapore has scarce manpower resources for its continuing economic development and a superfluity of lawyers would be a misallocation of scarce resources" (1993: 2). The report emphasized that lawyers, then numbering about 2300, were not productive in the same way as economists or engineers.

The report addressed only local lawyers, however, and it did not purport to disturb the legal community providing "offshore" legal services from law firms located in Singapore. But very few Singapore locals were then working in the international firms, which mainly served the region rather than Singapore (Int. S-1). There was a dual legal system reminiscent of the colonial system. Singapore firms would get referrals for the local aspects of the transactions in Singapore, but the practice was limited and the numbers were small. The recommendations of the report were enacted into law in 1993 and helped to limit the growth of the domestic legal profession and take the pressure off for a more substantial professional role.

Just a few years later, around the time of the Asian financial crisis, the government changed its tune toward the number of lawyers. The attorney-general, Chan Sek Keong, chaired a Legal Services Review Committee that reported to the minister for law, S. Jayakumar, both leading legal allies of Lee Kwan Yew and the PAP. The review concluded that there was a need to upgrade "the legal expertise of Singapore law firms" (Legal Services Review Committee 1999: iv), including through joint ventures with offshore law firms and "scholarships to Singapore lawyers for the acquisition of legal expertise in offshore laws" (1999: v). The goal was to enhance the competitiveness of Singapore as a financial center through this "infrastructure support for international banking and financial institutions" (1999: i). In January 2001, then, there was a follow-up "Report on the Supply of Lawyers in Singapore," again chaired by the attorney-general. The new conclusion was that "there is a shortage of lawyers in Singapore" (2001: i). Lawyers are now seen as essential to the growth of Singapore as a financial center.

The enclave of foreign law firms converted relatively late into international business law. The two founding law firms, which are still quite important in Singapore, are Drew & Napier and Allen & Gledhill. Allen & Gledhill "has a history that spans over 130 years in Singapore" (Int. S-5). The division of labor in law meant that they represented the interests of "old British houses of interest in Singapore," while Shook Lin & Bok, another local pioneer, represented "all the local houses" (Int. S-5). For a long time the strategy that placed law and lawyers at the margin of state power was also one that was economically quite profitable for the firms. In exchange for its political quiescence, the legal profession was guaranteed prosperity through its monopoly over the rapidly growing market of conveyancing and mortgaging, which also tied the firms directly into the growing economy of Singapore. The presence of British lawyers also reinforced the notion that Singapore, despite some of the activities of the state, was bound by the rule of law—even the British common law. The bar was also given some professional prerogatives that were reminiscent of its colonial role.

The emergence of an international corporate bar thus benefited from the support of political leaders responding to their own priorities for the Singapore state and economy. As noted above, the reconversion of Singapore from an entrepôt into a financial center began to change the attitude toward a more positive sense of the role of lawyers in economic development. Still, it was necessary to convert a bar that survived on routine and highly profitable conveyancing work into a more entrepreneurial group. Borrowing the strategy used to acquire other technologies possessed by foreign entities, the government in the report of 1999 proposed joint ventures with the expatriate law firms. While there are risks for the weaker party in such an arrangement, the government made sure that it had the power to approve or reject each potential alliance.

The joint ventures were thus arranged marriages by political leaders seeking to build law firms that could fly the Singapore flag in transnational corporate law. The joint venture proposal built on a relatively bad experience with the English firm of Freshfields, which had been granted a full license to practice Singapore law in the mid-1980s. The license was then withdrawn after a few years. According to one prominent Singapore lawyer, Freshfields was thought to have too much of a competitive edge:

> And it was felt that simply for public policy consideration you could not have
> a legal community that . . . is made up and dominated basically by one English

firm, for example, and no local firms at all. Also inadvertently, I think a memorandum was released from within the Freshfields's organization which actually had a very scathing remark which was considered to be racist in nature. That was basically effectively saying that no local lawyer would ever make it into the partnership, that would be worthy of becoming a partner. (Int. S-5)

International developments redounded to the benefit of the expatriate firms. Various events, including issues with the stock market and a crisis involving Pan Electric were,

in a sense, a wake-up call also. And, you know, everyone started focusing on how to go about . . . getting your securities market right again, expanding its depth, expanding its breadth, you need the expertise. So in a sense, everyone realized that there was work to be done there. And one of the firms that began to see its phenomenal growth there was actually, for example, Allen & Gledhill. In the two years following the Pan Electric debacle in Singapore, Allen & Gledhill went from a law firm which had only about 30 lawyers in practice at that time to a law firm that was close to 100 lawyers within that two years. And a lot of it can be attributed to Pan Electric and the work that flowed from that, both to restructure their securities houses, the insolvency work, the rescue operations, the attempt to put the securities market back in place. And because they were doing that, they attracted the attention of . . . the most famous of our local lawyers in the . . . financial services field. (Int. S-5)

According to the same interviewee with a long view of Singapore practice, a prominent Singapore lawyer with international law firm experience, Lucien Wong, then moved from Drew & Napier to Allen & Gledhill. In the new setting, "basically he spent the next I would say five years building what would be a credible local financial services practice in Allen & Gledhill. And once, you know, someone begins to open up a pathway, others follow" (Int. S-5). Drew & Napier, according to this lawyer, was content with a litigation practice at the time: "Drew & Napier is probably still considered to be the premier litigation practice. And I think the focus at that time was increasingly on developing . . . general litigation, commercial litigation practice" (Int. S-5). But the expansion of these and other Singapore firms really depended on the governmental initiative: "the sophisticated corporate work that you see only developed in the last 10 years. With the development of the work, you know, it was actually in a sense forced upon, because sooner or later the government kept telling us we had to open up our entire market" (Int. S-5).

Among the local firms that have moved into the elite of the corporate law firms is the firm of Rajah & Tann. It is very much a local firm, tracing its roots to the movement for independence in the 1950s. Its survival as a firm gives some indication also of the elimination of politics among Singapore lawyers. Rajah had been a leftist activist:

> Because he did not see eye to eye with Lee Kwan Yew. And he left the People's Action Party at a time to join the Socialists. So he was in a sense at that time famous or infamous, depending on whose version you get, as a Communist in Singapore, which would explain essentially why this firm is in this particular building, the Bank of China Building. Because in the early days, the Bank of China was a very strong supporter of P. T. Rajah. And it was a very small practice at that time. But they were very, very supportive. I think they were concerned that because he was famous as a local Communist that in a sense . . . , our living may have been compromised. And so the Bank of China basically became his anchor client for a very, very long time. So because of the historical ties, we continue to be in this building, even though the practice has fundamentally changed, especially in the last five years, I would say. . . . If you were to take it back even just I would say 12 years back, this was just a firm of about five lawyers. (Int. S- 7)

With aggressive leadership, including a period of alliance with Andersen Legal, Rajah and Tann has moved to the elite of the corporate bar in the renovated corporate sector in Singapore.

The prosperous and growing corporate sector in Singapore, however, falls in line with the governmental policies that produced it. The legal profession remains subordinate and weak as a political force. There is neither cause lawyering nor even the noblesse oblige that one sees among the Hong Kong legal elite discussed below. Law is in the service of trade and commerce and a state devoted to trade and commerce. Lee Kwan Yew gained power in part by investing in the move for independence and in representing relatively marginal groups against state power. Those who followed him have prospered whether in the practice of law or in the judiciary. But they have been shut down every time they sought to build a political role as a voice against authoritarian state policies. As in Malaysia, the bar in Singapore had good international ties, and the dissidents themselves also had good international ties. But the legal elite in Singapore had no presence in the field of state power or, with a few exceptions close to Lee Kwan Yew, in the growing state economic entities. Even worse than in Malaysia, the bar carved out virtually no role as spokespersons against authoritarianism.

Hong Kong's Corporate Compradors

The development of corporate law firms in Hong Kong is in many respects parallel to the story in Singapore. We have so far not dealt with Hong Kong, but we can provide the basic introduction here. In Hong Kong as in Singapore, the legal profession evolved very much out of the colonial setting as an entrepôt. There was some investment in courts and laws growing out of the dual system established with colonialism, but the mission of the courts was to provide judicial outcomes to commercial disputes. The situation in Hong Kong likewise involves expatriate law firms focused on highly profitable conveyancing in a setting with scarce and valuable real estate, but it also involves some Chinese firms that grew up to serve the growing Hong Kong Chinese family businesses moving into transnational commerce (Dezalay and Garth 1996). Furthermore, U.S. firms and large British solicitors firms have also been in the Hong Kong market since at least the 1990s and the opening to China. There is now a very large contingent of corporate lawyers from countless major law firms in Hong Kong. At the same time, unlike in Singapore, the legal profession has retained the division between solicitors and barristers, and the corporate law firms are very much identified with the solicitor side. Solicitors have focused on expanding their business and even taken stands against the leaders of the bar who have become visible proponents of democratization.

The activities of the British-oriented bar, echoed by the British-oriented law school, Hong Kong University, have promoted more professional involvement in politics and the state. The bar has promoted more English education and training in professional values. But the pragmatic ruling coalition in Hong Kong is much more oriented toward U.S.-style law and to the kind of practice that characterizes the solicitors firms that the ambitious students seek to enter (Jones 2008). The recent reform of legal education therefore is deemed to be more U.S. oriented but without the U.S. emphasis on public interest law. The corporate law firm sector in Hong Kong is very much allied with the pragmatic business-oriented ruling elite keeping smooth relations with Beijing. The corporate bar is therefore very much in the mold of the traditional Hong Kong compradors, as Carol Jones notes, who saw their mission as facilitating trade and commerce while also enriching themselves (2008).

Hong Kong: Late Conversion of Lawyers into Opponents of Authoritarian Government

Hong Kong was the prototypical entrepôt from its inception in 1841 (Dezalay and Garth 1996: 252). The traders dominated the colony, and law represented little more than a façade. Initially the traders were expatriates, but they were joined by Chinese compradors who built up their own businesses. The justices of the peace were also from the British merchant class. There was some further investment in the courts in the nineteenth century, promoted by "the small but growing body of intellectuals who received some Western education, and the better-off Chinese who were building up their businesses" (Tsang 2004: 55).

The colony was long dominated by merchants, and the legal profession remained relatively small. As Carol Jones notes about Hong Kong's colonial history, "the bar and the judiciary hardly ever tried to check state power" (Jones 2007: 112. Despite a few dissidents, the core of the legal profession "remained solidly conservative, pro- [colonial] government, and pro-capital" (2007: 113). Exceptions included some lawyers who mobilized against the government's use of preventive detention in the late 1960s (Jones 2007: 113). Hong Kong was also an outpost in the Cold War, which meant that practices such as preventive detention and deportation were accepted by the British—especially since applied both to communists and nationalists (2007: 113). There was little internal "political or legal opposition" to the "highly repressive society" of the 1950s and 1960s. In the mid-1960s the International Commission of Jurists and some Hong Kong activists argued against the summary deportations, and the Bar Association in 1968—with about fifty members—publicly criticized the government for failing to meet international standards. The solicitors branch did not join and in many cases deplored the bar's stance. But according to Jones, this period of relative legal activism "was soon forgotten" in the 1970s as the colonial government reinvested in legitimacy, including in the legal system.

The legal profession grew relatively slowly. By 1971, there were only some 150–200 solicitors, half of Chinese descent, and about fifty barristers (Dezalay and Garth 1996: 254; Jones 2007: 116). The real estate boom of the 1970s provided very lucrative conveyancing work, as in Singapore, and there were also some firms specializing in litigation. The legal system improved substantially in the 1970s, partly in response to the 1960s activism and to anticolonial riots that also took place in the 1960s. By the end of the 1970s, as Jones points out, "Hong Kong people lacked political accountability, but they had gained legal accountability" (2007: 120). The legal system improved and was generally respected in the 1980s. The 1970s also brought tremendous prosperity and economic growth to Hong Kong. Lawyers prospered, but again there was very little "cause lawyering" nor a positive reception to such lawyering among a judiciary that was still largely expatriate and "silent on controversial state/individual issues" (Jones 2007: 122).

The treaty promising the return of Hong Kong to China in 1997 was then signed in 1984, reawakening some legal activism and opposition to authoritarianism. The bar in particular began to get involved in democracy promotion. Many members of the bar had been educated overseas, had overseas ties, or were expatriates. Members of the bar in Hong Kong prior to the opening of the law faculty at Hong Kong University in 1969 in fact had all been educated abroad, which meant that they tended to come from elite families if they were not expatriates. Indeed, as Jones also notes, even the Hong Kong University law faculty was very much an imitation of elite British law faculties with Oxbridge advisors and British-trained academics (Jones 2008: 19). As was true of the Malaysian bar, the bar in Hong Kong was very British in orientation and also with "continued social power due to their association with the values of disinterestedness and noblesse oblige" (Jones 2008: 21). And once the democracy movement got underway, it was natural that the Hong Kong University faculty of law joined the fray as a human rights–oriented law school.

The most famous of the new democracy advocates among the bar was Martin Lee. The circumstances of Lee's transformation were described by someone close to him as follows: "Martin is a criminal lawyer basically. He's not political at all. And even when he became the Chairman of the bar in the late 70s or early 80s, the bar was concerned [with other issues] . . . So it is only in '82, we started final position negotiation [for the return of Hong Kong to China]. Now the bar becomes more and more vocal from that point" (Int. HK-1). Lee was picked for the drafting committee "because he has been the bar chairman . . . [and] seems to be a seasoned lawyer, . . . [but] no one knows about his political orientation. He didn't know that, as well" (Int. HK-1).

For Lee and others, the early 1980s "becomes a breeding ground for a number of people. . . . a whole new generation of lawyers. . . . And in a way they're forced into the picture, when you are debating on the Constitution of Hong Kong, naturally the lawyers will play a leading role. . . . Martin Lee had come out as a very strong advocate for democracy. . . . Sort of everyone becomes a leader in the political sense, eventually" (Int. HK-1).

The Hong Kong bar was labeled as radical despite its long tradition of a distance from politics. The bar could do this in part because it is acceptable to "take a high profile in public life. . . . [T]he bar has no difficulty about that. And indeed, the more high profile they become, it seems the more busy they become" (Int. HK-1). So "Martin ran for the legal functional constituency at that time. And as a result, he was at that time doing . . . the first complex commercial crime [trial] in Hong Kong. . . . you are printing money basically . . . [I]n the last ten years, Martin now has a bit more time to get back to his legal practice" (Int. HK-1). The political activism did not hinder his prosperity at the bar. Again in the words of an activist, "So whatever political stance they take, if you want the top people in the field to do your case, there is not a lot of choice" (Int. HK-1).

Political activism within the bar was not necessarily inconsistent with a booming legal practice. The situation was no doubt different for the solicitors. Jones notes that the Law Society included mostly locally born Chinese who were too timid and materialistic to resist the Chinese, and they lacked the option of going abroad. The newly democratic advocates also had a certain anxiety about the practice of law in Hong Kong post-1997: "Barristers and solicitors not fluent in written Chinese worried about the possible erosion of judicial independence under Chinese rule as well as about the need to cope with laws written in Chinese" (So 1999).

The pro-democracy movement had little success, however, in the move towards the transition to China. As Alvin So noted, "In the late 1980s, the prodemocracy forces were in disarray. The service professionals' populist democracy proposal was defeated and the big business-people's corporatist democracy was written into the Basic Law" (1999: 181). The movement then gained some power in response to the Tiananmen Square incident in 1989. The event changed the dynamic somewhat and led to the change in position by the British and, in particular, by the Hong Kong governor Chris Patten (So 1999: 181). Patten, appointed in 1991, brought a reversal of British policy in favor of more democracy and investment in the rule of law. Although a top-down initiative, "Patten's proposals had opened up a new political space to push anew the democracy project" (So 1999: 197). Law faculty activism also picked up, notably precipitated by the appointment of Yash Ghai to the University of Hong Kong law faculty (So 1999: 133). As a human rights scholar of international standing, his involvement in the debates brought attention to the issues in Hong Kong looking toward the handover to the Chinese.

The new focus of at least some sectors of the profession was therefore on the rule of law, democracy, and the independence of the judiciary. After winning election to Legco (a representative institution with some limited powers) in 1995, for example, Martin Lee said, "This may be our last-ditch effort to build enough democracy into Hong Kong's still undemocratic colonial legacy to preserve the rule of law, our way of life and Hong Kong's role at the heart of the Pacific Rim" (So 1999: 213). Patten's initiatives had boosted the prestige of the democracy professionals who, while gaining few concessions in the last years prior to the handover to China, did succeed in building some democracy/rule of law movement—overcoming "the traditional image of political apathy of Hong Kong Chinese who were only interested in economic well-being" (So 1999: 215).

At the same time, however, the power over Hong Kong is elsewhere, in China, and there is no local state as such that will provide opportune outlets for lawyers investing in the Hong Kong state. Indeed, the push is to be apolitical, and there is a growing new fraction of the legal elite and academia closely tied to businesses embedded in China. The relatively small bar has carved out a role, and at times can help speak for other groups gaining power in Hong Kong. The courts, in addition, continue to operate at a very high level staffed by well-respected lawyers. But, as in Singapore, the corporate bar is completely subservient to political power whether in Hong Kong or in China.

Conclusion

Legal capital divorced from social capital cannot stem authoritarianism on its own. The same finding is evident in settings outside of Asia.

Javier Couso, for example, shows that the well-established "legal complex" in Chile, once confronted by Pinochet and the military, was unable to resist the "wholesale destruction of a century-old liberal tradition" (Couso 2007: 333). Lawyers were very much part of the process of constructing the Chilean state, but at the same time the legal institutions as such were fairly easy to walk over when the state was secured by an authoritarian regime. The general pattern is that even well-functioning and well-established legal institutions, including law firms, bar associations, courts, and legal education, cannot by themselves hold back authoritarianism without strong connections outside the law. Malaysia, Singapore, and Hong Kong make clear this general finding.

CHAPTER THIRTEEN

Corporate Compradors Doubling as Sponsors of a New Generation of Social Justice Entrepreneurs: Indonesia, Philippines, India, and South Korea

T his chapter explores the emergence of a U.S.-oriented social entrepreneurship role among Asian elite lawyers in a number of countries, drawing in particular on the model of public interest lawyer that
gained prominence in the 1970s in the United States. As the previous
two chapters emphasized, the strategy of serving as champions against
authoritarianism was at best only partially successful in building the social credibility of lawyers. We see in this chapter examples of further investment into a new strategy with a ready-made international credibility.
The corporate compradors in varying degrees act as double agents by investing in the creation of a new generation of advocates for legal rights
of the poor, the environment, and other social causes. We see the social
entrepreneurship role emerge especially in countries most subject to the
influence of the United States because of historical reasons (the Philippines) or their strategic importance to the United States in the Cold
War (India, Indonesia, the Philippines, and South Korea). The link between public interest litigation in India, elite Indian advocates, and U.S.
influences was discussed earlier (chap. 11), and in this chapter we extend
that discussion to explore the creation of new and more meritocratic law
schools.

The emergence and even relative success of this new social entrepreneurial role is not inconsistent, we also note, with a story of local continuity. Especially where the legal, elite, as in India and the Philippines, is
strongly fortified with local familial, political, and social capital, the historical pattern of taking foreign approaches and deploying them for their
own devices is quite evident. The position of the legal elite and the capital that they represent is strengthened, not challenged.

Indonesia: A Small Elite Excluded from the State

When Sukarno's regime "began to collapse late in 1965," according to
Lev, the Indonesian advocates were understandably enthusiastic about
helping to end it and working to build a new regime, the New Order (Lev
1972: 286). Their numbers were small, and they were concentrated in
Jakarta, but they had "clear ideas about the changes that they wanted.
As it happened, in 1963, they had at last established a professional
organization—PERADIN...—which helped to amplify their presence....
[T]heir political credentials were impeccable" (Lev 1972: 286). As we
have seen elsewhere, this elite group of lawyers sought to become a voice
against the increasingly authoritarian political activities of Sukarno.
They began to define themselves as custodians of the rule of law and human rights. Lawyers associated with this group became the core of the
human rights movement in Indonesia under Suharto.

Adnan Buyung Nasution was one lawyer who played a major role in
promoting human rights against authoritarianism. Nasution is the son of
a successful journalist who both worked for a Dutch newspaper and also
took part actively in the movement for Indonesian independence. The father established the first Indonesian English language newspaper in Jakarta. He became an opponent of Sukarno when Sukarno moved to the
left, and his politics cost him his journalist position in the early 1960s.
Nasution himself graduated from the University of Indonesia, served as
a prosecutor from 1960 to 1964, and then studied international law at
the University of Melbourne after leaving the prosecutor position for his
own political reasons.

Another leader was Yap Thiam Hien, one of the founders of
PERADIN—which had very few ethnic Chinese as opposed to de-
scendents of the Javanese elite. A Peranakan (descendent of the early
Chinese in Indonesia), Yap was born into comfort and high status in 1913

in what is now Banda Aceh. According to Lev, at that time the "disability" of being a Chinese minority was "fading with changes in colonial policy" (Lev 1989). He had some hardships as a child, but he was given an elite colonial education: "After European primary school (ELS) in Kutaraja, Thiam Hien followed his father to Batavia, where he entered junior high (MULO), and then completed his secondary education, with scholarship assistance from the government, in . . . Yogyakarta" (Lev 1989). At the end of World War II at the age of thirty-two, he worked his way to Holland on a Dutch repatriation ship. Once in Holland he was admitted to the Leiden law school, where he graduated in 1947. He practiced law in a Chinese law firm and initially became active in ethnic politics.

Yap invested his major efforts, however, in the law. Again, according to Lev, "It was largely in PERADIN, . . . the Indonesian Advocates Association, where among other senior advocates he discovered the professional fellowship and values that allowed him to break out of the constraints that surrounded the ethnic Chinese community" (Lev 1989: 108). By the time of the 1965 coup, again in Lev's words, Yap believed "that the defense of minority rights made sense only as part of a struggle for the rights of all citizens" (Lev 1989: 108). A prominent human rights award is named after Yap Thiam Hien, who was very active internationally in the International Commission of Jurists and elsewhere.

The group of advocates these individuals represented opposed Sukarno and hoped for a transformation in the Suharto regime. Their actual role was relatively marginal in the resistance to Sukarno and in the new regime that replaced it. Nasution, for example, reportedly helped to "mobilize all the graduates in the universities in Indonesia to support the movement to topple the regime" (Int. Indon.-2).[1] He even served in Parliament before becoming discouraged with the Suharto regime. But this group of elite advocates was too small and weakly institutionalized to regain much strength as champions of resistance to authoritarianism. They lacked the kind of ties to state and economic power necessary to assume a more potent position. They did not have the power in the Suharto regime that they would have liked. Under Suharto, however,

1. The authors conducted interviews in each of the countries studied. In order to protect the confidentiality of the interviewees, the interviews are identified only by country and number. The countries are abbreviated as follows: HK, Hong Kong; India; Indon., Indonesia; K, South Korea; M, Malaysia; P, Philippines; and S, Singapore.

this group and others around it managed to rebuild a new corporate bar
and the seeds of a movement that led to a proliferation of NGOs under
Suharto and after his fall.

Corporate Lawyers as Elite Statespersons, Public Interest Lawyers, Brokers, and Modernizers

The revival of corporate law firms after the fall of Sukarno is part and
parcel of the development of public interest law in Indonesia, and it illustrates also the strong connections and division of labor among the descendants of the Javanese elite. It is part of a retooling toward the United
States dictated by the break from the Dutch colonial relationship and
the emergence of a powerful role for the United States as part of the
Cold War. The development of corporate law firms grew in part out of
the idea by Nasution to create a legal aid organization.

Pursuing an idea inspired from his earlier stay in Australia and the
emerging neighborhood law offices in the United States, Nasution decided to implement a plan to promote legal aid and human rights in
Indonesia. He was able to pitch the plan at a professional meeting of
PERADIN because, according to a source close to him, one evening
he came home to his father's house, and his father was playing chess
with "a lawyer of very high standing" who had also suffered under Sukarno (Int. Indon.-2). The lawyer was active in PERADIN and simply
said that, "We'll have a Congress next month, I will invite you as guest
speaker." Nasution's personal tie led then to the support of the elite bar
and then he also received support from inside and outside the government for the plan. The then-governor of Jakarta, Ali Sadikin, supported
the idea, as did at least one prominent general, and therefore Suharto
gave it his blessing.

In 1970, accordingly, Nasution created the Legal Aid Institute (LBH)
with the sponsorship of PERADIN. The key initial source of funding for
the LBH was not a foundation or government. Instead it was a private law
firm established by Nasution in order to serve foreign clients. The firm
itself grew out of an interdisciplinary business labeled Indo Consultant,
which involved Todung Mulya Lubis and the very prominent economist,
Professor Djojohadikusumo Sumitro, who has already been highlighted
in chapter 8. Sumitro was also part of the same Dutch-educated elite circle as Nasution and his father. The circumstances of the establishment

are interesting. In the late 1960s, according to a source involved in the events, when Nasution was already talking about establishing a legal aid organization, he got the idea to start a law firm from Professor Sumitro, who in effect said, "You must think of your family. You cannot work for the people unless you have your own income" (Int. Indon.-2).

Sumitro told Nasution he would help him and set up a lunch with Professor Mochtar, who was a key friend of the United States as already noted. Mochtar was still the dean of Padjaran University in Bandung. They agreed to go ahead with the support of Indo Consultant. Sumitro, however, soon became a minister in the government. This original group then split and Nasution created Adnan Buyung Associates, which used resources from the representation of foreign clients to help support the LBH. Mochtar also quickly went into government, becoming Suharto's minister of justice and later minister of foreign affairs.

Around the same time, in 1970, Frank Morgan, a graduate of Stanford Law School, came to Jakarta with the belief that the liberalization under the 1967 Foreign Investment Law would open up places for corporate lawyers. He visited the Minister of Justice seeking to start an expatriate practice, but the Minister said that he could practice law in Indonesia only if he could "find some Indonesians" (Int. Indon.-6). He then contacted Mochtar who agreed to make an alliance. They joined forces with Kirkland, Kaplan and Associates, a U.S. firm based in Thailand, but that arrangement did not work and they soon thereafter split. The new firm became MKK, and it remains prominent with Morgan and Mochtar still very visible at the law firm.

Another important Indonesian law firm started in 1967, when Ali Budiardjo, a prominent member of the Socialist Party (PSI) with an equally prominent father, asked Mardjono Reksidiputro, just back from education in the United States, to form a law office. Their first client was Freeport Indonesia (Int. Indon.-7), a leading mineral exploitation multinational in Indonesia. As with respect to the other lawyers we have mentioned, these individuals were direct descendants of the rather small Dutch-educated legal elite. With another law firm led by Professor Sudargo Gautama, these firms were the only ones in the early 1970s to cater to foreign investors. They all also avoided litigation—tainted by the decline of the courts—to maintain a respectable ethical posture. Not surprisingly, these law firms prospered with the rise of foreign investment, self-consciously imitating U.S. law firms and keeping a distance from the corruption associated with the government.

The LBH, closely linked to the individuals who became the nucleus of the corporate bar, also became the key point of reference for legal and political reform among U.S. academics. It later became the recognized leader of the human rights movement in Indonesia (Lev 1998). Nasution recruited idealistic young lawyers and developed the office, and the activities also began to generate more friction with the government. As the government became more repressive, Nasution decided to try to expand to other areas in Indonesia and for that purpose invited foreign notables, including Daniel Lev and Paul Modito (who had moved to the Netherlands), to "give lectures about the rule of law and democracy" (Int. Indon.-2).

The government, nevertheless, decided to forbid that expansion, and in January 1974, after a student rally against Suharto, Nasution was one of a number of individuals arrested. He was detained for two years without trial. When he came out, partly through pressure from the international community, he managed to rebuild the LBH and, with the active support of local bar associations, expanded the program ultimately to have eighteen offices throughout Indonesia.

During the 1980s, in fact, the LBH was able to gain substantial foreign funding, including from USAID and the Ford Foundation (Mohamad, Harsono and Hamid 2003: 80). When Nasution moved to the Netherlands in 1985 after the government took away his license to practice law for defending an opposition leader, another prominent lawyer with LBH, Todung Mulya Lubis, took over. Mulya Lubis was also well-known internationally and had studied at Berkeley with a scholarship from the Ford Foundation. For the next four years, the LBH was administered by Mulya Lubis. Nasution then came back in 1993 to run the institute and solve various problems associated with the successor to Mulya Lubis.

The vision of advocacy institutionalized in the LBH was reflected also in activities of other activist lawyers. The government sought to weaken PERADIN and, for that purpose, established a competing organization, and it also sought to discourage defense lawyers in political cases. But even under Suharto, "there is seldom, if ever, a shortage of lawyers who step forward to do so [speak out against abuse of power], and their ranks are constantly replenished by new young recruits" (Lev 1998: 441). The small elite corps therefore also kept alive the antiauthoritarian position of the bar, led by prominent lawyers such as Nasution and Yap.

The LBH played a major role in promoting more general "civil society" activity in Indonesia as well. Its global visibility, in particular, attracted considerable attention to governmental repression in Indonesia, and many activists trace their roots to the LBH (Clarke 1998: 41). The LBH, as we have noted, reflected the Indonesian legal elite. It is indicative that, according to Pompe, Nasution rejected a highly qualified applicant to chair the LBH in the late 1980s because, "he was a bit of a peasant, course in speech and behavior" (2005: 389).

According to a study of NGOs under Suharto, there was some liberalization in the period 1989–94 because of a more tolerant attitude among some part of the ruling elite (Davis 2008). The NGOs were in part political opposition, but they were allowed to survive for several reasons. One was the background and structure of the NGOs. According to Davis, "Under the New Order, advocacy NGOs were able to avoid confrontation since they 'did not claim to organise a struggle for political power, nor to mobilise a mass base.' . . . They were run by directors, were loosely-structured, middle class and issue-and task-oriented, and were largely seen to be 'apolitical' (or at least less dangerous than other kinds of politically-oriented organisations) and driven by overseas financial support" (Davis 2008, citing E. Aspinall, "Political Opposition and the Transition from Authoritarian Rule: The Case of Indonesia," unpublished thesis, Australian National University, Canberra 2000, p. 128). They could draw on the flourishing international human rights movement and the power of foreign capital within Indonesia.

The fact of the middle-class roots of the NGOs also helps explain why they were tolerated. The connections of the NGO leaders to corporate law firms serving international investors and businesses is notable, but another key is that there were also ties between these individuals and the groups that had come to set economic policy in Indonesia. As Robison and Hadiz demonstrated (2004: 60–66), the coalition of social groups that profited from and supported the Suharto regime (and survived it) was broad and diversified. The core of this coalition was constituted by the technocrats who built an alliance with the army (and the ethnic Chinese) to build highly prosperous enterprises that relied on government contracts, licenses, and low rate loans. This coalition was consolidated by a system of clientelism and patronage cemented by matrimonial alliances and joint ventures (Robison and Hadiz 2004: 62).

The leaders of many NGOs active after the Reformasi period can be traced to LBH (including Indonesia Corruption Watch and Judicial Watch). As one of the alumni of LBH stated, "you can find LBH" also in other human rights and environmental NGOs (Int. Indon.-8). This still relatively small group of lawyers leads the charge for corporate law responsive to the U.S. Corrupt Practices Act and, more generally, to the ways of doing business in the United States. They were also important contacts for the long-established USAID program of law and development (from the 1990s until recently) termed ELIPS (Economic Law and Improved Procurement Systems Project). These lawyers are also the key players in the NGOs and foundations seeking to reform Indonesian governance. They were major actors, for example, in the effort to create a new bankruptcy court that would restructure businesses in the wake of the Asian financial crisis.

A recent article on NGOs in Indonesia after Suharto highlights the NGOs that have come to play a role in the new focus on governance (Davis 2008). The article notes the role in the current period: "Instead of criticising the government for limiting democratic freedoms as they did under the New Order, in the post-Suharto era they seek to combat corruption and promote open and accountable practices." The article thus highlights the "highly respected Indonesia Corruption Watch (ICW)" as "one of the standard-bearers of this new governance agenda." ICW was established by the LBH and led by Teten Masduki, who had worked at the LBH since 1990. Bivitri Susanti, the executive director of the Centre of Law and Policy in Indonesia, comes from the same network of legal activists. The important Partnership for Governance Reform that was established in 1990 to coordinate funding and work on issues of governance, for another example, lists Bambang Widjojanto, until recently the director and one of the founders of the LBH, as its legal advisor. He is also listed as one of the founders of Tifa, which "focuses its attention on five Programs, namely Human Rights, Local Governance, Civil Society and Democracy, Pluralism and Media." Among the founders were two other alumni of the LBH, T. Mulya Lubis, a former chair, and Budi Santoso. Both have U.S. law degrees as well. In short, the world of the LBH is very prominent indeed in today's NGO milieu in Indonesia, including those focused on judicial reform and coordinated by the Asia Foundation.

According to one of the new generation of NGO leaders, furthermore, almost all "power lawyers" in Indonesia are graduates of the LBH. The LBH, he stated, "creates a prestige credential" and provides "excellent training for litigation" (Int. Indon.-9). The credential also provides a way to "say no" to corruption and to develop "good relations with the press" (Int. Indon.-9). And one of the leaders of a corporate law firm to-day noted that "many young lawyers" in the firm were or had been active in the NGO sector (Int. Indon.-10).[2] One young lawyer even stated that the LBH credential—or something comparable—is the essential ticket to gain credibility with U.S. clients and lawyers. It helps keep the elite of the profession above the masses of lawyers charged with corruption and poor legal ethics. There is no elite law school, and public interest prac-tice is also the best ticket to a scholarship to study abroad. The combi-nation of corporate and public interest, fostered also by strategic uses of the media (e.g., Lubis's media contacts with Tempo and Makarim's with AKSARA), helps build a reputation for virtue.

These NGOs continue to provide a certain reformist credibility that helps promote the legitimacy of the Indonesian state abroad. The legal elite—as seen through the discussion of these NGOs—remains highly in-ternationalized and connected to the United States. Individuals gain for-eign degrees that build their expertise and connections abroad, and the NGOs are attuned to the evolving international agenda. The recent ar-ticle by Ben Davis on NGOs makes very explicit the responsiveness of the elite Indonesian NGOs to the evolving priorities of the donor com-munity (2008). Bivitri Susanti, the executive director of the Centre of Law and Policy in Indonesia, was thus quoted as saying that, "'For me it is rather interesting that after the fall of Suharto we have such an open space; a new playing field, but now there are other factors that limit our engagement . . . we still depend on our foreign donors' money" (Davis 2008). Furthermore, "The emergence of the good governance agenda has created many new winners and losers among the NGO community. The winners are renovating their organisational structures in response to new demands, while those who ignore these demands are fighting to maintain their position" (Davis 2008).

This group helps therefore to create a whole new market of gover-nance consistent with the new hegemonic processes. Serving as brokers between international institutions, the local media, and NGOs, these

2. The connection between the sectors is evident also from a lawyer at the Asia Foun-dation promoting Indonesian reforms. The lawyer started working at the Makarim firm, could still return, but decided to go into foundation work after having "been there and done that" with corporate law (Int. Indon.-11). Similarly, one current corporate lawyer ob-served that when she graduated from law school, prior to the fall of Suharto, graduates of the top law schools sought to work with the corporate law firms, but, "with the crisis in Indonesia, . . . people [came] to the NGOs more" (Int. Indon.-12).

elites contribute to the importation of international expertise directed toward a new form of legitimacy—where personally based relations and exchanges of services are redefined as clientelism and crony capitalism. The promotion is fueled by creation of a market for a new virtuous professional elite characterized by personal mobility between and among NGOs and donor agencies—and corporate law firms—that facilitates the circulation and pooling of ideas and the elaboration of consensual diagnoses of "problems" and acceptable remedies. The group speaks for the international reform agenda against the power of the Indonesian state, but it is also connected to the state through relations with the military and the elite technocrats who promoted Indonesia's economic policies under Suharto.

The new network of NGOs serves also as training ground—substituting for obsolete and impoverished law schools—as well as an alternative early career path (particularly when administrative and professional jobs are disqualified and so poorly paid that it justifies complementary sources of financing). These alternative careers are very sought after because they offer many opportunities for contacts to media, to professional elites, and to networks that lead to foreign scholarships and training. They are also prestigious because they have a noticeable academic component. Research-oriented NGOs serve as think tanks for the media, politicians, and international agencies. Yet the linguistic and cultural competence required by this market reserves access to a relatively small elite already introduced in these circles through family relations—akin to the older generation of the elite bar continuing to serve indirectly as gate-keepers.

Instead of looking at the double role of these wealthy legal entrepreneurs reinvesting in civic virtue as a strange paradox, in sum, one can analyze it as another example of a division of labor between two poles of a state oligarchy held together by positions in or around the state, their common financial interests, and personal connections—from family and matrimony to quasi-family in the sense of clientelism and patronage. The cosmopolitan legal intelligentsia is very much part of that world even if they occupy a marginal position—still a profitable niche—as brokers for foreign investors and international financial institutions. This group succeeded in creating a world of law firms and NGOs that produces a new generation of elite activists oriented to the U.S. This new modernizing elite is reinvesting in the state while serving as the point of entry for transnational ideas and interests.

Philippines: Revamping Elite Lawyers as Promoters of Legal Empowerment

As in Indonesia, the legal elite in the Philippines is closely integrated into U.S. legal and intellectual markets. As we saw in chapter 11, the legal elite played a major role in engineering the transition to democracy, but the result was not a major change in Philippine governance. Scholars continue to characterize the government as a form of crony capitalism ruled by the traditional oligarchy. *Trasformismo* was a term used by scholars to explain why the "people power" that toppled Marcos did not lead to a more open and democratic system of governance (Hedman and Sidel 2000). Unlike the situation in Indonesia, in addition, the legal elite never lost its position in the field of state power. Authoritarian government and much of the legal elite thrived together.

There was, however, some change that was part of the relegitimation of law and the legal elite after Marcos. We can trace this process in the careers of some of the younger leaders of antiauthoritarianism. As was the case in Indonesia, we see the creation of a new generation investing in a more entrepreneurial, U.S.-oriented public interest law as a way to further build the social credibility of law and lawyers.

Carlos Medina, for an example of one such activist, followed political work against Marcos by returning to the Ateneo Law School to become executive director of the Human Rights Center, established in 1986, funded by the Ford Foundation, and modeled on the Columbia Law School human rights center. He took the initiative to tap what an observer termed the "unharnessed potential of law students" (Int. P-12). Redirecting internships from apprenticeships abroad—the Ford Foundation's model—to activism at home, he turned the center into a leading producer of lawyers for the emerging Alternative Law Group—itself an outgrowth of the legal aid activities begun with Free Legal Assistance Group (FLAG) and discussed in chapter 11. The program expanded outside the Ateneo to other law schools with good success records on the bar exam (meaning the most elite schools only), and the role of professionalism was also emphasized.

The students worked only on legal services to the poor and not with more general developmental NGOs. The goal was not only to help create a new cadre of activists, of which some ten percent of the alumni of the program became, but also to gain influence in the "mainstream" for advocacy on behalf of economic, social, and cultural rights. One activist, for example, stated that the network of graduates of the Human Rights Center programs could stop governmental appointments, produce legislation, and influence Supreme Court decisions—despite some opposition among the legal establishment to the "leftist" reputation of human rights advocacy (Int. P-15). Graduates can also be found among the corporate law firms. Through these activities the Ateneo produces missionary lawyers imbued with progressive legal ideals and closely linked to the elite of the profession.

Saligan, created in 1987 and one of the major institutions of the Alternative Law Group (ALG), provides a good example of this Catholic activism. The first president was Father Bernas, then the president of the Ateneo and a leader against Marcos as already noted. Early funding came from the Asia Foundation and Roman Catholic foundations from Norway and the Netherlands, facilitated by Father Bernas (Int. P-15). The two lawyers who began in the office were at that time connected to the Archdiocese of Manila Labor Center. The office is on the Ateneo campus. Although there is no formal link to the Ateneo, there are strong informal ties.

The history of Saligan also tells much about the process of reinvesting in and revitalizing the law. One of the founders, Roberto Arevalo Gana, grew up in an affluent family and received a Jesuit education from start to finish (Saligan 2002: 60). While in law school, "he helped law students sustain their spiritual lives" (Saligan 2002: 60) and decided to engage in public service to help the poor. Despite the more lucrative options available to him as one of the bar's "top notchers" in 1986, he elected to begin teaching at the Ateneo and work for the Ateneo Center for Social Policy. A year later, he and other friends established Saligan, and he became the executive director in 1995. Before dying in a plane crash in 1998, he was credited in Saligan's publication with "translating radical insights about structural justice long advocated by NGOs into conservative legal discourse" (Saligan 2002: 61).

Not surprisingly, the next generation of NGO leadership was recruited from among the interns at the Ateneo Human Rights Center. One of the leaders described how he had worked in one of the major corporate law firms and enjoyed it. Nevertheless, something told him "that he did not want to continue" (Int. P-15). He prepared his family for the shift in lifestyle and moved to Saligan. His work reportedly is well respected by the legal elite, and he could go back to his corporate law firm if he chose, but he appears to have settled down for a career in alternative law.

Saligan as an organization has been concerned with the rights of labor, women, peasants, fishermen, and the urban poor, and with issues of local governance and agrarian reform. It is probably the largest ALG organization, with a full-time staff of about thirty-six along with the student volunteers. The personnel tend to average five years in office, and alumni of Saligan reportedly can be found in the government, in corporate law firms, and studying or working in NGOs abroad. The essential mission of the organization, according to one of its current leaders, is to use "law as a tool for change" (Int. P-15). Saligan's lawyers work with "people's NGOs" as "part of our advocacy," and it is welcomed by those who "appreciate the relevance of working with law" (Int. P-15). Saligan engages in education, including publishing and using paralegal training to build the "capacity of leaders," litigation support, including test cases, and lobbying.

Saligan draws on a network of some twenty-five volunteer lawyers to augment its staff, but Saligan leaders still do not feel that they are very visible in the circles of the integrated bar—"most lawyers do not know we exist" (Int. P-15). Similarly, according to a social science observer, "in ten years alternative law has still not penetrated the mainstream of the legal profession" (Int. P-16). According to the leader we have quoted often, the "developmental perspective" of Saligan and the Ateneo Human Rights Center still clashes with the more "politically correct" traditional legal aid (Int. P-15). Nevertheless, the prominent role of Saligan is further confirmed by its involvement in the Supreme Court and Asia Foundation's "top-down" plans for court reform. The world of Saligan intercepts in many ways with elite corporate law in the Philippines.

The rise of the ALG goes with an increasing professionalization of the NGO world, exemplified by the Caucus of Developmental NGO Networks (CODE-NGO) established in 1990 and funded initially by the Canadian International Development Agency (Caucus of Developmental NGO Networks 2002). The genesis of CODE-NGO was a concern by established NGOs in the late 1980s that NGOs were the "in" thing, that many were "fly-by-night," and that it was necessary to "protect the integrity of longstanding NGOs" (Int. P-17). There was a further lingering divide between leftist NGOs and those who would disavow violence as a political tactic. The CODE-NGO has rules of conduct designed to "establish rigorous standards that would enable development NGOs to police their own ranks" (2002:5).

This moral and institutional refurbishing of the position of law in the

Philippines is also evident in careers bridging the Ateneo and the University of the Philippines. One rising political star now in the administration had planned as a teen to go into engineering or business, or even to serve a government akin to the Marcos one, which he admired. A Catholic Action trip between semesters to the countryside introduced him to social injustice and moved him to study philosophy and engage more with politics. Still, when a friend invited him to listen to a speech planned by Benigno Aquino upon Aquino's return to Manila in the late summer of 1983, he did not even know who Aquino was. Then Aquino was assassinated, and the attempt to blame it on a lone assassin alienated the student. He became committed to political change, and he found "fertile ground" with Catholic organizations at the University of the Philippines (Int. P-18). He knew that he was "not a Communist," and he sought an "alternative politics" between campus radicalism and Marcos dictatorship—of "faith doing justice" (Int. P-18). Moving through a succession of political coalitions, he sought leadership of the student sector and succeeded in "breaking" the "monopoly" of the left during the period 1985–87—working with an organization named Bandila as a "middle force" (Int. P-18). He became one of the first student leaders to endorse the campaign of Corazon Aquino. Bandila supported his leadership, and he gained further support from Jesuits who came to the university and urged their former students to vote for him. He then attended law school while participating in activities toward the drafting of the new constitution.

After some further political activity, he knew he had to convert from "mass movement politics" (Int. P-18). Fortunately, "Salonga took him under his wing" and invited him to join his political party, the Liberal Party. He later became part of the Liberal Party's think tank, focusing on youth issues, and he then moved into a legal position in the government. He has many friends, not surprisingly, in the Alternative Law Group, but he criticizes them for "not engaging the rest of the profession" (Int. P-18). He is moving to "cross-cutting" issues such as ethics for lawyers and judges. Libertas is one professional organization working on such issues—including helping to protect Chief Justice Davide from the impeachment charges brought by his political enemies.

The movements in law are complemented by movements in business. The Philippine Business for Social Progress organization was created in 1970—a time of particular rural unrest—by fifty prominent business leaders representing Philippine and multinational businesses (not typically from the Chinese business community) (http://www.pbsp.org.ph/). It was modeled after the Venezuelan "Dividendo Voluntario para la Comunidad," involving Royal Dutch Shell and using "self-taxation for its poverty alleviation programs" (Int. P-3). In the early 1970s, according to one of the participants, the debates were between "community organizing" and "charitable relief" (Int. P-3). The idea of the activists was that business principles could be used for social development. At the time there were no NGOs as such—"civil society was the church," and the "proponents" for reform likewise (Int. P-3).

The organization, led by very young and "idealistic program officers" (Int. P-3) drew on the teachings of Herb White—a follower of Saul Alinsky—to encourage community organization. Numerous grants were given out, but there was always "strict analysis" of the proposals and "accountability." By definition, communist organizations, which avoided "transparency," were not the recipients. The projects needed to focus on "developmental needs" and not "political needs." They worked with the Ford Foundation and USAID as well. They took initiatives with proposal development and moved intensively into "capacity building," training leaders and training those who could train leaders.

After 1983, as with respect to the legal and religious elite, the business people on the board turned actively against Marcos. The organization remains highly visible in issues of corporate social responsibility, and those who have passed through or been trained continue to make an impact. One of the young idealists, for example, Ernest Garilao, went on to a degree from the Kennedy School at Harvard and to manage the land reform process with significant results under President Ramos. According to Riedinger, Garilao brought his NGO experience to focus on land "reform's impact on its beneficiaries" (1995: 184). As a professor at the prestigious Asian School of Management, Garilao continues to work on issues of corporate social responsibility.

Finally, we can trace the same kind of developments among representatives of the Philippine left. The Institute for Popular Democracy (IPD), for example, is an organization long connected to the left. It was established in 1986, and it has moved to become a well-funded NGO and think tank involved in local government, the NGO community, and general "governance" reform. The trajectory is significant. From involvement with groups highly critical of any state involvement, the IPD now works closely with local governments, including on issues such as how best to tax and spend in order to find a "fiscal space" for reform (Int.

P-1). One of the projects is to develop machinery and capacity for access to transparent rules and to legal experts in order to overcome the "legal problems" that constitute some of the "biggest obstacles to good government" (Int. P-1).

The move of the IPD is consistent with the movement of its executive director since 1996. Joel Rocamora is the son of a provincial lawyer. He earned his doctorate at Cornell early in the 1970s and then returned to face martial law. Radicalized by an arrest that labeled him a communist, he became active against Marcos in the underground until forced to emigrate in 1976. He continued his anti-Marcos work from within the United States and the Netherlands, returning in 1992 and authoring a book on the struggle within the Communist Party about politics and political tactics. The book forcefully argued for an abandonment of the failed policies of armed struggle. Upon his return, he first worked as a political analyst at the Ateneo Centre for Social Policy and Public Affairs, and then he moved to the IPD. He is one of the leaders of a political party currently seeking to transform and open up Philippine politics.

The new generation of leaders responsible for the post-Marcos developments therefore uses the rediscovered and revamped legal virtue in the name of change on behalf of the underprivileged. From one perspective, what we see in this chapter is reminiscent of chapter 11. Those who come to leadership positions are descendants of and close to the traditional legal elite. Their leadership also excludes those whose credentials are not good enough or whose positions are immoderate. It is indicative that a published brochure from Saligan celebrates the ability of a leader of Saligan to turn radical insights into "conservative legal discourse." These leaders also police the NGO community and other organizations from groups that are not transparent or are "fly-by-night." In this respect, these elite activists help to reinforce a political and social structure that looks very much like what has endured in the Philippines throughout the twentieth century. This is a new generation of the same people who again profit under the new reformed state—and even protect those among the legal elite who profited most under Marcos. The activist story is, in short, consistent with the *trasformismo* perspective. The return of law looks to many observers as the return of the status quo. We could say that in some sense everything that the Ford Foundation and Asia Foundation did, for example, "worked" in the Philippines, but there was no major change in the structures of state power. It worked for the local elites at the same time it operated according to international criteria.

The process does bring some change, however. The terms of legitimacy change in subtle but important ways. It is true that roughly the same group is in power as before, but the children of the old elites and those who work with them are not precisely the same as their predecessors. Some of the dynamic can be traced into recent events, such as the failed impeachment in 2003 of Chief Justice Davide—in retaliation for his role in the Estrada impeachment. The Davide impeachment effort was led by legislators very much identified with the politics of guns, goons, and lawyers, but they were not successful with direct tactics of retaliation against those who enforced the law against their friends. Those who resisted knew that a reputation for integrity and a commitment to legality could have more value in the current period than it may have had in the past. Leaders of NGOs invest in the legitimacy of the new civil society organizations, and the response to earlier social unrest has moved the terrain of law and legal rights deeper into the issues that affect the disadvantaged in the Philippines. The system is thus made more legitimate as the supply of and demand for law is strengthened. It is therefore true that the longstanding Philippine oligarchy has been reinforced, but the cost has been a little more investment in law and in legal processes.

The rapid development of reformist NGOs linked to members of the elite also fit perfectly with developments in the United States. The Ford Foundation "funded more than a dozen ALGs" in the period 1989–1996 (Golub 2000: 198). The Asian Development Bank moved from a relatively tentative investment in law and legal reform in the 1990s more generally to an embrace of "legal empowerment" through NGOs in the Philippines and elsewhere in the past five years. Legal empowerment has indeed emerged as one of the latest strategies in law and development, favored by the World Bank, the United Nations, and other development organizations. The idea is that it moves beyond what its proponents saw as an excessive focus on "the "top-down," state-centered approach [that] concentrates on law reform and government institutions, particularly judiciaries, to build business-friendly legal systems that presumably spur poverty alleviation" (Golub 2003: 3).

Promoting the virtues of legal empowerment, Golub highlights the work of "the approximately two dozen Philippine legal services NGOs collectively known as Alternative Law Groups (ALGs) [, who] have contributed to scores of national regulations and laws concerning agrarian reform, violence against women, indigenous peoples' rights, environmental protection, and a host of other issues." He notes the need to use this strategy in part because of the failure of efforts to build the rule of law through court reform: "The ALGs largely have not worked through the Philippine courts for several reasons: judicial conservatism and corruption; the suitability of administrative, legislative, and other noncourt mechanisms to address partner populations' needs; and the fact that these populations are more legally self-sufficient when noncourt approaches are used" (2003: 30).

The close relationship between the Philippines and the United States makes it difficult to determine the source of this approach. The market in ideas is too closely intertwined. What is clear is that the U.S. approach and this revamping of the law in the Philippines both bring a new focus on legal rights and on politically respectable civil society groups located around the state. The U.S. reformist agenda directed at the Philippine state and in favor of the rule of law and activist legal NGOs matches well with the new Philippine generation of legal elites.

India: Elite Investment in the Production of Public Interest Lawyers

The issues connected with the Emergency in India and the subsequent Supreme Court switch to public interest activism brought forth discussion of the need for a "socially relevant legal education" that could attract bright lawyers to the opportunities to promote law on behalf of the disadvantaged (Int. India 10). A number of prominent Indian academics, working with the Supreme Court and its bar, came up with an idea ostensibly to increase the number of public interest lawyers and, again, to rebuild the prestige of the legal profession—the creation of a new law school. Well aware of the Ford Foundation's interest in public interest law and human rights, they turned to the foundation as well. The Ford Foundation earlier in India, in addition, had been quite successful in building new business schools with substantial autonomy from the state educational bureaucracy, and that made the new law school idea seem even more feasible. The Bar Council argued also that a new and self-consciously elitist law school could enhance the prestige of the profession given that some 480 new law schools had been created in the period after 1960. The rank and file of the legal profession and the law schools that produced them had very poor reputations among the legal elite.

The Ford Foundation went for the idea of a "moral law school" and made the grant that allowed the National Law School at Bangalore to be created. The first class graduated in 1992, and now there are similar law schools in four other places in India. According to a former dean, however, only a very small percentage of the graduates have gone on to public interest careers (Int. India 11). They have been deterred by the "low salaries" in public interest law and attracted by the much higher salaries in the corporate sector. The law school actually sought to ban on-campus interviewing at the beginning, but the students organized meetings with potential employers at a nearby hotel to make sure that they could find opportunities in corporate law. Many of the graduates also have gone on to further education in the United States. The largest group in the first class went to Arthur Andersen's law firm in India, no doubt because of high salaries but also because it was not controlled by the traditional legal-familial elite. The firm was closed down in India, however, by local litigation challenging foreign law firms (well before the Enron events killed Andersen Legal completely). The graduates have therefore tended to go into the solicitors firms, some offices of advocates, and to in-house counsel with the new breed of more U.S.-oriented Indian corporations. Again from the perspective of a former Ford Foundation official, the aspiration to "build a human rights and social justice" law school was defeated. It instead produced "brilliant young technicians for corporate law" (Int. India 8)—lacking enough "mentoring" or "commitment" to public service to fulfill the original ambition.

As with respect to Indian business school graduates, as suggested by the move to Andersen in the first class, the law graduates did not have an easy time getting a strong place in a field where opportunity is shaped more by family ties than academic achievements. It remains very difficult to become an elite advocate without a father and most often grandfather who was a leader in the bar, and the solicitors firms (even though the profession is not formally divided) were until very recently limited in the number of partners they can make—twenty—by an old imported law—which strengthens the importance of family ties. The relatively meritocratic law graduates have to find their way in that world and in doing so are providing new and meritocratic legitimacy to a family-dominated profession and also providing talented workers who can at least hope to achieve the elite status of those already at the top of the bar.

Again the story is perhaps of failure according to the criteria used by the sectors of the Ford Foundation that supported these reform-minded grants, but the actual story is more complex. The reform agenda was at best only partly shared by the Brahmin legal elite, which mainly wanted to enhance its own position, legitimate its role, and encourage some meritocratic entrants to enhance the prestige of the profession. The reformers were no doubt also sincere in hoping to encourage more public interest advocacy, which also enhances the image of the elite. From their perspective, the new law schools have been at least moderately successful.

More generally, this combination of great visibility, social activism, and high status law schools, accompanied by considerable media attention, served to provide a kind of cover for compromises in the political field that permitted the notables of the bar to revive their traditional double game—profiting handsomely in both the political and the legal fields. In this respect, it is significant that the Supreme Court has been relatively absent—except in some corruption cases—from the political debates and social conflicts that accompanied the processes of opening the economy and deregulation of the past ten-fifteen years. According to a former law minister, "the Court reaffirmed often that questions of political economy were not appropriate for judicial competence and that they ought to intervene therefore only with extreme reticence" (Int. India 2). This attitude of reserve might have been questioned. As he added, "the socialism written in the constitution imposes on the state a permanent obligation to address the social needs of the weakest in society" (Int. India 2). The prudence of an elite profession close to economic power kept the dismantling of the interventionist state outside the judicial arena. The elite of the bar itself quite naturally profits considerably from commercial cases and the processes of economic liberalization.

The extraordinary prosperity of the commercial bar through economic liberalization is a reminder that the bar has never sacrificed the development of its legal market to political ambitions—succeeding at different times in different ways to combine the two ambitions. The renewed investment in legal virtue epitomized by public interest litigation and by the more meritocratic and elite law schools also does not change much of the fundamental character of the highly stratified Indian bar. In particular, family ties and alliances continue to cement together the elite of the legal field by linking together social and even professional interests that may momentarily diverge. Neither public interest litigation nor the new law schools has challenged the role of family capital in reproducing the most elite members of the profession.

The value of specific family capital of course changes over time, as do the values of other forms of capital linked to success in the Indian legal field. As in other countries, the value of international capital has probably gone up, and the new law schools may over time increase the value of meritocratic capital in the legal field. As elsewhere, scandals that reveal law too much in the instrumental service of business can boost the fortunes of those more heavily invested in virtues associated with noblesse oblige. But the Indian story illustrates that family capital remains deeply embedded in the history and structure of the legal field. The opportunity to navigate the legal field successfully depends on the acquisition of forms of capital that are far more available to those with the requisite family capital.

As was the case in the Philippines, the revamping of the virtue of the legal elite produced more continuity than change. Elite lawyers had enough power to resist major change and remain in a central social position. Nevertheless, there was an impact. The profession was made somewhat more meritocratic, the courts were more open to the poor and their claims than before, and the careers of the new generation of the legal elite depended on a different mix of public interest advocacy and corporate representation than before the Emergency.

South Korea: A High-Risk Strategy with a High Yield on Investment

Lawyers in Korea had to contend with major handicaps. They were sidelined by the military regimes because both their knowledge and institutions had been too closely identified with the Japanese occupation. The strictly limited recruitment and very low bar passage rate tended to channel entrants toward activities focused on narrowly legal matters as prosecutors, judges, and litigators (Dezalay and Garth 2007). The compensation for private lawyers was very high because of the monopoly that the small number of practitioners had.

The process of building the credibility of lawyers in South Korea therefore started with very little capital except prestige and a relative lack of identification with the military regimes in South Korea. A number of South Korean lawyers adopted a strategy of relatively high risk linked closely to strategies adopted in the United States. As Tom Ginsburg noted, beginning in the 1980s, in particular, "small groups of activist lawyers drew on and adapted American social activist strategies to use the law for social change" (2007: 50). This group could link to "heroic lawyers" in earlier periods who sought also to use the Korean Bar Association, "to fight against the military dictatorship" in the 1960s (Jae Won Kim 2007: 60–61). Lawyers who sought to defend targets of the repression of the Park regime, particularly after martial law in 1972, did not have much success, and they were themselves often arrested and persecuted, but the activities "kept alive the cherished ideal of lawyers as guardians of human rights and inscribed a positive image of the lawyer in the public eye" (Jae Won Kim 2007: 62).

In the 1970s, they could link up to the emerging international human rights movement. As Seong-Hyun Kim stated, "the US government began to express concerns about the Korean government's human rights violations and put pressure on it" in the 1970s (forthcoming). There was also a Korean office of Amnesty International (KAI) founded in 1972. Under the Park regime, such activity was very difficult and risky, and Amnesty itself was closed down twice by the government (Seong-Hyun Kim, forthcoming).

The activities in the 1970s suffered also from the limited commitment by the United States to human rights issues. Cumings observes that

> President Jimmy Carter had built up hope that the United States might do something about Park's dictatorship, human rights violations, and the terror. He visited Korea in June 1979, in the midst of a rare downturn in the economy. But by then Carter's advisors had persuaded him to direct his human rights efforts toward Latin American and communist dictatorships, and not toward "strategic" allies like Korea and the Philippines. (Cumings 1998: 384; see also Brazinsky 2007: 228–29)

Still, the heroic efforts of some lawyers had built the reputation of the Korean Bar Association as a critic of authoritarian power, and that reputation played an ironic role in the transformation that took place in the 1980s. According to Jae Won Kim, the reason for the sudden increase in the number of lawyers allowed to pass the bar examination in the early 1980s—a doubling from one hundred to two hundred—was a desire by the Doo-Hwan Chun regime to "reduce the privilege of lawyers and thus

weaken the Korean Bar Association" (2007: 63).[3] The new lawyers, however, became "a major force of human rights lawyers" (Jae Won Kim
2007: 63).

In the 1980s, lawyers used the cause of human rights to gain new positions in the field of political power. The five or six lawyers defending
dissidents, including Young-Rae Cho and Won-Soon Park, formed an
informal organization in 1985, called Chun Bo Pae, to coordinate the
caseloads (Ginsburg 2007: 52). After mass demonstrations in 1986 led
toward democratization, the lawyers formalized the organization into
Minbyun, with more than fifty lawyers initially (Ginsburg 2007: 52;
Seong-Hyun Kim, forthcoming; Goedde 2009). As Seong-Hyun Kim
notes,

> members of this group experienced in their university life the rigid dictator-
> ship of President Park, the coup d'état of new military group, and the mas-
> sacre in KwangJu. They studied more "scientifically (that is, with Marxist
> theory)" . . . By becoming lawyers, they had as their mission national inde-
> pendence (from imperialism), democratization, and national unification.
> (forthcoming)

The group included Moo-Hyun Roh, who became the president of
South Korea from 2003–5. Roh was born in 1946 to a farming family in
southeastern Korea. A high school graduate who never went to college,
he served in the Korean army and then passed the bar from study on his
own in 1975. He made his political career in Pusan (Ginsburg 2007: 54).
In 1977, he became a regional judge and then practiced tax law. He became a human rights lawyer in 1981, when he defended students who had
been tortured for possession of illegal literature.

The activist lawyers have played a major role in South Korean politics. According to Ginsburg, the "activist lawyers have become the establishment" (2007: 54). For Goedde, similarly, the story is of "human
rights lawyers turned lawyer-statespersons" (2009: 82). Seong-Hyun Kim
writes, "some members [of Minbyun] became high-ranking bureaucrats"
and he names a minister of justice, the chief director of the National In-

---

3. Tom Ginsburg says, in contrast, that the reasons for the increase are "murky," and
that, "It is tempting to trace both developments [including another expansion later in the
1980s in bar passers] in part to the contemporaneous shift toward liberalization in economic and financial spheres, which led to greater demand for business lawyers" (2007: 47).

telligence Service, ex-Korean CIA, the chair of the Reform Commission of the National Tax Service and others, and he notes that many different parties are also represented (forthcoming). In 2007, according to Goedde, Minbyun had 550 members, which "represents about seven percent of the attorney population of about 8,000 in the same year" (2009: 76). More recently, Minbyun has "diversified its activities into research, publication, movements for legal reforms, and international solidarity" (Ginsburg 2007: 54).

Although lawyers had long been excluded from power in South Korea, the Malthusian recruitment process had enabled them to accumulate extremely valuable symbolic capital. Indeed, especially at the regional level, many lawyer activists were absorbed into the political parties that developed after the move to democratization (Seong-Hyun Kim, forthcoming). Lawyers, in short, made great strides in the Korean context serving as champions against authoritarianism.

The small but expanded legal profession in South Korea also moved from antiauthoritarianism into activism through NGOs with expanded reform agendas. The leaders of the most prominent of these organizations began in the struggles for democracy. As Seong-Hyun Kim (forthcoming) observes, "The roles of professionals as watchdogs for conglomerate capital and political power are increasingly emphasized, and lawyers are considered professionally capable of guiding Korean society towards more moderate and reasonable ways." In addition, he notes, some of the leaders even became "media stars" through their activities. The two pivotal organizations in the development of civil society in Korea are the Citizen's Coalition for Economic Justice (CCEJ), founded in 1989, and the People's Solidarity for Participatory Democracy (PSPD), established in 1994. Both groups show how dissent in Korea was pulled in the direction of U.S.-style civil society.

The CCEJ, which is considered to be the first of the South Korean "civil society" organizations, was thus "modeled on the American civil rights movement" (Seong-Hyun Kim, forthcoming). It was founded by important and well-known activists from the social movements of the 1970s. The goal, according to one of the founders, was to promote the law versus the radicalism that many intellectuals supported. The need was for "legal" strategies "within the regime" (Int. K-1). It was a response to those who "merely criticized," and the idea was that a way to moderate "antiestablishment" social movements was to "bring more professionals into the movement" (Int. K-1). The CCEJ thus was a group of professionals consisting of professors, lawyers, religious leaders, journalists, and managers of firms, and it suggested a more modest and professional "civil movement" rather than a radical one (S. Lee 1993). The CCEJ is a large membership organization now in Korea with considerable influence and interchange with the government.

The PSPD was created in 1994 by a group that defined itself to the left of the CCEJ. Won-Soon Park, the founder, was a well-known human rights lawyer in the 1970s and 1980s. He went abroad to take courses at the London School of Economics and then went to Harvard in the early 1990s (Seong-Hyun Kim, forthcoming). In 1994, he founded the PSPD as a group of activists, lawyers, economists, and scholars. According to one of the founders, Park sought to turn law from a "tool of dictatorship" into a tool of "democracy" and the "rights of people" (Int. K-2). PSPD gradually lost its ideological tilt and helped provide the model for future organizations in South Korean civil society. It also grew substantially and again provided a pool of personnel for reformist governments. In particular, many from the PSPD were recruited into the Moo-Hyun Roh government that gained power in 2003.

After reforms enacted in the wake of the Asian financial crisis with an eye toward strengthening minority shareholder rights, in particular the shareholders' derivative suit, the PSPD became the leading user of this legal device. While not particularly sympathetic to the ostensibly neoliberal aims of the reforms, the PSPD sought to weaken the power of the chaebols through these actions and efforts to make their conduct more transparent. Corruption has similarly been a major focus of the PSPD's activities. The effort to weaken the government-chaebol alliance, in this way, contributes to weaken the historically strong Korean state (Choi and Cho 2003; Ohnesorge 2003).

These law-inspired civil society organizations more recently have matured in the sense that all political sides draw on the approaches that they developed. According to Goedde, "There has been a shift in ideology, such that now any group of lawyers disagreeing with the incumbent administration can use the law to challenge the state. No matter what their political background, lawyers who find themselves at odds with the state can mobilize the law as a weapon to fight the state (2009: 87–88).

An opposition that was often Marxist and anti-American in the 1980s was therefore attracted to the programs and approaches promoted by the retooled legal elite in the United States.[4] As Ginsburg observes,

> The United States played a key role in national defense, as a reference society, and in supplying liberal legal ideology and institutions as a model. The presence of the liberal metropole in the form of the United States meant that liberalism was present in the array of ideas available to reformers. (2007: 62)

More generally, the tremendous U.S. efforts to shape the Korean "modernizing elite" helped to integrate South Korean intellectuals into the U.S.-oriented marketplace of ideas. According to Brazinsky, whose recent book details the U.S. "democratization" strategy in South Korea, "efforts to reshape the very thinking of South Koreans were at times based on disturbing assumptions of cultural superiority, but they facilitated the emergence of elite groups that were determined to develop the economy and democratize the country" (2007: 6). When democracy came, U.S. legal approaches made sense to lawyers seeking to build their position and credibility in the newly reformed South Korean state.

Corporate Law Firms Complementing the Public Interest Bar

The typical career pattern for Korean lawyers has long followed that of Japanese lawyers. After succeeding in becoming one of the lucky few to pass the bar examination, the young lawyer embarks on a career as a prosecutor or judge, moving later to a highly lucrative private practice as a litigator. The idea of a corporate lawyer does not fit well with this model, and indeed, also as in Japan, the emerging corporate conglomerates tended to deal directly with the state rather than through law and lawyers. Today, there is a thriving Korean corporate bar blending Korean lawyers, other professionals, and expatriate lawyers, typically of Korean descent, who have passed a U.S. bar exam but are not licensed in South Korea. The Martindale-Hubbell listing for Seoul counts 1,585 lawyers, which is one of the largest Asian listings. It attests to a large

---

4. The Constitutional Court, created in 1987, soon adopted a relatively activist role. Along with other courts, according to Ginsburg, the Constitutional Court "became a locus of activity for the several thousand new civil society organizations that exploded onto the scene after 1987" (2007: 51; Yang 1993).

number of lawyers able to advertise and oriented toward international business. Again starting almost with nothing, this development is a remarkable story of growth and embeddedness in the international market of expertise.

As was the case for the other countries, these firms originated as recent embodiments of the dual justice system characteristic of colonialism. As noted in chapter 8, the Tae-Hyong Lee and Heung-Han Kim Law Firm opened in 1958 in order to provide "services to foreigners" (Seong-Hyun Kim, forthcoming). Heung-Han Kim was a judge of the Seoul district court who took advantage of ties to Il-Young Cheong, the chairman of the diplomatic commission of the Korean National Assembly, to study abroad in the United States in 1953. He returned to open a U.S.-style law firm in 1958. He joined with Tae-Hyong Lee, his mother-in-law and Il-Young Cheong's wife.

Despite the connection to the existing political leadership, the firm was not threatened by the military coup in 1961. In fact, as Seong-Hyun Kim shows, "the developmental state did more good than harm to his law firm. . . . Coca-Cola, Kraft Food, Ford, Lockheed Martin and others became Lee & Kim's clients. The firm changed its name to Kim, Chang & Lee (KCL) after Dae-Young Chang's participation" (forthcoming). The 1960s saw a number of other firms modeled after the first law firm. Currently, the largest by far is Kim & Chang, with 272 lawyers, followed by Whaw (Yun Yang Kim Shin &Yu), GwangJank (Lee & Ko), TaePyong-Yang (Bae, Kim & Lee) and Sejong (Shin & Kim), all between 125 and 140, according to Kim (forthcoming).

The various founders were licensed in South Korea, graduates also of American law schools, and former judges or prosecutors. School ties and family relations governed recruitment. Kim & Chang, the largest, "established an American style law firm with respect to business methods and recruitment" (Seong-Hyun Kim, forthcoming). It was established in 1972 by Young-Mu Kim, with a JD from Harvard Law School, and Soo-Gil Chang, "his friend from Seoul National University's Faculty of Law." They recruited young lawyers after their courses at the Judicial Research and Training Institute, taught them international practice, and encouraged overseas training. According to Seong-Hyun Kim, "These methods were rapidly diffused to other firms, and recently more and more young lawyers without experiences as judges and prosecutors have started their juridical careers from law firms. They are sent to American law schools to obtain an LLM and learn American legal techniques" (forthcoming).

The role and importance of these law firms has increased steadily, even though in the 1970s "corporate law practice in Korea was restricted within a small boundary that mainly covered international business transactions" (Lee 2007: 231). The demand for these services serving mainly foreign clients has long exceeded the supply. And the domestic demand has grown considerably since the Asian financial crisis. Before 1997, Kim & Chang was the only law firm with more than one hundred lawyers. In three or four years, the top four firms all exceeded one hundred (Lee 2007: 234). Structural adjustment and deregulation increased domestic competition. The chaebols began to depend more on lawyers rather than negotiating directly with public officials. Business has continued to grow, although the looming liberalization of the legal services market brings the specter of U.S. firms taking a share of the most substantial matters. The success of the firms, coupled with democratization, has led law graduates increasingly to begin their careers at the firms rather than as prosecutors or judges. Seong-Hyun Kim notes, for example, that, "In 1999, there were seven top bar exam scorers . . . in Kim & Chang, two in TaePyongYang, and one in Sejong and KCL" (forthcoming).

The number of Korean lawyers is augmented by the so-called foreign legal consultants. According to Seong-Hyun Kim, citing the Korean Ministry of Justice, "the number of foreign lawyers was 55 between 1992 and 1993 but increased suddenly to 119 in 1999, two years after the Korean financial crisis." Most were U.S. citizens. There is also a large and uncounted group of Korean citizens who have passed a U.S. bar exam and returned to Korea as legal consultants: "Eighty percent of foreign lawyers in Korea are estimated to be Korean American Lawyers." Many Koreans obtain JD degrees in the U.S. and even more receive LLM degrees. The Korean-American lawyers help to integrate the corporate law firm into the international market in legal services.

One area of strength for the Korean corporate law firms is lobbying. They have hired numerous former government officials. According to Seong-Hyun Kim, "The number of Kim & Chang's consultants was 44 on May 2006. . . . The most remarkable figure is Hyon-Jae Lee, who twice occupied the post of the Minister of Economy and Finance. And 23 former bureaucrats of the National Tax Service found their new jobs at Kim & Chang" (forthcoming). Law firms also are very active in consulting, "ranging from accounting and auditing to personnel management."

The major role that the corporate law firms have carved out in South

Korea translates also into increasing involvement in the state and in the world of NGOs. Seong-Hyun Kim notes, for example, that well-known activist Young-Rae Cho worked in Kim & Chang for eighteen months beginning in 1982. Jong-Bae Chon, the former minister of justice in the current government, "was also a lawyer at Kim & Chang from 1981 to 1985. In 1985, he participated in Cho's 'Public Interest Law Consultation Bureau'" (Kim, forthcoming).

Similarly, the large firms have played a larger role in politics, exemplified by "major roles in President Moo-Hyun Roh's very controversial impeachment case in the spring of 2004" (Lee 2007: 239). In Lee's words, "the large firms are becoming a kind of new power center" (2007: 239). The links to the United States are also strengthened by the fact that seventy-five percent of the lawyers in the four largest law firms who passed the bar between 1980 and 1990 have studied abroad, mainly in the United States (Lee 2007: 245). These lawyers again support an agenda that seeks to restructure the Korean state toward a role more akin to that of the United States, and at the same time they are also very well connected to the state.

The importance of the law firms and the civil society organizations as social institutions is being reinforced by the changes taking place in Korean legal education. Following an idea that originated in Korea (Int. K-1) and then traveled to Japan before moving back to Korea, South Korea has created graduate law schools with the expectation that most graduates will pass the bar. As in Japan (Saegusa 2009), part of the focus has been on the demand for more corporate lawyers stemming from globalization (Choi 2007). Larger law firms are also a way to build up the domestic market in case it is opened to foreign competition (Lee 2007: 239). But the consensus for reform was broader in South Korea than in Japan. The initial movement in South Korea was linked to Se-Il Park, one of the main founders of the CCEJ and later part of the government. And, as pointed out by Miyazawa, Chan, and Lee (2008: 357), one reason the reform in South Korea went further than Japan is that South Korea is more embedded in the U.S. marketplace of ideas.

The first class of the twenty-five graduate law schools, with two thousand students total, has just begun (Miyazawa, Chan, and Lee 2008: 354). One key factor to examine is the social make-up of those who attend the new schools versus those who have attended the undergraduate law departments (a subset of which still remain). The admission to the undergraduate law departments was based on written tests only, and those who succeeded were often from the lower middle class (Dezalay and Garth 2007). Now language skills, experience, and performance in personal interviews also figure into the equation. One very likely result will be that the system of law schools will be better able to translate Korean social capital into legal careers. As the opportunities for lawyers to invest in the state have grown, making legal capital potentially more valuable, so, too, it appears will be the opportunities to link legal capital more closely to familial and social capital.

As in Indonesia, the South Korean reform agenda has moved very closely toward the U.S. agenda even if, of course, pursued in a very different context. Lawyers are moving with relative ease back and forth into politics, corporate law, and public interest law, and the situation in South Korea has been aided by transformations in the courts and legal education. Given the lack of legal capital produced either by colonialism in the first place or by the later move toward independence, the South Korean developments are quite remarkable.

Conclusion

This chapter depicts two pairs of countries where, from very different historical bases, the elite of the legal profession succeeded in securing a relatively strong position while moving toward the U.S. model that links corporate law to a relatively moderate public interest law. India and the Philippines provide examples where the legal elite drew on durable colonial legacies which limited the impact of the new global agenda identified with the United States. South Korea and Indonesia, in contrast, started with very little legal capital, making the emergence of corporate law and legal entrepreneurship appear more surprising. The contrasts are explored in the next chapter, which concludes the book. It begins with a more general theoretical discussion. That discussion then sets the stage for brief comparisons of the experiences examined in the first three chapters of this part—showing the diverse set of Asian legal revivals.

CHAPTER FOURTEEN

Political Investment and the Construction of Legal Markets: Legal, Social, and International Capital in Asian Legal Revivals

This concluding chapter begins with a central finding of our research. The debate between those who focus on markets as the key to understanding the legal profession and those who counter with the argument that "politics matter" misses the central fact of the relationship between politics and markets. Put simply, the value and social credibility of legal expertise is determined by investments in (and profits from) state politics. One of the often-repeated observations in the countries we studied is how lawyers who were thriving economically suddenly shifted their political stance when their credibility was threatened by the state. The process can be quite complex. Lawyers in the Philippines for a time thrived under Marcos even after martial law, and the opposition among the elite was very limited. But the international and national delegitimation that occurred with the assassination of Benigno Aquino discredited the legal elite and the oligarchy to which it belonged. At that point, lawyers not previously thought to be highly principled retooled and reinvested in legal virtue. In Hong Kong, similarly, Tiananmen Square's delegitimation of the Chinese state, coupled with the impending return of Hong Kong to China—with a potential devaluation of the law as practiced by barristers working in English—helped, again, to make statespersons out of lawyers who had otherwise paid little attention to politics.

This kind of transformation does not necessarily come because the country becomes more authoritarian or repressive. Some lawyers mobilize when a combination of domestic and international developments challenges the reputation and credibility of the law and lawyers in the setting in which they practice. The position and credibility of law in the field of state power is threatened. The threat creates an opportunity for reinvestment in legal virtue.

Recent episodes triggering reinvestment are also echoes of the earlier colonial and neocolonial periods. In particular, as highlighted in earlier chapters, we have many examples of traders converting into statesmen promoting independence (chaps. 3 and 7), including especially in India but also in Indonesia, Malaysia, the Philippines, and Singapore, or into imperial statesmen (chaps. 4 and 6) represented best by the U.S. foreign policy establishment defining and legitimating U.S. imperial ventures. Similar conversions took place among the colonial elites in Britain and the Netherlands.

The timing of these episodes of conversion, whether historically or recently, suggests that the relationship between the market and politics can change quite dramatically depending on the particular histories and the local and international context. Political investments, as noted above, relate very closely to the particular contexts that convert ordinary lawyers exhibiting no taste for statesmanship into political actors of high moral virtue.

The case studies suggest a more general hypothesis linking the market and politics. Political investments and market capitalizations of that investment follow a cyclical pattern alternating investment in politics and exploitation of markets. Latin American developments illustrate a comparative variation on this hypothesis. Lawyers in Latin America were first the officers of the crown and became politicians and intellectuals only much later. Much later still, a group of these lawyers reconverted into brokers serving as compradors for foreign traders and investors, in particular from Britain and the United States. This investment outside the traditional neocolonial sphere reinforced the position of these lawyers as insiders-outsiders to the traditional legal elites. They could connect to the traditional legal elite and move into a strong market position profiting from, for example, the Venezuelan oil industry (Gomez, forthcoming; see also Dezalay and Garth 2002). The cyclical developments that take place in different situations require a more systematic reconsideration of both "politics" and "markets."

Politics Matter

A body of work seeks to provide an antidote to the emphasis on markets as the defining feature of the legal profession. The central point of this literature is simply that "politics matter" in the development and behavior of legal professions (e.g., Halliday, Karpic, and Feeley 2007). Our work supports that finding, but we disagree with the effort to link the legal profession to "political liberalism" (Halliday, Karpic, and Feeley 2007). Lawyers, as repeatedly seen, are very often found in collaboration with strong rulers of various types (see also Ginsburg and Moustafa 2008). One type is the strong local or national leader, represented by condottieri in Italy, caudillos in Latin America, bosses in the Philippines, or military leaders such as Pinochet or Suharto. Another example is represented by centralizing monarchies characteristic especially of European states in England, France, Spain, and Prussia. And another type of strong leader is found in later modernist or developmental states exemplified by Meiji Japan and South Korea. Some of these states are even led by lawyers, including Singapore under Lee Kwan Yew, the Philippines under Marcos, and Mexico in the long period of rule by the Institutional Revolutionary Party (PRI) prior to the election of Raul Salinas—the first nonlawyer after the Mexican Revolution early in the twentieth century. In these various cases the lawyers are definitely engaged in state politics, albeit in support of strong leaders rather than social democracies.

The market-oriented activity of lawyers in these examples tends to be concentrated in enclaves oriented toward different states or thriving with relatively small numbers of elite lawyers with marginal positions but monopoly profits. Obvious examples include Hong Kong, Indonesia, Singapore, and South Korea. In Singapore, for example, the law firms either handled basic litigation or conveyancing for Singapore clients, prospering from their monopoly, or focused on representing clients from abroad seeking to do business in Singapore. The example of the Philippines is in part an exception since, until the Aquino assassination, quite a few elite lawyers thrived in and in support of Marcos's authoritarian state and its relatively thin legal veneer.

This general observation of lawyers as servants of power can be extended to other situations where lawyers serve powerful social groups. Examples include the representation of large landowners in England, India, and the Philippines; the representation of leading merchant groups in India, Indonesia, and the Philippines; and, of course, Wall

Street law firms representing major businesses in the United States. This specific situation creates risks for lawyers too close to particular interests, and the violent conflicts in the period after independence in Latin America illustrate that risk. Such violent conflicts tend to push lawyers closer to the model of serving state power. But the service of strong economic powers can also be extremely profitable when violence and conflict can be limited because of a relatively homogeneous elite or some kind of agreement among elites about how to divide the spoils fairly—*sexenios* of Presidential rotation in Mexico, *café con leche* as a regional compromise in Brazil, *puntofijo* among elites in the late 1950s in Venezuela. Lawyers can also play a key and highly profitable role serving as brokers and mediators among competing interests such as the church and the state in Italy; landowners and the monarchy in England; or Catholic landowners, liberal traders and export-oriented entrepreneurs in nineteenth-century Latin America. The strong mediation role is not so common in our Asian examples.

In order to analyze these very different situations, it is essential to go beyond the professional ideology of lawyers as natural statespersons, politicians, or state architects. Instead, we refocus our inquiry on the reproduction of social hierarchies through investments in learning that translate into entry into state politics. The key institution in many instances is the faculty of law domestically or abroad. It typically serves as the training organization for high-ranking state officers and the midlevel bureaucracy, exemplified especially by France, Prussia, and Spain in Europe, and by Japan and South Korea in Asia. In other situations, the faculty of law serves directly as the breeding ground for lawyer-politicians, with Latin America generally conforming to this model and the Philippines best exemplifying it in Asia, or as the site for bonding or brokering between different clans. The *camarillas* in Mexico and the legal fraternities in the Philippines provide examples of this model. The different ethnic groups in Malaysia meeting and bonding at the Inns of Court in London is another example. The role of the faculties of law is much less when lawyers are strongly embedded in social and family networks (or when their role in politics is mediated through these networks). The prominent European model of the family reproduction of legal expertise is the bar in England, and the obvious Asian example is India.

As agents of the state, lawyers are directly involved in state policies and in fights for or around the state. They are involved in palace wars among different fractions of the ruling elite competing for control over state institutions—a competition that is later reconfigured into competitions such as that between lawyers and economists. We see these competitions on both sides of the colonial relationship. Lawyers could assert the virtues of legal legitimacy when, for example, the traders became discredited or challenged in a new empire, such as with the Philippines, or when imperial policies have lost some support through the activities of the economic exploiters, as in India or Indonesia. There are also international competitions between colonial and hegemonic societies. Both the British and the United States claimed and legitimated their empires as more benevolent than others. Elites in the United States came to believe in some form of dollar diplomacy and the rule of law as keys to civilizing the world and securing U.S. global power. In historical contexts ranging from colonialism to the international human rights movement, we see lawyers playing double roles as, for example, colonial tax collectors on one side and protectors of Indian locals on the other. The comprador concept captures this enduring double role.

A third state role is as reformer, modernizer, or promoter of social welfare, which can be characterized as the preventive management of social inequalities and tensions through a mix of strategies. One strategy is to redistribute some of the profits accumulated through control over the patrimonial state, as in the Philippines. Another is to form an alliance with a strong and populist regime, such as that of Juan Perón in Argentina. Lee Kwan Yew in Singapore provides an example of the development of an authoritarian welfare state. In Hong Kong there is an emerging alliance of legal elites with the Chinese state. Earlier there emerged an effort to promote popular calls for democratization in Hong Kong. Finally, the opening of the profession with night law schools and more meritocratic recruitment also helps promote the role of the lawyer as a spokesperson for minorities. Legal strategies can therefore reduce the risk of violent protest by providing channels for incremental political and social change on behalf of the minorities. Retooling legal elites, as we saw in India and the Philippines, in particular, may somewhat broaden both recruitment into the professional elite and the beneficiaries of legal rights strategies.

There is a contradiction, however, between the reproduction of social hierarchies and a project of social redistribution, particularly in times of economic crises. The demise of progressive lawyer-led regimes in Latin America and elsewhere in the 1930s provides an example of this kind of challenge for lawyers. Such a challenge became even more problematic when the stakes escalated through an intensification of competition between hegemonic states, as in the Cold War. Those tending to favor the left or a social reform agenda, in particular, such as Sukarno, found themselves identified with the Soviet Union in the Cold War competition for global hegemony, thereby further delegitimating their strategy in countries taking the anticommunist side. More generally, there are numerous potential problems linked to the double role that lawyers play as members or even leaders of the privileged and propertied classes and/ or the hegemonic societies on one side, and as brokers and mediators purporting to embody universal knowledge, the common good, and public service on the other side—all the while seeking to mediate different social interests. The formidable challenge is to be involved in political fights while seeking to occupy the high ground of an umpire above the political fray. These difficulties help to explain investments in the autonomy of legal institutions, such as the supreme courts, even if to some extent that autonomy contradicts specific involvement in state politics. Finally, challenges are exacerbated in these societies by the weakness of the local production of legal knowledge (see, e.g., Lynch 1981 on Columbia's importation of a commercial code irrelevant to agrarian society).

Legal Markets and the Economics of Symbolic Products

Just as it is too simple to assert that lawyers as such are bound to take a particular political position, whether in favor of or opposed to political liberalism, for example, it is incorrect to focus narrowly on the role of lawyers as protectors of a professional monopoly seeking, for example, to restrict entry into the profession. Before lawyers can assert or protect a monopoly, the monopoly must be constructed and legitimated. That process requires investment in state politics. States are in fact the key to establishing, legitimating, and enforcing a monopoly position.

There are many examples of notable lawyer-politicians establishing— and profiting from—a quasi-monopoly on state politics. The Congress Party in India is a prime example, but others include Indonesia in the early 1950s and the Philippines from at least the period of the U.S. colonial relationship. There are also examples where the service to the state is at the margins of state power, for example, by providing a legal facade for basically authoritarian policies, but such a position is not as rewarding, and economic prosperity may in fact depend on strictly limiting the supply of practitioners, as in Singapore and South Korea, or go to those serving mainly foreign clients in a kind of trading enclave. The profits depend on lawyers moderating their criticisms rather than moderating the state.

The best and most lucrative market for lawyers, serving as mediators, brokers, and umpires among different social groups, spaces, societies, or institutions, is by definition difficult to construct as a legal monopoly. The lawyers work on the borders and rely on social (cosmopolitan) capital, which is difficult to protect because it is impossible to patent. The difficulty is especially pronounced when there are other competing groups who can mobilize a similar array of resources, for example, the technocrat-economists serving as diplomats in Indonesia and the accountants who competed in professional services through multidisciplinary practices.

A truly economic approach to understanding a market of symbolic goods such as law needs to take into account not only the production of producers but also the production of consumers. Consumers must come to a belief in the value of law, even for the most basic one of resolving disputes (Michelson 2006). We therefore focus on professional hierarchies and two-tier legal fields structured to create and legitimate the value of law and lawyers. The professional elites in most instances build the value that redounds to the benefit of the rank and file, who also typically build up the position of the elite.

The combination of the focus on markets and politics suggests a combination of research strategies. One involves synchronic study of local turf battles and the competition between national states. It means examining, for example, lawyers competing with economists, or the foreign policy establishment against Reagan era challengers. It means looking at colonial competition between the old Europeans and the new approach of the United States, between the Soviet Union and the United States during the Cold War, or increasingly between China and the United States. The other involves diachronic examinations that explore the initial accumulation of legal capital through the acquisition of universal knowledge and then the reinvestment in politics to accumulate complementary social capital.

The hypothesis that stems from this research is that there is a cyclical pattern relating law and politics. The cycle is not inevitable or regular, but it describes how legal capital can be accumulated, squandered, and then revived. Phase one is the period of the initial investment in colonial and then independence politics exemplified perfectly by the Congress Party in India. This phase involves a combination of imported expertise and local social and familial capital later valorized through independence and transition politics. The process leads to homologation and institutionalization by the independent nation state through transnational links to hegemonic societies.

Phase two involves profiting from or even abusing the unique combination of legal, political, learned, and cosmopolitan resources accumulated in phase one. Phase two is characterized at times by strong opposition to lawyers and the clients whom they represent. Nehru, for example, referred to a "purloined constitution" in India. In this phase there are high risks of marginalization or even of a demise of the political capital of lawyers. It can be displaced by competitors such as economic-technocrats, populists, or a more meritocratic military. The negative impact on the value of legal capital is enhanced in situations where the legal capital has been linked to discredited state patronage, as in the Philippines.

Phase three is a rebuilding process that is in fact very similar to the first phase. Once again, local social capital and imported expertise are reinvested by lawyers in political morality. This general process, of course, involves path continuities and discontinuities, and it follows different rhythms and paces in different national spaces. The differences relate to variations in the initial starts, depending in particular on the colonial policies of investing in law and in state building, on the early relationships to trade or a variation of moral imperialism, and on subsequent internal and external developments. In the following pages, we recap the Asian stories with these factors of comparison in mind.

India and the Philippines: Legal Revivals on the Basis of Strong Colonial Investment and Enduring Social Capital

India and the Philippines provide the best examples of relatively strong initial legal investments in the colonial state, local elites, and the propertied classes. That investment paved the way for a leading role by well-connected legal elites in the movements for independence. What began with trading in India through the British East India Company moved into elite co-optation, elite reproduction through legal expertise, state building, and then independence through the Congress Party. The rel-

atively long duration of this process of legal investment allowed lawyers and legal institutions, in particular the high courts, to embed themselves within elite Indian social hierarchies, including notably the Parsi
community and the Brahmin caste. When challenged in the fifties and
especially during the Emergency period under Prime Minister Indira
Gandhi, the leaders of the legal elite were able to regroup, in part by taking advantage of close ties to the legal elite in the United States through
the Ford Foundation and other sources attentive to India's importance
in the Cold War. Seeking to revamp the legal elite's tarnished reputation
in the fifties and sixties when the contradictions of the close relationships to the state and to landowning elites led to political hostility, the
Supreme Court invested in the development of public interest litigation
and then went further into legal education reform to promote a more
meritocratic basis of entry into the professional elite.

Although no longer dominant among the general political leadership,
the legal elite was able to rebuild its strong position by reinvesting in
state politics and broadening somewhat the entry into the elite of the
profession. But it did so without threatening the dominant position of
legal elites in the courts and in law-related positions in the state or the
more general role of law in the reproduction of family capital.

The Philippines is the other example of a relatively long and sustained
period of legal investment in an elite that prospered under U.S. colonial
tutelage, which then led the government after independence. U.S. training and expertise were central to the reproduction of that elite. Again
there was investment in the courts, especially the Supreme Court. More
so than in India, however, law and lawyers became embedded in business, land, family capital, and the state. Lawyers occupied positions everywhere in the so-called Philippine oligarchy, aided at times by the
famous "guns and goons" also enlisted in political wars for the spoils of
the state. The capital of the legal elite declined in the Marcos era. The
legal fraternities played a role at times moderating the authoritarian regime, and Marcos relied on a thin legal cover to legitimate his actions,
but law was quite clearly in the instrumental service of his regime. The
legitimacy was relatively unchallenged within elite circles in part because the U.S. position in Vietnam and in the Cold War took the pressure off the authoritarian path elected by Marcos. Even President Carter
backed off supporting an opposition seeking to promote the banner of
human rights against Marcos.

After the legitimacy of Marcos evaporated domestically and internationally with the murder of Aquino and a reduction in Cold War intensity, matters changed. Faced with a potential mass movement on the left against the Marcos regime and the elite so closely connected to it, a small group reinvested in legal values and began to revive the prestige and stature of lawyers and the law. Drawing on the growing importance of the international human rights movement outside the Philippines, the reinvigorated and internationally connected legal elite was able to assume power and begin to rebuild the legal institutions broken down by Marcos.

The processes of reinvestment in the law and reconnection to cosmopolitan elites in the United States in effect brought the old legal oligarchy back to power, including those who had been central to the Marcos regime. But there was also an effort to develop a new generation of social entrepreneurs. As in India, the process of retooling the elite in this manner opened up to a new generation of lawyers, including some from outside the elite, offered more legal rights to the disadvantaged, and bolstered the legitimacy of the Philippine legal elite and the oligarchic state that it continues to serve. The connection between the corporate law firms and a new generation of NGOs has also grown as the new generation of the old elite consolidates its position.

In India the legal elite came more to occupy the position of mediator and broker among the groups competing for state power, while the Philippine legal elite again occupies positions throughout the fields of the state and the economy. But in both cases, drawing on their long-established domestic position and their strong ties to their counterparts in the United States, the legal elites as lawyers and advocates were able to rebuild the value of legal capital—and the corresponding market that thrives on the value of that capital. Moderate change occurred, but the legal elites were also well able to absorb foreign ideas and approaches and turn them to the advantage of themselves, their social world, and their clients.

Malaysia, Singapore, and Hong Kong: Legal Capital without Social Capital

These three examples are variations on the evolution of a trading entrepôt with lawyers mostly occupying relatively weak positions in the field of state power. Lawyers served from the start as brokers and compradors, but in none of the cases did they acquire the social capital necessary to sustain strong strategies of investment in state power. In addition, unlike the situation in India and the Philippines discussed above, and Indonesia and South Korea discussed below, the severing of the traditional colonial ties did not lead to replacement investment from the United States in conjunction with the Cold War competition with the Soviet Union. Malaysia, Singapore, and Hong Kong were not substantial recipients of foreign and philanthropic aid from the United States in the Cold War. The loss of the connection to the British was not compensated for by U.S. investment in law and the state.

In Malaysia the legal elite increasingly became divorced from state power. At the time of independence, elite representatives of the different ethnic groups—Indian, Malay, and Chinese—were united through a shared legal education abroad in England. They came together to support independence and to build the new state. The British had invested substantially in the judiciary, and legal institutions functioned fairly well. Legal legitimacy was central to Malaysia, and it united and provided legitimacy to the governing elite. The foreign-oriented corporate bar, composed of lawyers from Indian and to a lesser extent Chinese descent, therefore had strong connections to the state at the time of independence.

As the economy under Mahathir became increasingly dominated by the state, which was committed to building the economic power of the ethnic Malay working with Chinese businesses, the traditional bar represented by the major corporate law firms and the Bar Council declined in power. The credibility of law also declined as the legal system was increasingly used instrumentally to serve the state. Seeking to rebuild the legal credibility, the traditional bar sought to speak out and mobilize to resist authoritarianism, but the lack of connections to the economy and the state kept the legal elite in a marginalized position. Mobilizing on the basis solely of power within legal institutions was not enough to gain any real leverage against the Malaysian state. There are some signs that the different ethnic groups in the post-Mahathir era might regroup into a more unified legal elite tied to more than simply domestic and foreign legal capital, but the current situation represents mainly a kind of return to the trading origins. Law remains part of the legitimacy of the state, but the market for the traditional legal elite's services comes mainly through the legal advice they provide to foreign business entities and the litigation that they undertake in courts that, at this point, are not central to Malaysian state governance.

Singapore was part of the same British colony until the split after independence. The movement toward independence involved classic legal strategies as detailed in Lee Kwan Yew's autobiography, but he and the People's Action Party (PAP) built state legitimacy on the basis of a kind of authoritarian welfare state. Law and legal institutions were part of the façade of legitimacy, but legal capital lacked much value in the Singapore state and economy. Lawyers who sought to challenge the PAP and its policies, as in Malaysia but more so, lacked any position from which to build a credible attack. Again, they had legal capital but lacked the kind of history that linked legal capital and social capital in India and the Philippines. Lawyers were well compensated for their conveyancing work and their litigation activity, but they occupied and continue to occupy a very marginal position politically. There remains the possibility of political strategies designed to strengthen the credibility and therefore value of the law, but the platform of lawyers is so far too weak to make the strategy pay off.

Hong Kong, similarly, starts with a long history as a trading entrepôt and with no real local move for independence. The British again invested in courts and the common law, but the legal role for the divided bar in Hong Kong was mainly lucrative litigation for the bar and real estate conveyancing for the solicitors. What appeared to be an impending devaluation of legal capital with the return of Hong Kong to China opened up a space for members of the bar to reinvest to shore up the value of the law and lawyers. A few elite and thriving members of the bar began to invest in politics, and their activity did at times connect to the Hong Kong middle class and its own political concerns. They certainly succeeded in attracting attention to the integrity of the courts and the legal system, and to that extent helped shore up the value of legal capital. But, as in Malaysia and Singapore, the rather small bar—not joined by the solicitors and transnational law firms focused on trade and investment in China—does not have the domestic or foreign resources to challenge the controlling Hong Kong merchant alliance with the Chinese state.

Indonesia and South Korea: From Weak Colonial Investment to Renewed Strength in the Field of State Power

Indonesia and South Korea represent paradoxes in the sense that very weak colonial origins did not prevent a relatively strong position in the field of state power in recent years. Daniel Lev (2007) highlighted the failures of the Indonesian legal system when contrasted to the situation in Malaysia. His point was that the history of the British Empire and the role of elite lawyers in independence created a bar of some stature and courts that operated for the most part fairly in Malaysia. In contrast, according to Lev, "Indonesia has nothing at work in common with the Malaysian bar" (2007: 411). From our perspective, however, the weak colonial investment in the law and lawyers in Indonesia, coupled with the relative displacement of lawyers by U.S.-trained economists in the Suharto era, led nevertheless to a relatively strong position of elite lawyers in Indonesia investing in corporate law firms and in NGOs around the state. Legal institutions are certainly not thriving and are staffed by poorly trained and undercompensated judges and prosecutors. But elite lawyers who kept aside but profited from Indonesia's version of crony capitalism have moved into a relatively strong position.

The important position of Indonesia in the Cold War is part of the story. Indonesia attracted considerable attention from the United States. Linkages to the U.S. legal elite brought some strength to the descendants of the colonially trained advocates, and they have taken advantage of foreign and domestic connections to invest in Indonesian state politics and rebuild the value of at least elite legal capital. Ties to the military, the economists in the state, and foreign capital have given the new legal elite a relatively strong position when compared to that of the traditional Malaysian bar.

The South Korean story is similar. The colonial legacy from the Japanese placed lawyers in a very weak position in independent South Korea. Lawyers were marginal to the authoritarian state in the 1950s, but at the same time they were relatively prestigious because of the difficulty of passing the Korean bar examination. South Korea was also very well integrated with the United States because of the Cold War, and U.S.-oriented corporate law firms grew up mainly by serving U.S. clients. As the number of lawyers gradually expanded and the state became less authoritarian, legal strategies against the state and into U.S.-like NGOs built a substantial place for lawyers in the structures of state power. This investment connected to the changed political and economic environment as well. Here, too, despite inauspicious origins and decades of relatively marginal status in the field of state power, entrepreneurial reinvestment in the past several decades has built up the value of legal capital and connected it to success in politics and markets. As with re-

spect to Indonesia, there was little to build on initially. Political strategies linked to U.S. legal approaches were able to draw on the credibility that came with this U.S.-oriented political/legal investment. As with
respect to Indonesia, corporate lawyers and NGOS together bring U.S.
approaches to law and state. The new law schools that began in 2009 may
accelerate that phenomenon.

Asian Legal Revivals and the Future

These various forms of Asian legal revivals make clear that, in one way
or another, lawyers and the law figure in the construction of the state
and its legitimacy. The role of the law and lawyers is a function of path-
dependent histories, connections to imperial powers and the factions
competing to dictate imperial policy, connections to competing hegemonic powers exemplified especially by the Cold War, and the ability of
legal actors to link what they have to offer as brokers, mediators, dispute
resolvers, and legitimators, to those possessing economic and political
capital. The cyclical pattern means that, in any country, lawyers serving
and profiting from power may periodically lose credibility for their political alliances or their profiteering, which then opens up new space for lawyers to reinvest in legal idealism and the reform of the state—also drawing on the groups with whom they have historically or newly connected.

We therefore anticipate more Asian legal revivals, but also some declines. We are not predicting that Asian countries (or Latin American,
for example) are inevitably on the way to the rule of law and democracy.
Lawyers in varying ways will seek to build up the value of legal capital
through political strategies in the countries we have studied, but the success of those strategies will depend less on the passion and idealism of
the lawyers and more on the domestic and international capital to which
the lawyers connect. The relative successes in South Korea and Indonesia, for example, were hardly to be expected given the historical experiences of each, while the Malaysian relative collapse in the value of legal
capital came to many as a surprise.

The situation is different where a relatively high value for legal capital has been the product of more than a century of development, as in
India and the Philippines—or the United States. It is more difficult to
hold the value down indefinitely in these countries. But the same tools

that facilitate reinvestment and a revaluation of legal capital in these settings ensure that the newest wave of reforms that refurbish the legal elite will also bring, for example, the familial, international, and even church-related capital that is both embedded in and the source of law's power.

As we have seen throughout, in addition, the changing world political scene shapes the international resources available for the various legal revivals. The relatively sustained investment in academic exchange, developmental strategies, and various forms of technical assistance that came from the United States to India, Indonesia, the Philippines and South Korea as part of the Cold War helped build up the position and shape the strategies of potential legal elites. The Cold War also helped keep the pressure off these and other authoritarian regimes during the most intense years of global combat. The United States in fact helped to build economists as competitors for positions and expertise in the field of state power—prioritizing anticommunism, modernizing elites, and open door economies to counter Soviet influence. But U.S. investment in the legitimacy of its state allies, including legitimacy through law as well as economics, helped set the stage for particular legal and economic strategies consistent, once again, with all the basic tenets of dollar diplomacy developed in part through the imperial relationship with the Philippines—open markets, relatively weak states, and the rule of law.

The seeming strength of the U.S. approaches, seen not only in the countries we studied but also in other parts of Asia, including China and Japan, means that it is easy to find evidence of an ascending value for legal capital oriented toward the United States. The Japanese, for example, have moved in the direction of U.S.-style law schools designed in particular to staff their growing law firms and corporate law departments. Legal education reform in China has also moved in the direction of U.S-style degrees and teaching (Erie 2009), and corporate law firms have also emerged as a kind of legal elite (Peerenboom 2008). The United States, indeed, has invested considerable resources in rule-of-law initiatives in China (Gewirtz 2003), seeking even to find Trojan horses—legal aid organizations—that will enhance the importance of law (Stephenson 2000). But there is nothing inevitable about the future strength of legal capital in China or Japan, especially given geneses meant to confine and harness law to state power. It remains for researchers to undertake the careful tracing of links between lawyers and the forms of capital—economic, learned, political, social, and cosmopolitan—that might provide more insight into the future of law than either idealistic hopes or faith in the inevitable emergence of lawyer statespersons. The case studies show that, while legal capital by itself is relatively weak, there are circumstances where lawyers succeed in building it up through the absorption of other forms of domestic and international capital.

Works Cited

Abas, Tun Salleh, and Haji Mohamed. 1989. *The Role of the Independent Judiciary*. Kuala Lumpur: Promarketing Publications.

Abel, Richard L. 1981. *American Lawyers*. Oxford and New York: Oxford University Press.

———. 1988. "England and Wales: A Comparison of the Professional Projects of Barristers and Solicitors." In Richard Abel and Phillip S. C. Lewis, eds., *Lawyers in Society, The Common Law World*, 23–75. Berkeley and Los Angeles: University of California Press.

Abel-Smith, Brian, and Robert Stevens. 1967. *Lawyers and the Courts: A Sociological Study of the English Legal System, 1750–1965*. London: Heinemann.

Abinales, Patricio N. 2003. "Progressive-Machine Conflict in Early Twentieth Century U.S. Politics and Colonial State-Building in the Philippines." In Julian Go and Anne L. Foster, eds., *The American Colonial State in the Philippines*, 148–81. Durham: Duke University Press.

Abueva, Jose V. 1998. *Eugenio Lopez Sr.: Philippine Entrepreneur and Business Leader*. Quezon City: Leadership, Citizenship and Democracy Program, College of Public Administration, University of the Philippines.

ACCRA Law Offices. February 7, 2009. Available at http://www.accralaw.com/sub.php?p= about&s= beginnings.

Adams, Jad, and Phillip Whitehead. 1997. *The Dynasty: The Nehru-Gandhi Story*. London: Penguin Books.

Alford, William P. 2007. "Of Lawyers Lost and Found: Searching for Legal Professionalism in the People's Republic of China." In William P. Alford, ed., *Raising the Bar: The Emerging Legal Profession in East Asia*, 287–310. Cambridge: Harvard University Press.

Annuar, Mustafa K. 2002. "Defining Democratic Discourses: The Mainstream Press." In Francis Loh Koh Wah and Khoo Boo Teik, eds., *Democracy in Malaysia: Discourses and Practices*, 138–64. Richmond and Surrey: Curzon Press.

Antlov, Hans, and Jorgen Hellman, eds. 2006. *The Java that Never Was: Academic Theories and Political Practices.* Germany: LIT Verlag Berlin-Hamburg-Münster.

Auerbach, Jerrold S. 1976. *Unequal Justice: Lawyers and Social Change in Modern America.* New York: Oxford University Press.

Badie, Bertrand. 1992. *L'Etat importe: Essai sur l'occidentalisation de l'ordre politique.* Paris: Fayard.

Bauer, Joanne R., and Daniel A. Bell, eds. 1990. *The East Asian Challenge for Human Rights.* New York: Cambridge University Press.

Baxi, Upendra. 1980. *The Indian Supreme Court and Politics.* India: Eastern Book Company.

——. 2000. "The Avatars of Indian Judicial Activism: Explorations in the Geographies of [In]justice." In S. K. Verma and A. S. Anand, eds., *Fifty Years of the Supreme Court of India,* 156–209. New Delhi: Oxford University Press.

Beckert, Sven. 2001. *The Monied Metropolis: New York City and the Consolidation of the American Bourgeoisie, 1850–1896.* New York: Cambridge University Press.

Bell, David A. 1994. *Lawyers and Citizens: The Making of a Political Elite in Old Regime France.* New York: Oxford University Press.

Benton, Lauren. 2002. *Law and Colonial Cultures: Legal Regimes in World History, 1400–1900.* New York: Cambridge University Press.

Berman, Edward H. 1983. *The Ideology of Philanthropy: The Influence of the Carnegie, Ford, and Rockefeller Foundations on American Foreign Policy.* Albany: State University of New York Press.

Bertrand, Romain. 2008. "Des gens inconvenants: Javanais et Néerlandais à l'aube de la rencontre impériale." *Actes de la recherche en sciences sociales,* nos. 171–72, pp. 104–22.

Bhagwati, Jagdish N. 2002. *The Wind of the Hundred Days: How Washington Mismanaged Globalization.* New York: MIT Press.

Bhatt, V. V. 2008. *Perspective on Development: Memoirs of a Development Economist.* New Delhi: Academic Foundation.

Bilder, Mary S. 2008. "English Settlement and Local Governance." In Michael Grossberg and Christopher Tomlins, eds., *The Cambridge History of Law in America,* vol. 2, *The Long Nineteenth Century (1789–1920),* 63–103. Cambridge: Cambridge University Press.

Bird, Kai. 1992. *The Chairman: John J. McCloy and the Making of the American Establishment.* New York: Simon & Schuster.

——. 1998. *The Color of Truth: McGeorge Bundy and William Bundy, Brothers in Arms.* New York: Simon & Schuster.

Bourdieu, Pierre. 1993. "Esprits d'Etat: Genèse et structure du champs bureaucratique." *Actes de la recherche en sciences sociales,* nos. 96–97, pp. 49–62.

———. 1998. *The State Nobility: Elite Schools in the Field of Power.* Stanford: Stanford University Press.

———. 2002. "Les conditions sociales de la circulation internationale des idées." *Actes de la recherche en sciences sociales*, nos. 145, pp. 3–8.

Brazinsky, Gregg. 2007. *Nation Building in South Korea: Koreans, Americans, and the Making of a Democracy.* Chapel Hill: University of North Carolina Press.

Bresnan, John. 1993. *Managing Indonesia: The Modern Political Economy.* New York: Columbia University Press.

———. 2006. *At Home Abroad: A Memoir of the Ford Foundation in Indonesia 1953–1973.* Jakarta/Singapore: Equinox Publishing.

Brown, Nathan J. 1995. "Law and Imperialism: Egypt in Comparative Perspective." *Law & Society Review* 29:103–25.

Brundage, James. 2008. *The Medieval Origins of the Legal Profession.* Chicago: University of Chicago Press.

Burn, Barbara B. 1968. "A New Initiative in Asian Legal Development—Lawasia." *American Journal of International Law* 62:464–69.

Burrage, Michael. 2006. *Revolution and the Making of the Contemporary Legal Profession: England, France, and the United States.* New York: Oxford University Press.

Byres, Terence J. 1998. *The Indian Economy: Major Debates since Independence.* Delhi and New York: Oxford University Press.

Carothers, Thomas. 1998. "The Rule of Law Revival." *Foreign Affairs* 77(2): 95–106.

Caucus of Developmental NGO Networks. 2002. *Annual Report.*

Charle, Christophe. 2001. *La crise des societes imperiales: Allemagne, France, Grande Bretagne, 1900–1940: Essai d'histoire sociale comparee.* Paris: Éditions du Seuil.

Chibber, Vivek. 2003. *Locked in Place: State-Building and Late Industrialization in India.* New York: Princeton University Press.

Choi, Dai-Kwon. 2007. "Judicial Reform in Perspective with Particular Focus on Legal Education." In Dai-Kwon Choi and Kahei Rokomoto, eds., *Korea and Japan: Judicial Transformation in the Globalizing World*, 287–318. Seoul: Seoul National University Press.

Choi, Woon-Youl and Sung Hoon Cho. 2003. "Shareholder Activism in Korea: An Analysis of PSPD's Activities." *Pacific-Basin Finance Journal* 11(3): 349–63.

Clarke, Gerard. 1998. *The Politics of NGO's in Southeast Asia: Participation and Protest in the Philippines.* New York: Routledge.

Cohn, Bernard S. 1961. "From Indian Status to British Contract." *Journal of Economic History* 21:613.

——. 1996. *Colonialism and Its Forms of Knowledge—The British in India.* New York: Princeton University Press.

Conner, Alison W. 1994. "Training China's Early Modern Lawyers: Soochow University Law School." *Journal of Chinese Law* 8:1–46.

——. 2010. "China's Lawyers and their Training: Enduring Influences and Disconnects." In Albert Chen and John Gillespie, eds., *Legal Development in East Asia: China and Vietnam Compared*, chap. 11. New York: Routledge.

Coronel, Sheila S. 1995. In Jose F. Lacaba, ed., *Boss: 5 Case Studies of Local Politics in the Philippines.* Pasig City: Philippine Center for Investigative Journalism, Quezon City: Institute for Popular Democracy.

Coronel, Sheila S., and Philippine Center for Investigative Journalism. 2004. *The Rulemakers: How the Wealthy and Well-Born Dominate Congress.* Quezon City: Philippine Center for Investigative Journalism.

Couso, Javier A. 2007. "When the 'Political Complex' Takes the Lead: The Configuration of a Moderate State in Chile." In Terence C. Halliday, Lucien Karpik, and Malcolm M. Feeley, eds. *Fighting for Political Freedom: Comparative Studies of the Legal Complex and Political Liberalism*, 315–44. Portland and Oxford: Hart.

Crouch, Harold. 1996. *Government and Society in Malaysia.* Ithaca: Cornell University Press.

Cumings, Bruce. 1998. *Korea's Place in the Sun: A Modern History.* Boston: W. W. Norton.

Cunningham, Clark D. 1987. "Public Interest Litigation in Indian Supreme Court: A Study in the Light of American Experience." *Journal of the Indian Law Institute* 29:494–523.

Dahrendorf, Ralf. 1969. "Law Faculties and the German Upper Class." In W. Aubert, ed., *Sociology of Law*, 294–309. London: Penguin.

Davis, Ben. 2007. *Advocacy NGOs, Transnationalism and Political Space: An Indonesian Case Study.* Sydney: *The University of Sydney* (http://gerundelan .wordpress.com/2008/07/09/ngos-under-soeharto-regimes/).

——. 2008. "Back to the Drawing Boards: NGOs Are Having to Come to Terms with the Demands of the Governance Agenda." *Inside Indonesia* 93 (Aug–Oct) (http://insideindonesia.org/content/view/1116/47/).

de Dios, Emmanuel S. 1999. "From Sanciano to Encarnacion: Footnotes to a Genealogy of Economics in the Philippines." In V. Miralao and Cynthia Rose Banzon-Bautista, eds., *The Philippine Social Sciences in the Life of the Nation*, vol. 1, *The History and Development of Social Science Disciplines in the Philippines.* Quezon City: Philippine Social Science Council.

del Carmen, Rolando V. 1973. "Constitutionalism and the Supreme Court in a Changing Philippine Polity." *Asian Survey 13(11):* 1050–61.

Dezalay, Yves. 1992. *Marchands de droit: La restructuration de l'ordre juridique international par les multinationales du droit.* Paris: Fayard.

——. 2004. "Les courtiers de l'international: Héritiers cosmopolites, mercenaries de l'impérialisme et missionnaires de l'universel." *Actes de la recherche en sciences sociales*, nos. 151–152, pp. 4–35.

Dezalay, Yves, and Bryant G. Garth. 1996. *Dealing in Virtue: International Commercial Arbitration and the Construction of a Transnational Legal Order.* Chicago: University of Chicago Press.

——. 1998. "Le 'Washington Consensus': Contribution a une sociologie de l'hegemonie du neoliberalism." *Actes de la recherche en sciences sociales*, nos. 121–22, pp. 3–22.

—— 2002. *The Internationalization of Palace Wars: Lawyers, Economists, and the Contest to Transform Latin American States.* Chicago: University of Chicago Press.

——. 2006. "From the Cold War to Kosovo: The Rise and Renewal of International Human Rights Law as a Socio-Legal Field." *Annual Review of Law and Social Science* 2:231–55.

——. 2007. "International Strategies and Local Transformations: Preliminary Observations of the Position of Law in the Field of State Power in Asia." In William P. Alford, ed., *Raising the Bar: The Emerging Legal Profession in East Asia*, 81–106. Cambridge: Harvard University Press

——. 2008. "From the Foreign Policy Establishment to the Legalization of Foreign Policy." In Michael Grossberg and Christopher Tomlins, eds., *The Cambridge History of Law in America*, vol. 3, *The Twentieth Century and After*, 718–58. Cambridge: Cambridge University Press.

Dhavan, Rajeev. 2002. "Judges and Indian Democracy: The Lesser Evil?" In Francine R. Frankel, ed., *Transforming India: Social and Political Dynamics of Democracy*, 314–52. New Delhi and New York: Oxford University Press.

Drake, Paul W., ed. 1993. *Money Doctors, Foreign Debts and Economic Reforms in Latin America from the 1890s to the Present.* Wilmington: SR Books.

Epp, Charles R. 1998. *The Rights Revolution: Lawyers, Activists, and Supreme Courts in Comparative Perspective.* Chicago: University of Chicago Press.

Erie, Matthew. 2009. "Peripheries at the Center: Reforming Legal Education in the People's Republic of China." *Journal of Legal Education* 59:60–96.

Evans, Peter B. 1995. *Embedded Autonomy: States and Industrial Transformation.* Princeton: Princeton University Press.

FAC News. 2002. "Rais Yatim Eats His Words, Yet Again." September 13 (http://www.freeanwar.net/june2002/facnews130902a.htm).

Fasseur, C. 1992. "Colonial Dilemma: Van Vollenhoven and the Struggle between Adat Law and Western Law in Indonesia." In W. J. Mommsen and J. A. De Moor, eds., *European Expansion and Law: The Encounter of European and Indigenous Law in 19th- and 20th-century Africa and Asia*, 237–58. Oxford and New York: Berg Publishers.

Faulconbridge, James R., Jonathan V. Beaverstock, Daniel Muzio and Peter J.

Taylor. 2008. "Global Law Firms: Globalization and Organizational Spaces of Cross-Border Legal Work." *Northwestern Journal of International Law and Business* 28(3): 455–88.

Feeley, Malcolm, and Setsuo Miyazawa. 2007. "The State, Civil Society, and the Legal Complex in Modern Japan: Continuity and Change." In Terence Halliday, Lucien Karpik, and Malcolm Feeley, eds., *Fighting for Political Freedom: Comparative Studies of the Legal Complex and Political Change*, 151–93. Oxford and Portland: Hart Publishing.

Ferguson, Niall. 2004. *Empire: The Rise and Demise of the British World Order and the Lessons for Global Power*. New York: Basic Books.

Freeland, Richard M. 1992. *Academia's Golden Age: Universities in Massachusetts, 1945–1970*. New York: Oxford University Press.

Galanter, Marc, and Thomas Palay. 1991. *Tournament of Lawyers: The Transformation of the Big Law Firm*. Chicago: University of Chicago Press.

Gambe, Annabelle R. 2000. *Overseas Chinese Entrepreneurship and Capitalist Development in Southeast Asia*. New York: Palgrave Macmillan.

Gandhi, J. S. 1988. "Past and Present: A Sociological Portrait of the Indian Legal Profession." In Richard L. Abel, Philip S. Lewis, eds., *Lawyers in Society, The Common Law World*, 369–82. New York: Beard Books.

Gardner, James A. 1980. *Legal Imperialism: American Lawyers and Foreign Aid in Latin America*. Madison: University of Wisconsin Press.

Garth, Bryant. 2000. "James Willard Hurst as Entrepreneur for the Field of Law and Social Science." *Law & History Review* 18:37–58.

Gerwitz, Paul. 2003. "The U.S.–China Rule of Law Initiative." *William and Mary Bill of Rights Journal* 11:603–21.

Ginsburg, Tom. 2007. "Law and the Liberal Transformation of the Northeast Asian Legal Complex in Korea and Taiwan." In Terence Halliday, Lucien Karpik, and Malcolm Feeley, eds., *Fighting for Political Freedom: Comparative Studies of the Legal Complex and Political Change*, 43–64. Oxford and Portland: Hart Publishing.

Ginsburg, Tom, and Tamir Moustafa, eds. 2008. *Rule by Law; The Politics of Courts in Authoritarian Regimes*. Cambridge and New York: Cambridge University Press.

Go, Julian. 2003. "Introduction: Global Perspectives on the U.S. Colonial State in the Philippines." In Julian Go and Anne L. Foster, eds., *The American Colonial State in the Philippines: Global Perspectives*, 1–42. Durham: Duke University Press.

Goedde, Patricia. 2009. "From Dissidents to Institution-Builders: The Transformation of Public Interest Lawyers in Korea." *East Asia Law Review* 4:63–88.

Goh, Daniel P. S. 2008. "Genèse de L'Etat colonial: Politiques colonisatrices et resistance indigene (Malaisie Britannique, Philippines Americaines)." *Actes de la recherche en sciences sociales*, nos. 171–172, pp. 56–73.

Goldstein, Judith. 2001. *Legalization and World Politics*. Cambridge: MIT Press.

Golub, Stephen. 2000. "Participatory Justice in the Philippines." In Mary Mc-Clymont and Stephen Golub, eds., *Many Roads to Justice: The Law-Related Work of the Ford Foundation Grantees Around the World*, 197–232. New York: Ford Foundation.

———. 2003. *Beyond the Rule of Law Orthodoxy: The Legal Empowerment Alternative*. Carnegie Paper No. 41.

Gomez, Manual. Forthcoming. "Greasing The Squeaky Wheel of Justice: Networks of Venezuelan Lawyers from the Pacted Democracy to the Bolivarian Revolution." In Yves Dezalay and Bryant G. Garth, eds., *Constructing the Rule of Law in National and Transnational Settings: Recycling Social Capital into International Legitimacy and State Expertise*. New York and London: Routledge.

Gomez, Terence Edmund. 1999. *Chinese Business in Malaysia: Accumulation, Accommodation, and Ascendance*. Richmond: Curzon.

Gomez, Terence Edmund, and Jomo K. S. 1999. *Malaysia's Political Economy: Politics, Patronage, and Profits*. Cambridge: Cambridge University Press.

Gordon, Robert W. 1984. "The Ideal and the Actual in the Law: Fantasies and Practices of New York City Lawyers, 1870–1910." In Gerald W. Gawalt, ed., *The New High Priests: Lawyers in Post-Civil War America*, 51–74. Westport: Greenwood Press.

Halliday, Terence, Lucien Karpik, and Malcolm Feeley, eds. 2007. *Fighting for Political Freedom: Comparative Studies of the Legal Complex and Political Change*, 151–93. Oxford and Portland: Hart Publishing.

Hamilton-Patterson, James. 1998. *America's Boy: The Marcoses and the Philippines*. Pasig City: Anvil Publishing.

Harding, Andrew J. 1990. "The 1988 Constitutional Crisis in. Malaysia." *International & Comparative Law Quarterly* 39:57–81.

———.1992. "Public Interest Groups, Public Interest Law and Development in Malaysia." *Third World Legal Studies* 231–43.

Harbaugh, William H. 1973. *Lawyer's Lawyer: The Life of John W. Davis*. New York: Oxford University Press.

He, Weifang. 2005. "China's Legal Profession: The Nascence and Growing Pains of a Professionalized Legal Class." *Columbia Journal of Asian Law* 19:138.

Hector, Charles. 2003. "Mahathir and the Judges: The Judiciary During the Mahathir Era." *Aliran Monthly* 8. http://reocities.com/CapitolHill/embassy/6296/190903judiciarymahathirera.html

Hedman, Eva-Lotta E., and John T. Sidel. 2000. *Philippine Politics and Society in the Twentieth Century: Colonial Legacies, Post-Colonial Trajectories*. New York: Routledge.

Henderson, William D. 2007. "The Globalization of the Legal Profession." *Indiana Journal of Global Legal Studies* 14:1–3.

Henretta, James A. 2008. "Magistrates, Common Law Lawyers, Legislators: The Three Legal Systems in British America." In Michael Grossberg and Christopher Tomlins, eds., *The Cambridge History of Law in America*, vol. 1, *Early America (1580–1815)*, 555–92. Cambridge: Cambridge University Press.

Hilley, John. 2001. *Malaysia: Mahathirism, Hegemony and the New Opposition in Malaysia*. London and New York: Zed Books.

Hirschl, Ron. 2004. *Towards Juristocracy: The Origins and Consequences of the New Constitutionalism*. Cambridge: Harvard University Press.

Hodgson, Godfrey. 1990. *The Colonel: The Life and Wars of Henry Stimson, 1867–1950*. New York: Knopf.

Hussin, Iza. 2007. "The Pursuit of the Perak Regalia: Law and the Making of the Colonial State." *Law and Social Inquiry* 32(3): 759–88.

Hutchcroft, Paul D. 1998. *Booty Capitalism: The Politics of Banking in the Philippines*. Ithaca: Cornell University Press.

———. 2000. "Obstructive Corruption: The Politics of Privilege in the Philippines." In Mushtaq H. Khan and L. S. Jomo, eds., *Rents, Rent-Seeking and Economic Development: Theory and Evidence in Asia*, 207–47. Cambridge and New York: Cambridge University Press.

International Bar Association. 2000. *Justice In Jeopardy: Malaysia 2000, Report of a Mission*. London: International Bar Association.

Irons, Peter H. 1993. *The New Deal Lawyers*. Princeton: Princeton University Press.

Isaacson, Walter, and Evan Thomas. 1986. *The Wise Men: Six Friends and the World They Made*. New York: Simon and Schuster.

Jayasuriya, Kanishka. 1998. "Corporatism and Judicial Independence within Statist Legal Institutions in East Asia." In Kanishka Jayasuriya, ed., *Law, Capitalism and Power in Asia: The Rule of Law and Legal Institutions*, 147–73. London and New York: Routledge.

Jones, Carol A. G. 1994. "Capitalism, Globalization, and Rule of Law: An Alternative Trajectory of Legal Change in China." *Social & Legal Studies* 3:195–221.

———. 2007. "'Dissolving the People': Capitalism, Law and Democracy in Hong Kong." In Terence Halliday, Lucien Karpik, and Malcolm Feeley, eds., *Fighting for Political Freedom: Comparative Studies of the Legal Complex and Political Change*, 109–50. Oxford and Portland: Hart Publishing.

———. Forthcoming. "Legal Education in Hong Kong: Producing the Producers." In Stacey Steele and Kathryn Taylor, eds., *Legal Education in Asia*. New York: Routledge.

Kabaservice, Geoffrey. 2004. *The Guardians: Kingman Brewster, His Circle, and the Rise of the Liberal Establishment*. New York: Henry Holt.

Kang, David C. 2002. *Crony Capitalism: Corruption and Development in South Korea and the Philippines.* New York: Cambridge University Press.

Kantorowicz, Ernst H. 1997. *The King's Two Bodies: A Study in Mediaeval Political Theology.* Princeton: Princeton University Press.

Karnow, Stanley. 1989. *In Our Image: America's Empire in the Philippines.* New York: Random House.

Karpik, Lucien. 2000. *French Lawyers: A Study in Collective Action 1274 to 1994.* Oxford: Oxford University Press.

Kim, Jae Won. 2007. "Legal Profession and Legal Culture during Korea's Transition to Democracy and a Market Economy." In William P. Alford, ed., *Raising the Bar: The Emerging Legal Profession in East Asia.* Cambridge: Harvard University Press.

Kim, Seong-Hyun. 2003. "Diplomatie economique autour du contrat du TGV coréen: Une sociologie de grand contrat international." Unpublished thesis, L'École des hautes études en sciences sociales.

———. Forthcoming. "The Democratization and Internationalization of Korean Legal Field." In Yves Dezalay and Bryant G. Garth, eds., *Constructing the Rule of Law in National and Transnational Settings: Recycling Social Capital into International Legitimacy and State Expertise.* New York and London: Routledge.

Konefsky, Alfred S. 2008. "The Legal Profession: From the Revolution to the Civil War." In Michael Grossman and Christopher Tomlins, eds., *The Cambridge History of Law in America,* vol. 2, *The Long Nineteenth Century (1789–1920),* 68–105. Cambridge: Cambridge University Press.

Konig, David Thomas. 2008. "Regionalism in Early American Law." In Michael Grossman and Christopher Tomlins, eds., *The Cambridge History of Law in America,* vol. 1, *Early America (1580–1815),* 144–77. Cambridge: Cambridge University Press.

Kostal, Rande W. 1994. *Law and English Railway Capitalism, 1825–1875.* Oxford and New York: Clarendon Press/Oxford University Press.

Krishnan, Jayanth K. 2004. "Professor Kingsfield Goes to Delhi: American Academics, the Ford Foundation, and the Development of Legal Education in India." *American Journal of Legal History* 46:447–99.

———. 2005a. "From the ALI to the ILI: The Efforts to Export an American Legal Institution." *Vanderbilt Journal of Transnational Law* 38:1255–88.

———. 2005b. "Transgressive Cause Lawyering in the Developing World: The Case of India." In Austin Sarat and Stuart Scheingold, eds., *The Worlds Cause Lawyers Make,* 349–82. Stanford: Stanford University Press.

Kumaramangalam, Mohan. *1971. Constitutional Amendments: The Reason Why.* New Delhi: All India Congress Committee.

Kusum, K. and S. K. Verma, ed., 2000. *Fifty Years of the Supreme Court of India, Its Grasp and Reach.* New Delhi: Oxford University Press.

Lardinois, Roland. 2008. "Entre monopole, marché, et religion: L'emergence de l'état colonial en Inde, années 1760–1810." *Actes de la recherche en sciences sociales*, nos. 171–72, pp. 90–104.

Larson, Magali Sarfatti. 1977. *The Rise of Professionalism: A Sociological Analysis*. Berkeley and Los Angeles: University of California Press.

Lee, Kuk-Woon. 2007. "Corporate Lawyers in Korea: An Analysis of the 'Big 4' Law Firms in Seoul." In Dai-Kwon Choi, ed., *Korea and Japan: Judicial System in Transformation in the Globalizing World*, 219–50. Seoul: Seoul National University Press.

Lee, Su-Hoon. 1993. "Transitional Politics of Korea, 1987–1992: Activation of Civil Society." *Pacific Affair* 66(3): 351–67.

Lee, Tahirih V. 1993. "Risky Business: Courts, Culture, and the Marketplace." *University of Miami Law Review* 47:1335–414.

Legal Services Review Committee. 1999. *Report*. Singapore: Attorney-General's Chambers.

Legemann, Ellen Condliffe. 1989. *The Politics of Knowledge: The Carnegie Corporation, Philanthropy, and Public Policy*. Chicago and London: University of Chicago Press.

Leue, H. J. 1992. "Legal Expansion in the Age of the Companies: Aspects of Justice in the English and Dutch Settlements of Maritime Asia, c. 1600–1750." In W. J. Mommsen and J. A. de Moor, eds., *European Expansion and Law: The Encounter of European and Indigenous Law in 19th- and 20th-century Africa and Asia*, 129–58. Oxford: Berg Publishers.

Lev, Daniel. 1972. "Judicial Institutions and Legal Culture in Indonesia." In Claire Holt, ed., *Culture and Politics in Indonesia*. Ithaca and London: Cornell University Press.

——. 1976. "Origins of the Indonesian Advocacy." *Indonesia* 21:135–69.

——. 1989. "In Memoriam: Yap Thiam Hien (1913–1989)." *Indonesia* 48:107–10.

——. 1998. "Lawyers' Causes in Indonesia and Malaysia." In Austin Sarat and Stuart Scheingold, eds., *Cause Lawyering: Political Commitments and Professional Responsibilities*, 349–430. New York: Oxford University Press.

——. 2000. *Legal Evolution and Political Authority in Indonesia: Selected Essays*. Hague and Boston: Kluwer Law International.

——. 2007. "A Tale of Two Legal Professions: Lawyers and the State In Malaysia and Indonesia." In William Alford, ed., *Raising the Bar: The Emerging Legal Profession in Asia*, 383–414. Cambridge: Harvard University Press.

Likosky, Michael B. 2005. *The Silicon Empire: Law, Culture, and Commerce*. London: Ashgate Publishing.

Linnan, David K. 1999. "Indonesian Law Reform, or Once More unto the Breach: A Brief Institutional History." *Australian Journal of Asian Law* 1:1–33.

Lopez, Leslie. 2007a. "Surprise Resignation rocks top Malaysian law firm." *The Straits Times*, January 8.

——. 2007b. "Johari May Help Check Fall-Out From Resignation of Firm's Managing Partner." *The Straits Times*, April 14 (http://walkwithus.wordpress .com/2007/04/14/shearn-delamore-unfazed-by-cecil-abrahams-exit/).

Lydgate, Chris. 2003. *Lee's Law: How Singapore Crushes Dissent*. Melbourne: Scribe Publications.

Lynch, Dennis O. 1981. *Legal Roles in Columbia*. Uppsala: Scandanavian Institute of African Studies; New York: International Center for Law and Development.

Machado, K. G. and Rahim Said. 1981. "The Malaysian Legal Profession in Transition." In C. J. Dias et al., eds., *Lawyers in the Third World: Comparative and Developmental Perspectives*, 248–72. Uppsala: Scandinavian Institute of African Studies. New York: International Center for Law in Development.

MacDougall, John James. 1975. "Technocrats as Modernizers: The Economists of Indonesia's New Order." PhD thesis, University of Michigan.

Magallona, Merlin M. 2000. "A Brief Report on Legal Education in the Philippines." Presented at AALS Conference of International Legal Educators, May 24–27, Florence, Italy.

Malatesta, Maria. 2002. *Society and the Professions in Italy, 1860–1914*. Cambridge: Cambridge University Press.

Malcolm, George A. 1957. *American Colonial Careerist: Half a century of official life and personal experience in the Philippines and Puerto Rico*. Boston: Christopher Publishing House.

Manapat, Ricardo. 1991. *Some Are Smarter than Others: The History of Marcos' Crony Capitalism*. New York: Aletheia Publishing.

Martines, Lauro. 1968. *Lawyers and Statecraft in Renaissance Florence*. Princeton: Princeton University Press.

McCoy, Alfred W., ed. 1993. *An Anarchy of Families: State and Family in the Philippines*. Madison: University of Wisconsin, Center for Southeast Asian Studies.

Michelson, Ethan. 2006. "The Practice of Law as an Obstacle to Justice: Chinese Lawyers at Work." *Law & Society Review* 40(1): 1–38.

Mines, Mattison. 2001. "Courts of Law and Styles of Self in Eighteenth-Century Madras: From Hybrid to Colonial Self." *Modern Asian Studies* 35:33–74.

Minger, Ralph Eldin. 1975. *William Howard Taft and United States Foreign Policy: The Apprenticeship Years, 1900–1908*. Urbana: University of Illinois Press.

Miyazawa, Setsuo, Kay-Wah Chan, and Ilhyung Lee. 2008. "The Reform of Legal Education in East Asia." *Annual Review of Law and Social Science* 4:333–60.

Mohamad, Goenawan, Andreas Harsono, and Sandra Hamid. 2003. *Celebrat-*

ing Indonesia: Fifty Years with the Ford Foundation 1953–2003. New York: Equinox Publishing.

Mommsen, Wolfgang J., and Jaap de Moor, eds. 1991. *European Expansion and Law: The Encounter of European and Indigenous Law in the 19th- and 20th-century Africa and Asia*. Oxford and New York: Berg.

Nair, Sheila. 1999. "Constructing Civil Society in Malaysia: Nationalism, Hegemony, and Resistance." In K. S. Jomo, ed., *Rethinking Malaysia*, 84–106. Hong Kong: Kuala Lumpur.

New Straits Times. 2001. "Group Campaigns on Platform of Reforming the Bar Council." *New Straits Times (Malaysia)*, November 18.

———. 2007. "Urgent need to reform judiciary." *New Straits Times (Malaysia)*, February 21.

———. 2007. "CJ's reaction surprises legal fraternity." *New Straits Times (Malaysia)*, February 23.

Ocko, Jonathan K., and David Gilmartin. 2009. "State, Sovereignty, and the People: A Comparison of the 'Rule of Law' in China and India." *Journal of Asian Studies* 68(1): 55–133.

Oguamanam, Chidi, and Wesley Pue. 2006. *Lawyers' Professionalism, Colonialism, State Formation and National Life in Nigeria, 1900–1960: "The Fighting Brigade of the People."* Available at Social Science Research Network (http://ssrn.com/abstract=953313).

Ohnesorge, John K. M. 2003. "The Rule of Law, Economic Development, and the Developmental States of Northeast Asia." In Christoph Antons, ed., *Law and Development in East and Southeast Asia*, 91–130. London and New York: RoutledgeCurzon.

———. 2007. "The Rule of Law." *Annual Review of Law and Social Science* 3:91–114.

Palkhivala, Nani A. 1974. *Our Constitution Profaned and Defiled*. New Delhi: Macmillan India.

Palkhivala, N. A., L. M. Singhvi, M. R. Pai, and S. Ramakrishnan. 1999. *Nani Palkhivala: Selected Writings*. New Delhi: Viking/Bhavan's Book University.

Paul, John J. 1991. *The Legal Profession in Colonial South India*. Bombay: Oxford University Press.

Peerenboom, Randall. 2008. "Searching for Political Liberalism in all the Wrong Places: The Legal Profession in China as the Leading Edge of Political Reform?" *La Trobe Law School Legal Studies Research Paper No. 2008/7*.

Perez-Perdomo, Rogelio. 2006. *Latin American Lawyers: A Historical Introduction*. Stanford: Stanford University Press.

Pistor, Katharina and Philip A. Wellons. 1998. *The Role of Law and Legal Institutions in Asian Economic Development, 1960–95. Final Comparative Report. Revised Text*. Prepared for the Asian Development Bank, March 1998.

Pitts, Jennifer. 2005. *A Turn to Empire: The Rise of Imperial Liberalism in Britain and France*. Princeton: Princeton University Press.

Pompe, Sebastian. 2005. *The Indonesian Supreme Court: A Study of Institutional Collapse*. Ithaca: Cornell Southeast Asia Program.

Powell, Michael J. 1988. *From Patrician to Professional Elite: The Transformation of the New York City Bar Association*. New York: Russell Sage Foundation.

Prest, Wilfred R. 1986. *The Rise of the Barristers: A Social History of the English Bar, 1590–1640*. Oxford: Clarendon Press.

Price, Pamela G. 1989. "Ideology and Ethnicity under British Imperial Rule: 'Brahmins,' Lawyers and Kin-Caste Rules in Madras Presidency." *Modern Asian Studies* 23:151–77.

Priest, Claire. 2008. "Law and Commerce, 1580–1815." In Michael Grossman and Christopher Tomlins, eds., *The Cambridge History of Law in America*, vol. 1, *Early America (1580–1815)*, 400–46. Cambridge: Cambridge University Press.

Pue, Wesley W. 1997. "Lawyers and Political Liberalism in Eighteenth- and Nineteenth-Century England." In Terence C. Halliday and Lucian Karpik, eds., *Lawyers and the Rise of Western Political Liberalism: Europe and North America from the Eighteenth to Twentieth Centuries*, 167. Oxford and New York: Clarendon Press, Oxford University Press.

Quezon, Manual L., III. 1996. "On the Road to EDSA." *TODAY Newspaper* (EDSA Anniversary Supplement), February (http://www.tribo.org/history/edsa.html).

Ransom, David. 1975. "Ford Country: Building an Elite for Indonesia. In Steve Weissman, ed., with members of the Pacific Studies Center and the North American Congress on Latin America, *The Trojan Horse: A Radical Look at Foreign Aid*, 93–116. Revised edition. Palo Alto: Ramparts Press.

Reksodiputro, Mardjono. 2003. "Challenges to Legal Education in Indonesia" (http://www.aseanlawassociation.org/docs/w3_indo.pdf).

Riedinger, Jeffrey M. 1995. *Agrarian Reform in the Philippines: Democratic Transitions and Redistributive Reform*. Stanford: Stanford University Press.

Robison, Richard and Vedi R. Hadiz. 2004. *Reorganising Power in Indonesia: The Politics of Oligarchy in an Age of Markets*. New York: Routledge.

Rosen, George. 1985. *Western Economists and Eastern Societies: Agents of Change in South Asia, 1950–1970*. Baltimore: Johns Hopkins University Press.

Rosenberg, Emily S. 1982. *Spreading the American Dream: American Economic & Cultural Expansion 1890–1945*. New York: Hill and Wang.

———. 2003. *Financial Missionaries to the World: The Politics and Culture of Dollar Diplomacy 1900–1930*. Durham: Duke University Press.

Rudolph, Lloyd I. and Susanne H. Rudolph. 1965. "Barristers and Brahmins in

India: Legal Cultures and Social Change." *Comparative Studies in Society and History* 8:24–49.

—— .1987. *In Pursuit of Lakshmi, The Political Economy of the Indian State.* Chicago: University of Chicago Press.

——. 2001. "Redoing the Constitutional Design: From an Interventionist to a Regulatory State." In Atul Kohli, ed., *The Success of India's Democracy,* 127–62. Cambridge: Cambridge University Press.

Rueschemeyer, Dietrich. 1997. "State, Capitalism, and the Organization of Legal Counsel: Examining an Extreme Case—the Prussian Bar, 1700–1914." In Terence C. Halliday and Lucien Karpik, eds., *Lawyers and the Rise of Western Political Liberalism: Europe and North America from the Eighteenth to Twentieth Centuries,* 207–28. Oxford: Oxford University Press.

Sacriste, Guillaume and Antoine Vauchez. 2007. "The Force of International Law: Lawyers' Diplomacy on the International Scene in the 1920s." *Law and Social Inquiry* 32:83–107.

Saegusa, Mayumi. 2009. "Why the Japanese Law School System Was Established: Co-optation as a Defensive Tactic in the Face of Global Pressures." *Law and Social Inquiry* 34:365–98.

Santa Maria, Dina. 2006. "Eugenio Lopez Sr.'s A Legacy of Service" (http://www.newsflash.org/2004/02/sb/sb004182.htm).

Sathe, S. P. 2002. *Judicial Activism in India: Transgressing Borders and Enforcing Limits.* New Delhi: Oxford University Press.

Saligan. 2002. *Fifteen Year Report.* Manila: Saligan.

Salonga, Jovito R. 2001. *A Journey of Struggle and Hope: The Memoir of Jovito R. Salonga.* Quezon City: University of the Philippines Center for Leadership, Citizenship, and Democracy and Regina Publishing.

Sarat, Austin and Stuart Scheingold, eds. 1998. *Cause Lawyering: Political Commitments and Professional Responsibilities.* New York: Oxford University Press.

Scalapino, Robert A. 1964. "Environmental and Foreign Contributions: Japan." In Robert E. Ward and Dankwart A. Rustow, eds., *Political Modernization in Japan and Turkey.* Princeton: Princeton University Press.

Schmitthener, Samuel. 1968–69. "A Sketch of the Development of the Legal Profession in India." *Law & Society Review* 3:337–82.

Scully, Eileen. 2008. "The United States and International Affairs, 1789–1919." In Michael Grossman and Christopher Tomlins, eds., *The Cambridge History of Law in America,* vol. 2, *The Long Nineteenth Century (1789–1920),* 604–42. Cambridge: Cambridge University Press.

Seah, Datuk George. 2004. "The Hidden Story" (http://www.aliran.com/oldsite/monthly/2004a/4m.html).

Seow, Francis. 1994. *To Catch a Tartar: A Dissident in Lee Kuan Yew's Prison.* New Haven: Yale University Press.

———. 1997. "The Politics of Judicial Institutions in Singapore." Lecture at University of Sydney, April (http://unpan1.un.org/intradoc/groups/public/documents/ apcity/unpan002727.pdf).

Setalvad, Motilal C. 1999. *My Life: Law and Other Things*. Delhi: Universal Law Publishing.

Shamir, Ronen. 1995. *Managing Legal Uncertainty: Elite Lawyers in the New Deal*. Durham: Duke University Press.

———. 2000. *The Colonies of Law: Colonialism, Zionism and Law in Early Mandate Palestine*. Cambridge: Cambridge University Press.

Shapiro, Martin. 2008. "Courts in Authoritarian Regines." In Tom Ginsburg and Tamir Moustafa, eds., *Rule by Law: The Politics of Courts in Authoritarian Regimes*, 326–36. Cambridge and New York: Cambridge University Press.

Sidel, John Thayer. 1999. *Capital, Coercion, and Crime: Bossism in the Philippines*. Stanford: Stanford University Press.

Silk, Leonard, and Mark Silk. 1980. *The American Establishment*. New York: Basic Books.

Silver, Carole. 2007. "Local Matters: Internationalizing Strategies for U.S. Law Firms." *Indiana Journal of Global Legal Studies* 14:67–93.

Silverstein, Gordon. 2008. "Singapore: The Exception That Proves Rules Matter." In Tom Ginsburg and Tamir Moustafa, eds. *Rule by Law: The Politics of Courts in Authoritarian Regimes*, 73–101. Cambridge and New York: Cambridge University Press.

Simpson, Bradley R. 2008. *Economists with Guns: Authoritarian Development and U.S.-Indonesian Relations, 1960–1968*. Stanford: Stanford University Press.

Smith, Tony. 1994. *America's Mission: The United States and the Worldwide Struggle for Democracy in the Twentieth Century*. Princeton: Princeton University Press.

So, Alvin Y. 1999. *Hong Kong's Embattled Democracy: A Societal Analysis*. Baltimore: Johns Hopkins University Press.

Southworth, Ann. 2008. *Lawyers of the Right: Professionalizing the Conservative Coalition*. Chicago: University of Chicago Press.

Staples, Eugene S. 1992. *Forty Years, A Learning Curve: The Ford Foundation Programs in India 1952–1992*. New Delhi: Ford Foundation.

Steinmetz, George. 2007. *The Devil's Handwriting: Precoloniality and the German Colonial State in Qingdao, Samoa, and Southwest Africa*. Chicago: University of Chicago Press.

———. 2008. "Le champ de l'état colonial." *Actes de la recherche en sciences sociales*, nos. 171–72, pp. 122–43.

Stephenson, Matthew C. 2000. "A Trojan Horse Behind Chinese Walls? Problems and Prospects of U.S.-Sponsored 'Rule of Law' Reform Projects in the People's Republic of China." *UCLA Pacific Basin Law Journal* 18:64–97.

Stokes, Eric. 1959. *The English Utilitarians and India.* Oxford: Clarendon Press.

Sui, Cheong Mei and Adibah Amin. 1995. *Daim: The Man Behind the Enigma.* Selangor Darul Ehsan: Pelanduk Publications.

Taylor, Veronica. 2005. "New Markets, New Commodity: Japanese Legal Technical Assistance." *Wisconsin International Law Journal* 23:251–81.

The Committee on Restricting the Supply of Lawyers. 1993. *Report on the Legal Profession.* Singapore. Chaired by the Attorney-General of Singapore.

The Third Committee on Restricting the Supply of Lawyers. 2001. *Report on the Supply of Lawyers in Singapore.* Singapore. Chaired by the Attorney-General of Singapore.

Thomas, Tommy. 2001. "Human Rights in Asia in 21st Century." *Aliran Online* (http://www.aliran.com/oldsite/hr/tt4.html).

Thompson, Mark R. 1995. *The Anti-Marcos Struggle: Personalistic Rule and Democratic Transition in the Philippines.* New Haven: Yale University Press.

Tomasic, Roman. 2003. "Asian Economic Crisis and Legal Institutions: A Tale of Two Cities." In Antons, Christoph, ed., *Law and Development in East and Southeast Asia,* 358–87. London: RoutledgeCurzon.

Tremewan, Christopher. 1994. *The Political Economy of Social Control in Singapore.* New York: St. Martin's Press.

Trubek, David M. and Marc Galanter. 1974. "Scholars in Self-Estrangement: Some Reflections on the Crisis in Law and Development Studies in the United States." *Wisconsin Law Review* 1974:1062–102.

Trubek, David M. and Alvaro Santos, eds. 2006. *The New Law and Economic Development: A Critical Appraisal.* Cambridge: Cambridge University Press.

Tsang, Steve Yui-Sang. 2004. *A Modern History of Hong Kong.* London and New York: I. B. Tauris.

Wallerstein, Immanuel Maurice. 2000. *The Essential Wallerstein.* New York: New Press.

Wee, Vivienne and Chan Yuk Wah. 2006. "Ethnicity and Capital: Changing Relations Between China and Southeast Asia." *Journal of Contemporary Asia* 36:328–49.

Weingast, Barry R. 1997. "The Political Foundations of Democracy and the Rule of Law." *American Political Science Review* 91:245–63.

Westad, Odd Arne. 2005. *The Global Cold War: Third World Interventions and the Making of Our Times.* Cambridge and New York: Cambridge University Press.

Willrich, Michael. 2003. *City of Courts: Socializing Justice in Progressive Era Chicago.* Cambridge and New York: Cambridge University Press.

World Bank. 1993. *The East Asian Miracle: Economic Growth and Public Policy.* New York: Oxford University Press.

Worthington, Ross. 2001. "Between Hermes and Themis: An Empirical Study of the Contemporary Judiciary in Singapore." *Journal of Law and Society* 28:490–519.

Yew, Lee Kwan. 1999. *The Singapore Story: Memoirs of Lee Kuan Yew.* Princeton: Prentice-Hall.

———. 2000. *The Singapore Story: Memoirs of Lee Kuan Yew, Vol. 2: From Third World to First, 1965–2000.* Princeton: Prentice-Hall.

Yang, Kun. 1993. "Judicial Review and Social Change in the Korean Democratizing Process." *American Journal of Comparative Law* 41:1–8.

Zimmerman, Warren. 2002. *First Great Triumph: How Five Great Americans Made Their Country a World Power.* New York: Farrar, Strauss, and Giroux.

INDEX